# How Prayer Heals

Books by Walter Weston:

*Pray Well: A Holistic Guide to Health and Renewal*
*Healing Others: A Practical Guide*
*Healing Yourself: A Practical Guide*
*How Prayer Heals: A Scientific Approach*

# How Prayer Heals

## A SCIENTIFIC APPROACH

WALTER WESTON

HAMPTON ROADS
PUBLISHING COMPANY, INC.
for the evolving human spirit

Cover design by Mayapriya Long
Cover art by Frank Riccio

For information write:

Hampton Roads Publishing Company, Inc.
134 Burgess Lane
Charlottesville, VA 22902

Or call: (804)296-2772
FAX: (804)296-5096
e-mail: hrpc@hrpub.com
Web site: http://www.hrpub.com

If you are unable to order this book from your local
bookseller, you may order directly from the publisher.
Quantity discounts for organizations are available.
Call 1-800-766-8009, toll-free.

Library of Congress Catalog Card Number: 98-72216

ISBN 1-57174-092-9

10 9 8 7 6 5 4 3 2 1

Printed on acid-free paper in Canada

# Table of Contents

# Preface

Prayer is such a private activity that we seldom realize that many people besides ourselves pray. Yet, two-thirds of Americans report that they pray daily. And across our planet, billions of people in most cultures, races and religions pray daily.

If anything unites all humanity, it is prayer. Prayer is the universal means by which human beings petition God to intervene in their lives. Prayers for the sick—any place on Earth—take on universal characteristics that transcend religious beliefs.

When a loved one is ill, the person praying would obviously use plain words that simply ask God to grant healing. An example: "God, my mother is sick. Please heal her." Any prayer expressing compassionate love introduces the power of God into the life of the world for the purpose of bringing healing and wholeness to hurting people.

The religious diversity of humanity is immense. Yet the above assumptions make non-sectarian religious prayers for healing and wholeness not only possible but also practical. In practical terms, there is no such thing among Christians as a Catholic, Orthodox, Baptist or Methodist prayer for healing. Nor are there uniquely

Christian, Muslim, Hindu, Jewish, Shinto, or primitive or tribal prayers for healing. The core intention of their prayers is universal.

The almost universal belief that God heals through prayer makes this book needed. It also makes this book timely. Timely because, around our planet, holistic medicine is becoming popular in medical circles. Within a few years, holistic medicine will be practiced in every hospital in the United States. In the midst of this holistic health revolution, the world's oldest holistic healing method is being excluded. That holistic healing method is prayer for healing. The implications of this are immense for the world's religions and will be thoroughly explored.

If the power of prayer is to be used in holistic medicine, and in your home, then a new paradigm—a new model for healing with prayer is needed. This book creates that new paradigm with a new way of looking at prayer and healing. This new paradigm is based upon science—the science behind healing. It tells us how prayer works.

Why do we need a new paradigm? Because our present popular beliefs about prayer and healing are inaccurate and incomplete, they block our willingness to accept healing prayer; they hinder our ability to understand healing and its immense potential; they hamper our capacity to practice healing and produce positive outcomes; they prevent us from using healing technology to transform all life on Earth.

Our new scientific paradigm addresses each of these issues. Its purpose is to provide a more accurate picture of prayer and healing; to persuade our culture to trust this more accurate and helpful picture of healing; to lift healing prayer into the mainstream of American life; to make every American household comfortable with healing prayer; and finally, to make every hospital and health care professional open to healing prayer as a basic tool of holistic medicine.

## We Begin in the Bottomless Pit

At the present time, about ninety percent of Americans would rather die than try healing prayer. Most of the rest view healing prayer as a last resort, to be used only after all other conventional and alternative medical approaches have failed them.

In spite of any public lip service, healing is shunned. People feel shame and embarrassment, fear and anger, about healing. They do not know why. No one discusses this mysterious response toward healing.

Yesterday, a man called me about his secretary, Allison. For two months the pain of shingles had tormented her. The pain was now so intense that even the strongest pain medications offered little relief. Her boss asked, "Do you think you can help Allison?"

I assured him: "Yes. The pain of shingles is stress related. It will take less than an hour to remove all of her stress and heal her shingles. She has a ninety-five percent chance of being symptom–free within forty-eight hours."

He agreed to pay for the healing session in her home. He later called back. Allison refused the treatment. Why? She offered no explanation.

Allison is like most Americans. Healing remains the most misunderstood, disbelieved, ridiculed and rejected phenomenon in American life.

So, we begin this book in the bottomless pit, in the abyss of utter cultural rejection. Can we overcome humanity's seemingly innate blindness toward the true nature of healing? Can I convince you of the truth of healing's new scientific paradigm? Can I excite you about healing's immense potential for bringing wholeness to all humanity?

## The Emperor's New Clothes

In the children's story of *The Emperor's New Clothes*, the emperor's subjects roared approval as he paraded past them in his "new clothes." Then a little boy observed, "Mother, he is not wearing any clothes." His mother shushed him. That has remained my favorite story since childhood.

When I entered the healing world more than three decades ago, I tried to rationally understand healing. So, as I observed healing wherever it was practiced, I would often ask questions like that little boy did about the emperor. I was seeking the truth. My eyes and my mind saw cracks in the cultural beliefs surrounding healing. But everyone hushed me, scolding me as disrespectful and heretical.

Years later, after earning my doctorate in prayer and healing research, the scolding continued. Sometimes the ridicule comes from the most unlikely sources. An unbelieving physician, who had stated earlier that healing was impossible, sternly corrected me. I had said, "Scientific research shows that healing is a process."

The physician replied, "You're wrong! Everyone knows that healing happens instantly."

I replied, "I am talking about conclusive scientific evidence that healing is rarely instant. It is a process. Are you willing to look at the evidence?"

He responded, "Who cares?" And walked away.

I do not want you to walk away from this book. As a rule you act logically and intelligently in your thinking. Should this new paradigm of healing make you feel uncomfortable in any way, think it out. Your mind may be wearing the cultural blinders that seem to have contaminated most people's responses.

WHY CARE?

Why read this book? Because you are about to embark upon one of the most exciting journeys of your life. You are about to learn a new way of looking at prayer, disease, health, wholeness, human beings, relationships, personal renewal, cultural regeneration, man, and God. Healing uses a new paradigm, a new model for looking at reality that offers more effective ways of approaching these issues. That is what new paradigms are all about: developing new models for the next step in human evolution. That is what your exciting new journey is all about.

This is one of the greatest stories ever told. Step by step the plot will thicken. We'll set forth the new scientific understanding of prayer and healing. Then, we will use this knowledge to unveil one new paradigm after another. These paradigms offer new hope and new life to you and all humanity.

It all begins with the science behind prayer and healing.

*Walter Weston,*
*April 1998*

# 1

# Characteristics of Healing Prayer

Years ago, the women of my local church formed a prayer chain to pray for the sick. Several months into its operation, the leaders noted that no one was reporting healings. I investigated.

I privately interviewed a few members of the prayer chain, and asked, "What do you do when you receive a call for healing?"

The standard answer was, "I wish the ill person the best and call the next member of the prayer chain."

I inquired, "Do you pray for healing?"

Again, the standard answer, "I would like to, but I do not know how to pray for healing."

We addressed the problem with a six-session course in healing prayer. Believing that people learn best by doing, I divided the eighty people into prayer circles of eight. As they were learning healing prayer, they were asked to share their personal needs with their prayer circle and to pray daily for each other.

A written survey at the last session confirmed the merits of what they had practiced. Seventy-five percent reported physical healings, eighty-three percent emotional healings, eighty-seven percent interpersonal healings, and ninety-five percent being filled with the presence and peace of God.

Those people in Delaware Avenue Church learned the first lesson in how God heals. You must first learn how to pray for healing. Their prayer chain developed a citywide reputation. Their prayers produced consistent, positive healing outcomes.

## The Value of Spoken Prayer

The mention of spoken prayer frightens most persons. We have privatized our prayer lives, praying alone, silently and secretly. Though two-thirds of Americans report praying daily, fewer than one percent of married couples have ever prayed aloud with a spouse for his or her needs.

There is an uneasiness about praying aloud, almost a shame and embarrassment about it. And no wonder! We have no experience in doing it. We have no opportunity to learn how. I may have the only course in America designed to teach people to pray aloud.

When churches conduct courses on healing, they take it for granted that everyone knows how to pray. Outside of organized religion, I know of no healing technique that even mentions prayer. Healers usually belittle any suggestion that they pray. This is because they do not know how to pray aloud. I, myself, remain convinced of the value of spoken healing prayer.

When I work in silent group healing, the introduction of spoken prayer dramatically increases the group's energy and success. For that reason, spoken prayer has always been heartily welcomed by those with whom I share it, for the focus and power it brings to the group effort. Regardless of the attitude of healers, prayer remains the primary means by which most of humanity seek God's presence, power, and wholeness.

In absent prayer, of course, you can pray silently. But the best way to pray for the sick is in person. To pray silently for the sick is not nearly as effective as praying aloud. In all my books, I teach people how to pray aloud. I also provide prayer models for the reader's use.

Prayers for healing are the easiest to say. They have one focus: healing. The simplest healing prayer is, "God, my son is sick and hurting. Heal him in body, mind, and spirit. Thank you. Amen."

## Eighteen Reasons for Using Spoken Prayer

1.  Spoken prayer forces the pray-er to focus intentionally upon what she or he is thinking and doing.
2.  Spoken prayer establishes an emotional and spiritual link between pray-er and healee, or a sense of unity among those gathered.
3.  A spoken prayer can express acceptance and compassion.
4.  Spoken prayer uses vocal frequencies which possess healing power.
5.  The words used in spoken prayer have meanings which program and empower healing energy.
6.  Spoken prayer can express a theology of God's love and healing. This expresses the pray-er's intentions and is God's Word for the prayer.
7.  Spoken prayer can affirm the healee's life journey, his or her hurts, fears, and struggles; his or her faith, hope, and trust; and the sacredness of his or her life.

8. Spoken prayer can acknowledge and accept brokenness, forgiveness, reconciliation, and renewal.
9. Spoken prayer is the most reliable means for attuning the pray-er to both God and the healee so that all are united as one, enhancing the effectiveness of the healing energy.
10. Spoken prayer can command healing in God's name.
11. Spoken prayer can fixate the desired healing results.
12. Spoken prayer can thank God for the healing that is taking place.
13. Spoken prayer can praise God, from whom all blessings flow.
14. Spoken prayer enhances the significance of healing touch.
15. Spoken prayer is, historically, the most powerful medium for channeling God's power and miracles.
16. Spoken prayer is the best means for building spirituality and for increasing an awareness of God's spiritual presence in family, groups, community, and nation.
17. Spoken prayer is the best means for creating healing group energy fields.
18. Spoken prayer produces a sense of God's presence, love, joy, peace, and unity among all those who use it. This is one of the most consistently blissful experiences known to humanity, resulting in a yearning for more. Our hearts are restless until they find their peace in God, and spoken prayer provides a direct path to that peace.

## The Uniqueness of Healing Prayer

Healing prayer is different from any other form of prayer. Personal prayer styles tend to be passive. Healing prayer takes on a different and far more forceful style. This is true because in healing prayer one is acting to bring the power of God into human lives. The power of God's light and love is battling with the forces of chaos, which are made known through evil and darkness. This is not a time for being timid or passive. Healing prayer uses God's power to overcome the evils of physical illness, destructive emotions, and alienated relationships. Though the basic tool is love, the battle demands a forceful style.

Most people are not familiar with the forceful style of healing prayer. When they attempt to make the necessary transition into the healing prayer style, they tend to retain the passive personal style. They remain uncomfortable with forceful prayers. This discomfort goes beyond accustomed style.

Traditionally, most people have viewed prayer as involving expressions of appreciation and the making of requests. In other words, their prayer content has always involved thanking God and asking God for specific blessings. As channels for God's power, we need not ask. The healing power is always present and available. In healing, we are called to use that power forcefully. People who are new at praying are uncomfortable with this new style of forceful prayer; but, to the experienced healer, most people's personal prayer comes through as wishy-washy.

Here are some examples. One style of prayer pleads, "God, if it is your will . . . ?" Most persons assume that we do not know the will of God for a specific person's illness. However, God created and wishes his power be used to recreate and make people well. We do not doubt that God wishes everyone to receive appropriate medical care. If healing prayer is seen as a constructive way to bring healing, then we can express it in a forceful way through our prayers.

Another way of praying humbly requests healing from God. "God, I ask you to please heal Bill." This style assumes that God is like a great heavenly computer granting some requests for healing while denying others. The scientific evidence suggests a different approach, one that recognizes that we are partners with God during the practice of healing prayer. When we unite with God for healing prayer, it inevitably results in an unlimited supply of healing energy moving through us to the person for whom we are praying.

This brings us to the forceful style of healing prayer. This involves a blessing or a command for wellness. Most religious traditions offer similar ritual blessings in a commanding style. It is usually called a blessing, but the form in which it is stated is a command in God's name.

In baptism—in my Christian tradition—we forcefully say, "John Smith, be baptized." In joining the Church, we forcefully state, "John Smith, be confirmed as a faithful member." In benedictions, we forcefully bless, "The power of God be present with you—" Believers feel comfortable with each of these styles. In a similar context, to pray forcefully, "God, use me as a channel for healing;" "God, I open myself to being a channel for healing;" "God, heal John;" "In God's name, be healed;" or "In God's name, I command the spirit of illness to depart—" makes sense.

The ongoing resistance to offering a blessing or a command for healing comes from the reluctance of most persons to accept the concept and the role of priesthood. Anytime we pray effectively, we are acting as a priest, bringing the power of God into the life of the world. The only time that God can act to bring about healing is when a person is willing to become a channel for God's healing flow. Therefore, in healing prayer, as transmitters of God's healing power, we must forcefully command, "In God's name, be healed."

## How Dependable is Spoken Prayer?

Spoken prayer is one of the most powerful spiritual tools known to humanity. It is a more powerful spiritual tool than thought, meditation, visualization, centering and silent prayer. Historically it has proven its power as the basis for religious ritual. The spoken word is the best way for humans to communicate and draw closer. The spoken word in prayer can draw upon the wisdom of sacred writings. The spoken word is the basis of divine power in all religious ritual and is superior to thought, meditation, visualization, centering, and silent prayer because of this.

Think about it. If you were given time to inspire one hundred people gathered for religious purposes, what one method would you use? Standing and thinking, silent meditation, inner visualization, inner centering, silent prayer, or using the spoken word? The spoken word transmits energy that is both information-bearing and intelligent. God's power is expressed more effectively and consistently through the spoken word than through any silent activity taking part in the brain alone.

## A Few Cultures Do Not Use Prayer

A few Asian cultures do not utilize prayer. Chinese are skilled in using Wu Chi, a secular Ineffable Life

Energy. In Taoism, it is known as the Tao—the Way or the Voice.

There is little or no religious overtone in traditional Chinese philosophy regarding Ineffable Life Energy. Taoism says that the Tao existed before Heaven and Earth, carried out the process of creation, and exists within all things and life forms.

According to traditional Chinese medicine, the sun, moon, and stars radiate energy toward the Earth in a pattern that varies in ten ways, depending upon their relative positions during the year. The Earth changes its energy state with twelve different annual patterns, affecting all life. Therefore, the state of energy and blood flow in the human body is subject to influences of the Ten Energy Interferences from Heaven, and the Twelve Energy Changes from Earth.

The quality and nature of the Ineffable (meaning inexpressible, or too sacred to be spoken) Universal Life Energy in the human being is called the spirit. The spirit of each human being exists in the universe like a droplet of water in the vast ocean of universal life energy. When the human body is formed, the power of spirit is housed in the organs, where it directs and energizes various psychological and physiological functions. The one who attunes his or her spirit with the Universe can live long in health.

The Chinese use chi to balance the life energy throughout the body for health and longevity. To do so, they utilize techniques such as herbology, massage, acupuncture (inserting needles in the energy meridians), and tai chi (a martial art). These are complex cultural techniques that can take a lifetime to master.

In conversations with a few Chinese citizens, I have found a complete indifference to both God and prayer. Their secular way of utilizing Ineffable Life Energy works.

In a similar way, Western healers with the psychic ability to see and to manipulate the human energy fields for health see no reason for using prayer. Their way of utilizing life energy works. For the rest of us, praying is an easily learned skill for utilizing God's power or life energy. It, too, works. Offering a prayer for healing is called spiritual healing.

## Naming the Illness in Prayer

Fear and denial are common responses to the medical diagnosis of an illness. A century ago, the names of certain illnesses were expressed only in a hushed, secretive whisper. Cancer was one of those illnesses whose name created shame and terror among loved ones.

Not naming the illness is an expression of fear. It gives an illness far more power than when the condition is unveiled. Medical and mental health professionals have made great progress in diminishing the fear of illness through encouraging people to name the illness, talk about it, and become knowledgeable about its nature and treatment. Clinical studies reveal that a person has a better chance of coping with an illness and marshaling his own healing resources to fight for his life when the illness is named.

By naming an illness in prayer, we are removing fear as we acknowledge the presence of the illness. We are also offering the faith and hope that there is a power in the universe that is greater than disease: the power of God to heal. This enables people to transcend their fear.

## Naming the Emotions

In enabling people to cope with a crisis, it is crucial to deal with emotions. This is also true of spoken healing prayer. During prayer, naming the emotions of everyone involved expresses compassion, creates emotional empathy and oneness between pray-er and prayee, and empowers and attunes the healing energy. To avoid the emotions, as though this will cause them to go away, is faulty, magical thinking.

## The Need to Volunteer Prayer

It is rare for anyone to request a prayer. Any clergyperson knows that requests for prayer in the hospital or home setting are rare. On the other hand, when prayer is appropriately offered, it is overwhelmingly accepted with deep appreciation! Physicians who utilize healing prayer with their patients report only fulfilling experiences.

## Healing Prayer is a Gift of Love

Healing prayer remains a gift of love that must be offered without thought of a return—a generous gift offered with the intention to heal. Without this understanding, you are likely to give up. For example, one healer became irritated with a dear friend vowing never again to offer her healing. During four distinct health crises, he had volunteered healing to her, resulting in the alleviation of the symptoms in her painfully arthritic knees, an arthritic shoulder, and hip and knee damage incurred in a fall. During the current health crisis, she had told him, "I do not think your previous efforts were the reason I was healed." This produced his "never again" vow.

Like many others, this woman had great difficulty acknowledging the source of her seemingly impossible healing results. In order to allow herself to receive further assistance, she was impelled to make the illogical denial: a move based on the limitations of her conventional belief system.

This type of response is maddening to most healers, and is likely to continue to be an inhibiting factor for all those who offer healing prayer. Practitioners of healing must realize that, while their process is an effective and practical means for caring about people, it is different from others in that one's successful efforts may seldom be satisfactorily acknowledged, let alone appreciated.

## Guidelines for Offering Healing Prayer

Whether volunteered or requested, here are some guidelines for offering spoken prayer. Begin the transaction in a private place. Most will welcome your offer if it is made in private.

Offer the prayer privately. People are often uncomfortable about praying in public, although there are exceptions. Prayer can be offered by a family member within a family setting, or by a friend among a group of close friends.

Ask, "May I *pray* with you?" Never ask, "May I pray *for* you?" Many people will experience the latter request as demeaning.

Approach people as equals. Never imply that you have a better link to God or goodness than someone else.

Do not fear offering an unexpected prayer for healing. Such unexpected opportunities often produce rewarding results, even with someone you have just met.

## The Role of Faith and Belief in Healing

Of all the issues surrounding healing prayer, the importance of faith and belief during the healing encounter has been the most troubling for me. The public overwhelmingly believes that one must have great faith in God in order to be healed. This has been hammered into our minds by one television faith-healer after another. This belief, this requirement about faith, has then been repeatedly stated by the public to the extent that it has unfortunately become "a Law of Divine Healing."

Nothing antagonizes people more than my questioning the truth of this belief, but nothing hampers healing efforts more than this belief. This belief causes countless people to feel that God cannot heal them because they do not have enough faith, whatever that might mean. In many minds, faith implies being perfect before God. Few people view themselves to be godly enough, good enough, worthy enough, or faithful enough to be healed. Consequently, this belief has become the major obstacle hindering healing results.

In a similar manner, this belief has also become the major obstacle to people practicing touch-healing prayer. They do not view themselves to be godly enough, good enough, worthy enough, or faithful enough to offer touch-healing prayer. The truth is that the only qualification for offering healing prayer is a loving concern. The only qualifications for being healed are the desire to become well and a trust in healing prayer.

What is the true role of faith and belief in healing? There is no evidence that a pure faith in God alone produces any healing results. This type of faith can be used as a denial of the seriousness of one's condition.

However, the certain belief that one cannot be healed, for whatever reasons, greatly hampers healing efforts. And a sense of personal inadequacy for the task hampers the practice and effectiveness of healing prayer.

My dilemma as an author, researcher, and practitioner lies within myself. I grew up in the Christian Church. Since early childhood, I have been a believer. I have always prayed and felt God's presence during prayer. I have always felt close to God. His presence has always lived within me, transforming, guiding, and sustaining me.

In addition, I am an optimist, an idealist, a dreamer. I believe that all things are possible. I have known many peak experiences of God. I have observed and participated in many encounters that could be considered divine miracles. Therefore, I would have to consider myself to be one who lives with a firm faith in God. That is also my handicap in addressing the issues of faith and belief in healing. My handicap is in not understanding what is going on within people who have not shared a similar faith journey. It is from this perspective that we will explore the role of faith and belief in healing.

Let's first explore the belief that one must have faith in order to be healed. For me, faith in this context means a faith that one will be healed. Faith has also meant believing in what a particular faith-healing evangelist says. Both these images need to be rejected. Faith is a factor in healing but only if one takes some action on the basis of faith.

Dr. Herbert Benson's research indicates that having faith that one's actions will produce healing, works. This is a result of the placebo effect. This includes faith in a physician, a medication, a medical procedure, a healer, a healing process, a prayer, meditation, a special diet, or exercise. This type of faith opens one to the possibility of healing.

This type of faith is identical to that expressed by Dr. Bernie Siegel's "exceptional cancer patients," who recover from terminal cancer because they have faith that a change in lifestyle will make them well. In each instance, faith is a belief that one will get well through a specific type of action or practice. This type of faith can reprogram the body's energy field into the perfect blueprint, and elevate the level of subtle energies.

In another context, faith can be defined as "a trust in." In this context, a trust in the person offering healing is faith. A trust that healing prayer works is also faith. This type of faith opens one's energy fields to the healing flow, a crucial factor.

Belief that a specific healing approach works is important. Filipino healers report the need to spend extra time with foreign clients in order to deal with their belief systems. They must persuade clients that their healing activity causes no harm and actually works. Most persons either do not believe in healing, or are uncomfortable with the healing styles being practiced. These are barriers to the healing process because they block the flow of healing energy.

Another factor more important than faith in the healing encounter is attuning the healing flow. Attuning is simply accomplished through compassion and relationship: a oneness between the healer, the healee and God.

I think that often the issue of faith is a tiresome excuse for why the healer failed in his or her efforts to produce healing. Rather than looking within himself, the healer blames the ill for not getting well. I am not comfortable with this. As a professional healer, I have a responsibility to my client to use any number of techniques to open them to healing. These techniques include building relationship and trust, explaining the scientific data, caring for them, and opening their being to the flow with my hands.

This brings us to the beliefs of the pray-er. I see the beliefs of the pray-er as far more significant factors than the beliefs of the healee. The pray-er needs to believe in the sacredness of each person, in a God who heals, and in himself as a channel for healing. It helps when the healee trusts or believes that this particular person can be a channel for healing. Yet, experience has taught me that skeptical healees are more likely to be healed than believers. It is rare for cynics to be healed. Assurance that the healing process is taking place is a part of belief.

If an ill person believes he is not going to get better or is going to die, that belief will likely negate any effects of prayer. God's healing love energy intelligently produces healing, but it also respects free will. Any inner programming or script about the course of the illness is an important factor.

## Barriers to the Use of Prayers for Healing

We have seen that the capacity for prayer to produce physical healing has, traditionally, been one for which the general public has shown little understanding or support. Yet, public surveys report that the vast majority of people pray. During a medical crisis, it could be expected that most of those pray-ers would offer a prayer for physical healing. Thus, a majority of human beings have prayed for a physical healing.

With such actions affirming the belief in the power of God to heal, it would be logical to conclude that the public believes in healing prayer. The public, however, claims not to believe. Here we encounter one of the great social mysteries of our day, and the number one barrier to the effectiveness of healing prayer. People tend to believe that prayer heals only under certain limited circumstances: specifically, during a medical emergency.

During a life-threatening medical emergency, most persons will pray. Fearing the death of a loved one, they become open to miracles—any kind of miracle that will work. This miracle-readiness, which involves faith and hope, all but disappears after the medical emergency is resolved. If a healing miracle should occur while they pray in a state of miracle-readiness, few persons will talk about it afterwards—even privately with loved ones.

Once the medical emergency has passed, the survivor's loved ones, no longer in a state of extreme fear, seldom continue their prayers. If the ill one continues to live with a chronic or life-threatening illness—heart disease, cancer, stroke, diabetes, or emphysema—their loved ones tend to stop praying for healing.

I think that people are unable to make the connection between their prayers for God to rescue a loved one during a medical emergency and healing prayer. They did not observe that what they had offered was actually healing prayer. They had merely prayed for God to rescue a loved one. Therefore, they could not take the next step by continuing their healing prayers afterwards.

27

## The Ill Maintain a State of Miracle-Readiness

Usually, only the one who is ill maintains the needed state of miracle-readiness in which prayers for healing remain an effective option. Following the initial medical crisis, the ill continue to live in a condition of fear. This may produce the survival response, a state of faith, hope, and miracle-readiness based upon the belief that God will heal them.

Even today, upon learning that I practice healing prayers with the ill, the majority of those I meet register strong emotions of anger, fear, suspicion, shame, embarrassment, and rejection. You, too, must be prepared to face public opposition to your plans to pray for healing or self-healing.

The first barrier, therefore, to your pursuit of prayer as a healing technique is public opinion, as seen above.

The second barrier to your resolve involves your potential resistance to setting aside your present understanding, and adapting to a new perspective based upon objective research findings. Some of these findings may contradict what you have believed. You will be traveling on unfamiliar ground. The research data is designed to provide a new road map for your own understanding. The results will be the most convincing evidence you will need.

A third barrier—and probably the greatest of all—may be your belief that others are more qualified than you to offer prayers for healing. The truth is that all persons have the inborn potential to produce effective prayer results. Much of this barrier arises from the human inability to accept the role of a priest who acts for God. As a pray-er, you are acting as a priest bringing the power of God into the life of the world. Throughout history, humans have struggled with this identity of priesthood. Be aware that serving in the priestly role of pray-er has nothing to do with your goodness, worthiness, religiousness, age, education, or any other status. It is based solely upon your capacity to express love, and to take the intentional action of praying.

A fourth barrier is your lack of knowledge and experience in prayer. You may feel awkward at first. Most new endeavors require a practice time in order to become competent.

A fifth barrier is your image of how God works. Since earliest times, people have sensed that there was a power in the universe greater than themselves; the power they called God. That awareness of God is known as "spirituality." In other words, humanity has always possessed a spiritual nature or awareness. This sensing of God has always led to religious beliefs: an attempt to explain the universe in terms of how God works, and an attempt to tell humanity how to live life with God.

God created and recreates to make all things new. But in human affairs, God does not do this magically. God seldom intervenes in human affairs unless people ask for help. Much of the creative power of God at work is due to the actions of people who pray. The whole field of spiritual healing is united in the belief that a human being inevitably serves as the bridge between God and healing results. Prayer is a significant means by which God continues to create and to make all things new.

A sixth barrier involves belief. Doubt about the healing process is almost universal. The inner question is always, "Is anything really happening?" We all want something dramatic and immediate as a sign of what is quietly occurring within. Healing prayer remains a process that takes place over a time. Believe in the process. Through prayer, God is helping people get well.

A pleasant surprise awaits you. As you journey on your path of prayer for wholeness, you will be blessed far beyond what you had ever hoped. The powerful presence of God makes prayer encounters joyous and rewarding moments. Much of humanity is longing for both personal wholeness and spirituality. This book is committed to fulfilling your deepest spiritual yearnings. In the midst of this prayer journey, you will come to a deeper appreciation of the psalmist who declared, "Our hearts are restless until they find their peace in God."

# 2

# What Is Man?

As a child, God filled me with his Love and Life. It was in the Christian faith tradition. I was nine when I accepted Jesus Christ into my life. I was filled with spiritual bliss, the most beautiful experience I would ever know. It was love at first sight. I knew then that I always wanted to be filled with God's love and serve him.

I spent my tenth year reading the Bible. Every afternoon after school, I went to my bedroom and secretly read it until dinnertime. In those moments, God presence was near. Yet, I discovered spiritual bliss to be so fleeting. It would never last long enough. That became my quest: for God to live within me all the time.

This faith journey, or spiritual quest, was rocky. There were so many dead ends. I was looking for my sacred lover. It was like the search for Tennyson's Holy Grail. Every path turned to dust, to emptiness.

"O God, I have tasted the sweetness of your sacred lips. I have been intoxicated with the bliss of your touch. I yearn to be joined with your Love and Life forever.

"O God, teach me the secret of your joyous ongoing presence. Teach me how to have you within me every moment of my life. This is my quest. This is the goal of my heartrending journey.

"O God, like the Psalmist, my heart is restless until it finds its rest in Thee. I have sought you in church, in seminary, as a pastor. But, I catch only glimpses of your glory.

"O God, I have worked so hard **throughout** my quest. Will the dark night of my soul **never end?** Surprise me with the glory of your ongoing joy, love, peace, and bliss. Thank you."

## God's Surprise

It came unexpectedly, like a tornado in the night. It roared into my life near the moment of death. Its flames of glory swept away my previous life, my previous beliefs. It sent me into mental shock, in the midst of which I wept in utter joy. It filled me with a sacred bliss that changed my life forever. My quest was over, for God lives within me to this day.

It was God's surprise. It was God's blessing, an anointing in Spirit. It was God's curse, setting me upon an agonizingly painful path. It was God's joke on me—his poetic sense of humor—and He must be laughing still. Yes, be careful of what you seek because it might find you.

God's surprise occurred in 1966 on a summer's afternoon in Ohio. As a young pastor, I was visiting a parishioner in her home when I unexpectedly said, "I've got to go." I ran to my car and broke every traffic law in my three-mile drive. I ended up in the community hospital's parking lot. I did not know why I was there or what possessed me. I calmly sprinted to the hospital door.

As I entered the lobby one of my parishioners, Betty, hung up the phone and rushed into my arms. She was crying, and she said, "Thank God you're here. I have been phoning all over town for you. My husband, Alex, is dying." (I still blame Betty's love and prayers for her husband for all that was about to happen.)

I was feeling anxious as I ran through the corridors of the hospital to Alex's room. Dr. Bob was emerging from the room as I approached. Solemnly he stated, "Walt, I wouldn't give him more than half an hour to live."

Alex had had surgery for a ruptured appendix and a peritonitis infection had set in. He lay in his bed, his abdomen immensely bloated and his complexion a lifeless gray. After some pastoral care, I took his hand into mine and began offering a prayer for the dying. Almost immediately, I became spontaneously filled with God, a peak state of consciousness involving immense holiness, love, joy, and peace. Then, I felt energy descend upon my head and shoulders and flow down my arm into Alex's hand. I was sobbing in joy, tears freely flowing down my cheeks.

I continued praying throughout this experience. When I finished the five-minute prayer, Alex's eyes were wide in awe as he said, "Pastor, I felt something flow from your hand into mine."

I was still in mental shock as I looked at Alex. Then came another surprise. To my dismay, Alex was now healthy, his complexion and abdomen both normal. Then, the doctor returned and discovered that Alex's three-day-old surgical wound was completely healed and exclaimed, "Walt, this is impossible. This is impossible."

I have practiced this impossibility ever since.

## Impossible Bliss

Yes, the healing impressed me. I had not believed in healing nor did I have any knowledge of it. But, that is another story.

What really got to me was the impossible holy bliss that accompanied the healing. This was the fulfillment of my spiritual quest. I was troubled by the healing but joyous about the spiritual bliss.

I soon discovered that I entered a state of spiritual bliss during every healing encounter. This wonderful bliss would last a day or two. During this time, I was filled with my soul's yearning—God's glorious love, joy, peace, and bliss. It is within me as I write these words.

I suspect this spiritual bliss is the reason that I have been obsessed since that day with discovering everything there is to know about healing. God's surprise was not only my anointing to heal, it was also discovering the possibility of ongoing spiritual bliss.

## What is Man?

This first healing experience began changing my world-view and beliefs. It began changing my concept of the nature of man. What is a human being?

I had held the world-view of medical science. Human beings are biological in nature: flesh and blood.

I also held the biblical view. Humans are body, mind, and spirit. I took this to mean that we are physical, mental, emotional, and spiritual beings. I had never given much thought to what that might mean in practical terms. The book of Genesis states that we were created in the image of God. A psalmist said we were created a little lower than the angels, who have no physical bodies.

The Apostle Paul knew we had more than a physical body; he said we each also had a spiritual body. This spiritual body survives physical death.

As I lived with this abiding spiritual bliss, new experiences were happening within my physical body. No scientific or scriptural wisdom answered my new questions about what was happening within me.

I was constantly feeling this enormous energy just below my navel and in my diaphragm area. My family physician could offer no biological explanation for this.

During peak experiences of spiritual bliss, a bright white light often filled my mind. My ophthalmologist stated there was no optical basis for this.

When I began picking up the emotions of others, no existing models of the nature of man explained this phenomenon.

When I held the hands of the sick, I could feel an energy surge forth from my hand into theirs. Again, no existing model of man provided a rational explanation.

Time and again, the same questions arose: What within us makes these experiences possible? What is the true nature of man? Many of my readers already know the answers and where I am heading. Please be patient with me. Remember that these inner experiences began way back in 1966.

## The Impossible is Now Possible

Upon viewing that first healing, the doctor in bewilderment stated, "Walt, it is impossible! It is impossible!"

Humanity remains in awe of the impossible. So awed that humanity still responds in shame and embarrassment, fear and anger, about healing and spiritual bliss.

Terrified by people who performed the impossible, humanity burned millions of witches during a five-century period in the Middle Ages.

Today, our response is to shun healing. For thousands of years we have been conditioned to wear blinders. We unconsciously censor discussing it. We reject the naked truth. We have amnesia to forget healing encounters. We can't remember because remembering the impossible is mind-boggling and maddening.

But what if the impossible could be made routine? And what if causing the impossible, routinely, could lead to a Golden Age of health, peace, and prosperity for all humanity? What if understanding the impossible is the key to the next evolutionary step in human progress?

This is not conjecture. These possibilities arise from the science behind healing. Already the impossible can be made routinely possible, but we have a roadblock. This roadblock is our current cultural understanding of the nature of man as merely physical matter. Remove this roadblock, and human shame, embarrassment, fear, and anger toward the impossible will slowly die.

Our present understanding of the nature of man is incomplete. This incompleteness stops us from taking the impossible seriously; it hinders our ability to understand healing and its immense potential; and, it prevents us from using healing technology to transform humanity and all life on Earth.

Come and join me in my hope of making the Earth a much, much better place to live. Explore with me the new paradigm of what it means to be human.

## 3

# What It Means to Be Human

What if we discovered a new way of making people whole in body, mind, and spirit? What if this way merely used a new paradigm, a new model, of what it means to be human?

What if we could cure depression without the use of psychotherapy or medications? And do this in less than an hour?

What if we could restore any dysfunctional marriage without counseling? And do this in a few hours?

What if we could quickly remove the emotional trauma of the victims of physical, emotional and sexual abuse? And do this in just one hour?

What if we could cure cancer without surgery, radiation or therapy? And the patient would be cancer free within four months?

What if we could cure a criminal-hardened juvenile delinquent of his destructive values and behavior? And what if we could do this with only twenty hours of work?

What if we could go into a former war zone, like Bosnia, and permanently remove the hatred, fear, distrust, and hurts of every citizen? And do this in less than a year?

All these impossible miracles become possible when we develop a new paradigm for what it means to be human.

## The Current Inaccurate Model

At present, we scientifically view man as a physical body controlled by an intelligent mind that resides in the brain. This physical model is inaccurate and incomplete because it has never satisfactorily explained the nature of emotions and how they are stored.

This physical model is inaccurate and incomplete because it has never satisfactorily explained how spiritual awareness is possible; it prevents medicine from identifying and treating the root causes of most disease; it relies upon feeding knowledge into the brain as the primary approach to human development and problem solving; it can provide no effective means for healing emotional trauma, dysfunctional relationships, antisocial behavior, or unhappiness.

Finally, this physical model is inaccurate and incomplete because it ignores the full picture of the nature of man. The physical model is only the tiny visible picture of man. Hidden from our eyes is an enormous invisible component of man. For thousands of years, humanity has known and talked about this invisible component. This component has now been scientifically measured and quantified.

Yet, humanity rejects this new objective reality in the same way it rejects the impossible in the healing miracle. In the name of science and respectability, it denounces this new objective reality by putting evil labels upon it or by dismissing or ignoring it.

This is modern, cultural conformity which rejects the potential next step in human evolution. These are powerful, existing cultural institutions protecting the status quo to assure their future viability. This is ignorance blocking the path leading toward a possible Golden Age for all humanity.

## Ancient Wisdom—Modern Paradigm

In Bill Moyers' PBS special, "Healing and the Mind," chi, the vital energy, is used in China to heal persons through the use of the ancient healing arts of acupuncture, herbology, tai chi, and qigong. Moyers states that these, "Defy all the biophysical laws of the West."

The ancient Chinese healing arts work because the Chinese define the nature of man in a more complete way. Man is not just physical. He is given life through inner energy meridians. The goal of all these ancient Chinese medical approaches is to make the meridian system healthy by filling it with chi, or vital energy. This vital energy causes health in the physical body.

The Chinese chi has no religious roots in the Western sense. The Chinese view the chi as a secular vital energy that fills the universe, and not as God's Spirit. Yet, one cannot help but compare their vital energy to the sacred power of God's Spirit and the meridian system to the religious concept of the soul or spirit in humans.

In ancient India, mystics intuitively detected a different human energy system. It was composed of four energy fields which encompassed the body and seven major energy centers. Each energy field had a specific function in regulating the physical body, the emotions, the mind, and the spiritual. At physical death, the biological energy body was sloughed off, leaving the emotional, mental, and spiritual energy fields intact to continue life on the other side.

Unfortunately, the ancient Western religious traditions make no reference to the human body possessing energy fields. The Bible defines man only as a physical body. In the Jewish, Islamic, and Christian Old Testament, the word soul is used 755 times, but here soul means only the human person, life, or vitality. The general meaning of soul in the Bible is in reference to the physical body of man. The soul and the spirit are always an integral part of the physical body, the whole, and never stand alone, even in physical death. After death, the biblical viewpoint is that man is resurrected in a physical body, not a spiritual body. Only the Apostle Paul mentions, and only once, that humans have both physical and spiritual bodies.

Yet, by the Middle Ages, popular Western culture had borrowed from ancient Greek thought the concept of a soul (spiritual essence) that is separate from the physical body. Twenty-five centuries ago, the Greek philosopher, Socrates, stated that the body could not be healed without the soul (or spiritual essence) also being healed. This is the basis of today's holistic medicine.

Today, most Westerners believe that human beings possess a soul or spiritual essence that separates from the body and survives physical death. But, we have not seen another logical implication of this. If we have a soul or spiritual essence that survives death, then it also must be present before death. This soul or spiritual essence is present within us throughout life. It permits us to have

40

religious experiences and feel emotions and be physically healed using prayer and touch.

Scientists can now explore our spiritual essence. But because science is religiously neutral and can only identify and measure energy, life energy scientists refer to our spiritual essence as energy and explore the human energy fields that house our spiritual essence. In this new science of life energy, humans are both physical and spiritual (or energy) beings.

Yet, all of our educational, biological, physiological, and medical disciplines still state that the nature of man is entirely physical. As stated before, this physical model is inaccurate and incomplete because it ignores the full picture of the nature of man. The physical model is only the visible picture. Hidden from our eyes is an invisible component of man. For thousands of years, humanity has known and talked about this invisible component. This component has now been scientifically measured and quantified. These are the human energy systems of China, India, and Japan.

Most Westerners know humans are more than biological mechanisms, but we have failed to understand the immense significance of this truth. No United States university or government research laboratory conducts research in this area. We have ignored the spiritual essence of what most of us already know exists inside each human being. In doing so, we have missed one of humankind's great opportunities to resolve the many human issues facing humanity.

### Unreported Story

This does not mean no research has been conducted on human energy fields. During the past forty years, there have been more than a thousand unfunded scientific studies performed in order to prove the objective existence of healing phenomena. Some of this research has mapped out the human energy fields while others hint of the immense benefit of the existence of human energy fields for all humanity.

This is an unreported story. After all, we wear blinders when it comes to healing. Healing is the most misunderstood, unbelieved, ridiculed, rejected subject of our culture today. The mass media has ignored this research. After all, who cares?

Now is the time to care. This book reports on the science behind prayer and healing. In doing so, it makes the impossible possible. It sets the stage for the possible next evolutionary step for all humanity. It provides answers for many of the unresolved human issues of our day. It provides glimpses of a possible Golden Age of health, prosperity, and peace for all humanity.

Humans are biophysical beings possessing a measurable spiritual essence or energy fields. This is a new scientific and religious paradigm for the nature of man. This paradigm is the basis for the dozens of other paradigms you will be reading about in this book. This is the science behind healing, but it is also a wonderful gift to all humanity.

# 4

# Healing Prayer and Holistic Medicine

Eastern healing approaches fascinate Western medicine and the American public. This fascination began when the West first learned of acupuncture's amazing outcomes and the media reported it. This was during President Nixon's visit to China more than two decades ago. Since then, the West has been introduced to dozens of Eastern healing approaches, including tai chi, qigong, and oriental herbs.

As a Western healer, I welcomed this fascination with Eastern healing approaches. I thought that some of it would rub off and make Western healing approaches more attractive. I was mistaken. Instead, the Eastern healing approaches began to dominate the West, pushing Western healing approaches even further into obscurity.

When holistic healing centers began opening, those focusing upon Eastern approaches received the most publicity. When hospitals began opening holistic healing centers, they, too, adopted the Eastern model and purposely excluded Western healing approaches as unmarketable or inferior.

The reasons for excluding Western healing approaches from holistic centers are many and have their practical merits. Some of those reasons are given here.

The mass media has played a role. The dramatic outcomes of Eastern healing approaches have been hyped in the media, while the dramatic outcomes of Western healing approaches have been ignored.

Eastern healing approaches are considered secular, while Western healing approaches tend to arise from religious beliefs. Our secular medical community feels much more comfortable with secular approaches than those deriving from Western religion. After all, religion is religious, partisan, and self-serving while secular is non-religious and thus more altruistically trustable.

Eastern healing approaches boast a scientific basis while the scientific basis of Western healing approaches remains largely unknown. This book provides that missing scientific approach.

Eastern healing approaches do not use the word "healing." Healing is a taboo word in the West. A deep aversion exists for the word, healing. In actuality, all Eastern approaches are offering healing. Instead of the word healing, they use the word "holistic." They operate holistic centers, not healing centers.

Eastern healing approaches do not use prayer. Outside of a religious setting, the use of prayer has become a taboo in the West. Most Eastern-approach health care professionals laugh in ridicule at the idea of using prayer in holistic medical centers.

The result of all this is that American holistic medicine is presently dominated by the Eastern healing traditions of Asian cultures. Also represented in holistic medicine are new American secular healing approaches like Reiki, Therapeutic Touch and Barbara Ann Brennan's Healing Approach.

They all produce outcomes that conventional Western medicine cannot. I respect the validity of what they offer. I have learned to practice some of these healing disciplines. They work as well as healing using prayer and touch. Yet, Western healing approaches can do the same things, and may even go a step further in the outcomes of healing.

## What Holistic Medicine Really Is

Holistic medicine is not actually holistic in the Western sense. Most holistic medicine is healing, as in healing prayer. Its scientifically correct name is "energy medicine." That is also the correct scientific name for the use of prayer for healing.

Energy medicine is based upon the spiritual nature of man. In Eastern cultures, this spiritual nature is clarified by the presence of human energy fields which contain our spiritual essence. Eastern healing approaches work by transmitting a subtle energy that heals the human energy fields. The human energy fields then restore the health of the physical body. The same is true of Western healing approaches.

This recognition of the human energy fields completes our understanding of the nature of man as a whole person with both a biophysical and energy nature. Therefore, the term holistic medicine.

In contrast, conventional medicine works only on a simple biophysical model of man which is an incomplete and inaccurate model. It does not recognize the whole extent of man's nature. It is, therefore, not holistic.

## The Western Meaning of Holistic

In the Western conventional medical tradition, holistic means treating the whole person. Three generations ago, the first applications of holistic medicine were a medical hospital model that added mental health, pastoral care, and social services to hospital care. To become healthy, one must treat the whole person—body, mind, spirit, and relationships.

This was an immense advancement in health care. It is still the core model of holistic health care in hospitals today. It remains a competent working model that must not be displaced by a relatively one-dimensional model called holistic medicine. Holistic medicine is not holistic in the above sense of holistic.

## Undermining Western Cultural Values

America has exported much of its culture to the entire global village. Our movies, satellite TV shows, and rock music influence the whole global culture. Western medical and economic models dominate our planet. Middle class couples in many nations imitate Western marriage and family styles.

So, should we complain if the present secular holistic healing model might be undermining our cultural values? After all, in global competition, it is the survival of the most workable approach that usually dominates. How might our present holistic healing models undermine our traditional cultural values?

## They are Secular Holistic Healing Models

China is one of the few nations that has no ancient religious tradition. China remains secular in its world-view. Chi, their subtle healing energy, is a secular force, like gravity, that permeates Earth.

The dominance of these secular models is no accident. Thanks to the mass media, this secular model is the only one known by health care professionals and the American public. The use of the secular makes everyone comfortable.

In contrast, the Western holistic approaches have been rooted in Western religious traditions for centuries. But these Western religious holistic models find increasing distrust in public settings outside a religious context, because central to these models is the use of prayer.

In America, prayer is primarily practiced in private, mostly by believers within their families or religious communities. The Christian tradition is accepted by 85% of Americans. People in this religious tradition reject healing prayer and healing ministries almost unanimously. They may believe God heals, but do not practice touch-healing prayer. This is because of a deep shame and embarrassment about it, along with fear and anger. They have generally rejected the scientific data on healing. Many have dismissed holistic healing as evil or New Age. Thus, the secular model for holistic healing really had little competition, because the religious community expressed little interest in it.

## Secular Models Are in the Psychic Healing Tradition

The newly developed Western healing models which are used in American holistic centers are also secular.

47

They have emerged from the Western psychic healing tradition rather than the Western spiritual healing tradition.

In his classic book "The Medium, the Mystic, and the Physicist," psychologist Lawrence LeShan identifies two basic approaches to healing. In Type One Healing, there is a spiritual oneness or empathy between the healer, healee, and God that produces a sacred healing flow from the healer's hands, usually through the use of prayer. In Type Two Healing, the healer perceives a pattern of energy between his palms—a flow of energy. Nothing exists for this healer but his hands. Both types share two common behaviors. They enter an altered state of consciousness, and are focused on the healee by love and caring.

LeShan also identified three distinct groups of healers. Spiritual healers, the largest group, describe their work as prayer and believe their success is due to the intervention of God. This is practiced in most religions and cultures.

Spirit healers believe that spirits or spirit guides do the healing after the healer has set up a linkage between the spirits and the healee. This is primarily practiced in England, Brazil, the Philippines, and in spiritualism.

Psychic healers believe they are originators and transmitters of some form of energy that has healing effects. The healer has a flow of healing energy and concentrates on the healing flow entering the healee through his hands. Worldwide, they have traditionally been the minority in healing work, perhaps due to the needed psychic ability. The most competent psychic healers have clairvoyant abilities that enable them to see or feel subtle energy and

human energy field interactions. Spiritual and spirit healers may also, but this is not required to be competent.

## Comparison of Energy Healing and Spiritual Healing

| *Energy Healing* | *Spiritual Healing* |
|---|---|
| 1. Healer motivated by loving compassion | 1. Healer motivated by loving compassion |
| 2. Healer enters altered state of consciousness—centering | 2. Healer enters altered state of consciousness—prayer |
| 3. Healer emits the eight-megahertz healing frequency | 3. Healer emits the eight-megahertz healing frequency |
| 4. Healer has intuitive abilities to sense and manipulate the human energy fields | 4. Healer has the ability to pray aloud with healee while touching the physical body |
| 5. Healer manipulates human energy fields with his mind and hands, removing energy blocks and improving energy flow without touching the physical body | 5. Healer physically touches the body with his hands, transmitting a healing energy that freely flows throughout the body to wherever it is most needed |
| 6. Healing is a process that increases the healing rate and may require repeated sessions | 6. Healing is a process that increases the healing rate and may require repeated sessions |

All healers believe that God is the healer. The evidence indicates that healers in all three groups are transmitting a healing energy at the same frequency, and their
results are identical.

Psychic healers dominate American holistic centers. They are viewed as more competent because of their energy field sensitivity. All healing owes them a debt of gratitude because of their clairvoyant descriptions of human energy field interactions. They come through as secular, even though they are just as spiritual as other types of healers. All healers experience God and know the spiritual bliss accompanying healing encounters.

## A Secular Image Discredits the Power of God

By not using a religious or spiritual model, the secular holistic model discredits the practical value of religion and the power of God. In the Western religious tradition, healing is the most powerful expression of God's power. Healing transforms, renews, and empowers people. This is the central belief and proclamation of what God does in the Western religious tradition. By removing the sacred from holistic centers, we are destroying the image of God in American public life.

The secular image in holistic models is discrediting God's Power in America's major industry: health care. Health care was the last stronghold of religion in America's public sector. It could destroy the legitimacy of organized religion in the coming generation, and even threaten its continuing existence.

## The Secular Approach Hampers Experiencing God

Most Americans are on a spiritual journey. They are continually seeking to revel in firsthand experiences of God. Only when healing is practiced in a sacred context do people have the opportunity to know one of the most powerful means for having firsthand experiences of God. Profound experiences of God are a common side effect of healing prayer.

Also, I have found that most people suffering from a debilitating or life-threatening illness begin a spiritual journey. Often, this provides them with the most fulfilling moments with God that they have ever known. Linking their healing to God and the spiritual would continue to validate their new faith journey.

## The Secular Holistic Model has a Theology

Though not outwardly religious or even mentioning God, the American secular holistic model has a theology. This theology is a combination of Eastern religious philosophy and New Age thought. Holistic health care professionals may not even be aware of this. It is woven into the fabric of their healing training.

These beliefs undermine America's heritage by slowly altering the basic beliefs of our Founding Fathers and Western religious traditions. These beliefs are not necessary for successful healing outcomes. Americans are slowly being religiously brainwashed without knowing it. This theological relearning process is a subtle but powerful evangelistic influence throughout America.

## The Secular Holistic Model and Disease Cause

The secular holistic model is undermining the Western medical understanding of disease. Some of this new understanding of disease is beneficial and long needed. Humans do have a spiritual nature that is expressed in their energy fields. Body tissue does possess memory of trauma and disease. Disease does manifest itself in conscious energy entities: spirits of disease. Emotional pain is the major cause of disease.

But many other beliefs are invalid and untrue. This undermines the professional work of Western medical researchers, psychologists and sociologists, as well as the public's understanding of disease and its causes.

## The Secular Model Undermines Holistic Concepts

The secular model does not offer a supportive community, relational healing, or religious nourishment for the ill. These are already present values in the Western holistic health model.

## Finally, It Alienates Many Americans

Many of the above factors alienate many Americans. This denies them access to holistic health care services. It denies them the best opportunity they might have to become well.

Most Americans would feel more comfortable in a Western holistic healing model, and it is not too late to develop one. Yes, it would be grounded in healing prayer and touch. After all, prayer is used by all Western religious traditions. The prayers would have to be non-sectarian, but that is no problem. Prayers for healing take on a universal form that transcend theological differences.

Such a model would be based upon a scientific understanding of healing, rather than a theological model. Science is theologically neutral, but healing studies draw an accurate picture of healing which makes acceptable theological sense to all religions.

That is what this book is all about— how prayer heals. As you learn how prayer heals, you will also be introduced to a possible Western spiritual holistic healing model.

# 5

# The Human Energy Field Paradigm

A human energy field model is a must for any scientific basis in Western holistic medicine. This is a new paradigm for Western healing using prayer and touch. This human energy field model clearly explains how prayer works.

It makes the impossible appear possible. It explains religious miracles, yet makes them no less amazing or surprising. It opens the door to your acceptance of unfamiliar healing miracles.

For instance, if every emotion you have ever known is stored as knowledge in a human energy field, rather than in the physical brain, what is the significance of this paradigm?

It is extremely significant when you have a means for removing painful memories from this energy field. This means that every emotional trauma, from the time of your conception to the moment of your death, could be removed. Rather than being impaired by the accumulation of the emotional pain in your life, you would become emotionally peaceful. This frees you from the emotional obstacles that can trouble you and hinder your potential throughout a lifetime.

The only word that properly describes the implications of this comes from the mouth of the child-like Mary Poppins, supercalifragilisticexpialadosis.

Imagine an emotionally wounded child being freed to laugh, to play, to learn, and to grow normally—able to develop his full potential.

Imagine the victim of violence being released from the emotional trauma and able to resume a normal life.

Imagine a couple in a dysfunctional marriage able to put past wounds to rest, and thus capable of rebuilding their lost love, affection, and commitment.

Imagine a depressed person having her depression completely removed, and being restored to a life of happiness and satisfaction.

Imagine the implications for the mind-body connection in disease when the emotional conditions that contribute to the onset and maintenance of disease are removed.

These are a few of the hundreds of breakthroughs that are possible if we adopt a new Western paradigm for the nature of man. The complete and accurate paradigm is that man is both physical and spiritual. The spiritual body is studied by scientists as an energy body or an energy field. The existence of a human energy field turns what is currently impossible into the possible.

The science behind prayer and healing studied and defined these human energy fields. How are healing effects possible? Healing restores and strengthens the human energy fields. The healthy energy fields then cause the physical body to be healed. This explains, in large part, the miracle of healing. The science behind healing makes the miraculously impossible both rationally possible and believable.

## The Discipline of Energy Medicine

The Western fascination with Chinese energy medicine is merited. But Western observers have failed to make the connection that energy medicine is already being practiced in the West right under their noses. Though healing techniques vary, all healing approaches transmit the same quality of healing energy at the same frequency. Though Western energy medicine cannot do everything Chinese energy medicine does, it can do many things that Chinese energy medicine cannot.

All energy medical approaches seek to bring health to the human energy system, which in turn restores health to the physical body. An element of energy medicine is present in acupuncture, acupressure, homeopathy, herbs, fresh fruits and vegetables, food supplements, aromatherapy, music therapy, some massotherapy and chiropractic, physical exercise, the martial arts, tai chi, qigong, yoga, meditation, compassionate love, healing, and prayer.

For thousands of years, the Western energy medicine tradition has flourished with healing touch and prayer in their religious traditions. The new paradigm of the nature of man clarifies this. May this earn Western energy medicine more attention as well as a touch of respect.

## The Human Energy Field Paradigm

All sciences use theoretical working models. These are theories about how a phenomenon works based upon observation and intuition. Research is then conducted to confirm or to deny the elements of a working model.

Our theoretical working model about the nature of man is based upon scientific studies, practical observation, and the practice of healing. Our primary focus is a model based upon seven human energy fields or auras. Passing through them are the seven major energy centers shaped like tornado funnels.

These seven energy fields all exist in the same space in the body. This is possible because each has its own unique electromagnetic frequency, and like seven television stations, each with its own unique channel frequency, can exist in the same space. These energy fields radiate beyond the physical body, with the lowest frequency going about a quarter inch beyond the skin and the highest frequency radiating out to more than twenty-five feet from the skin.

Each energy field contains information, acts purposefully, and is essential for life. They duplicate the biological, mental, emotional, and spiritual components of human beings and interact with them.

Every human function has its counterpart in the energy fields, each at a different informational energy frequency. Emotions are stored as an energy form in the second energy field. Brain functioning exists in the third energy field as the mind. Spirituality exists in the fourth energy field. The three outer energy fields deal with higher consciousness, mature love, and sacredness. These latter three are not relevant here. The various qualities of human wholeness are present as intelligently acting energy information.

## The Physical Energy Field

At the lowest human energy field frequency is the physical energy field, the first energy field that extends just about a quarter inch beyond the skin. Here, every cell and organ of the physical body is duplicated.

The studies of Russian researchers indicate this energy field is a blueprint for the physical body. They use the analogy of a gelatin mold. Each physical organ is formed and sustained, just as hot liquid gelatin is shaped in a gelatin mold, by the energy blueprint of the energy field.

If the mold is distorted, the product of that mold will be distorted (and ill) in the same way. Energy fields shape the physical body the same way a gelatin mold shapes gelatin. They also interact with the physical body, affecting the energy blueprint.

Another way of looking at this is through the effects of a magnet upon iron shavings. A simple magnet has an energy field, invisible like the human physical body's energy fields. We know it exists because we can measure its effects as it either pulls metal objects to it or as it clings to iron objects.

The invisible energy field of the magnet takes visible shape when iron filings are placed upon paper above it. The magnet molds the iron filings into a visible pattern that makes a picture of its energy or force field. The invisible energy field of the magnet creates form just as real as the form of gelatin in a gelatin mold; or, just as real as the organic matter of the human physical body, molded by the human energy fields.

The first energy field, the energy blueprint, duplicates every cell and organ of the physical body, down to the basic cell structure. Human wholeness and health are present when each energy field is operating at healthy performance levels. When any of the seven energy fields becomes distorted or sick, the other energy fields reflect this, causing the physical body to become ill.

## The Other Energy Fields

When the second energy field—the emotional energy field—becomes distorted by painful memories and destructive emotional states, it sends that message to the other energy fields and causes illness. How do we make it whole again in order to restore physical health? If it remains distorted, no conventional or alternative medical treatment can restore health for long.

When the third energy field—the mental energy field—becomes distorted by faulty thoughts, attitudes, and beliefs, it sends those messages to the other energy fields to cause illness. How do we make it whole again in order to restore physical health?

When the fourth energy field, the spiritual energy field, becomes distorted by ineffective faith development, and then sends these messages to the other energy fields to cause illness, how do we make it whole again in order to restore physical health?

## This is a Spiritual Approach

Most people who practice holistic medicine are grounded in God. They have an active spiritual life, practicing various spiritual disciplines.

They are also creative idealists. They are visionaries who envision better ways for people to live. They are on the cutting edge in developing new holistic health care approaches. Being on the cutting edge has never been popular.

Social activists who fought for civil rights, the poor, and peace preceded them. The human potential and personal growth movement preceded them. These were past cultural cutting edges. They served their purposes and left their mark on American life.

Many holistic health care practitioners emerged from the ashes of these earlier movements. They were searching for a deeper meaning to life. They were searching for a new model for what it means to be human. They embraced the ancient truth that humans are not just physical. They grounded themselves in a spiritual journey. Out of this grew their new paradigm for the nature of man. Humans are biophysical with a spiritual nature that is rooted in the human energy fields.

They looked at conventional medicine with its physical model for humanity. They saw that this model was inaccurate and incomplete. They embraced the spiritual nature of man. They quickly accepted the spiritual model involving human energy fields. It made sense of their spiritual journeys. It offered new possibilities for successfully treating diseases that did not respond well to conventional medical care. They developed the various cutting edge disciplines of holistic medicine.

Like the early marchers in the civil rights movement, they were at first treated as troublemakers. Wellness doctor Bernie Siegel's earliest book was rejected by bookstore chains as impossible theory. You could only find this book in New Age bookstores. When sales skyrocketed, his books became mainstream bookstore bestsellers. Bernie Siegel's formerly impossible approach has now become a model for support groups with the ill.

This book is about holistic medicine or energy medicine, about the science behind healing. This book is about spiritual touch and prayer. This book is about new paradigms, new models. Because of early pioneers like Siegel, it will be stocked by the mainstream bookstores.

But will church people embrace it? Can Christians, Jews, and Muslims accept a new paradigm for the nature of man based upon a spiritual body that is described in terms of energy fields? Before answering that question, let's discuss the benefits of accepting the new paradigm.

This book will make your prayer life blossom. It will teach you how to find spiritual bliss. It will teach you to fill your home with God's love and peace. It can help your church become spiritually revived. The science behind prayer and healing presents the greatest present hope of creating the kingdom of God on this earth.

# 6

# The Science Behind
# the Power of Prayer

Jesus said, "Someone touched me; for I perceive that power has gone forth from me." (Luke 8: 46) This is one of the most instructional verses in scriptures. Jesus is describing the power emitted during healing encounters. Everyone on a prayer journey comes to know the sacred power of God filling him or her with holiness, love, joy, and peace. This is the sacred power of prayer.

Everyone involved in healing is aware of the power of God in the midst of a healing encounter. Both the toucher and the touched feel a warm energy flowing from the toucher into the touched. It may feel like heat or like energy or both. In a group setting, the whole room often becomes uncomfortably warm with the heat that is being released during touch-healing prayer.

The toucher may also feel a pleasant combination of warmth and energy flowing throughout his or her whole body, from the top of the head to the tip of the toes. When the touched person senses a tingling throughout his body, a complete healing has usually occurred.

Most people are not analytical about what is happening. This is how the healing power of God has always felt. It is a wonderful feeling. So, just enjoy God's presence within you.

Others of us have a practical curiosity. We have sought a scientific understanding of what is happening in healing prayer and touch. And, if we investigate, we discover that there is already a scientific understanding of healing touch and what is occurring.

## Research on Healing Energy

Forty years ago, the father of healing research, biologist Bernard Grad, proposed the existence of an energy to explain the experimental effects of healing touch. Long before Grad began his research, healers had reported energy flowing from their hands into the healee. Grad observed that human beings act like electrical capacitors for healing energy. This means that healers have the ability to accumulate the energy and then release it to the healee. Aeronautical engineer and healer Ambrose Worrall observed that this energy acts like electricity in flowing from a high potential source to a person or object of lower potential. This means the healee is able to receive the energy because he is energy deprived and needs it. When a healer touches a healthy person, no energy is transmitted because there is no need for it.

Research on the healing effects of touch and prayer was first called life energies research. Now it is called subtle energy research, because the energy is light and not obvious.

As a non-scientist, I prefer to call it healing energy. This is more descriptive of what it does. I think the best theological words for it are "sacred energy," or "God's healing love energy." More on this later.

## What is the Source of the Energy?

Subtle energy scientists are comfortably silent about the source of the healing flow. They are objectively studying an energy that produces healing outcomes. Religious questions are not permitted within the realms of science.

I will always call this transmitted healing energy the power of God or God's healing flow. But the research data has dramatically changed my childhood view of how God works to heal.

Healing has little to do with faith in God. I have had successful healing outcomes with many skeptics, and even with atheists. Healing is empowered by loving compassion and intention. While healing is always a religious experience that leads me into a state of spiritual bliss, some healers do not work in a religious context. Beginning with inner centering, they work with the intention of helping the sick become well. While I always pray, many healers offer no prayer. This disclosure may be troubling for some readers.

Throughout history, the source of the healing power has been a contentious issue. The attitude has often been that if the source does not come from my trusted religious tradition, then do not accept it, because it is evil or satanic. I have received healings from many non-Christian persons. My healers were loving, compassionate persons who can be found in any culture or religion. I have successfully practiced healing with Jews, Muslims, Hindus, Native Americans, new agers, witches, agnostics, and even atheists. God is open to everyone being healed.

What about those who heal in a non-religious context? Healing is first and foremost empowered by loving concern. Anytime we love and intend to offer healing, the power of God works through us. No other qualification is necessary. God works through anyone who offers love. A scriptural verse from my own religious tradition explains this: "God is love, and those who abide in love abide in God, and God abides in them." (I John 4:16)

Objective research reports that almost all cultures and religions believe that God heals. People in most cultures and religions pray. Natural healers are found in every culture and religion. These facts may be unsettling, yet they remain true.

The Chinese experience is also unsettling for religious people. For thousands of years, China has been a secular society. Yet, they practice healing. They do this through what they believe is a secular energy, chi, which permeates the universe. Religious people cannot help but compare chi with their God who permeates the universe. From my religious perspective, the Chinese have discovered God in their chi energy but their secular society has developed no vocabulary nor thought pattern that can make this sacred connection.

## How Healing Works

The last chapter introduced the new paradigm that humans possess a spiritual nature. This spiritual nature is possible because of the existence of human energy fields in which their spiritual nature resides. This energy is able to influence all living organisms because all living organisms have energy fields that receive the healing energy and utilize it effectively.

Healing through prayer and touch imparts an energy into the human energy field. This energy is the power of God, but for research purposes it is known as life energy or subtle energy. It is measurable at a specific electromagnetic frequency.

This energy repairs and recharges the human energy fields, or spiritual nature. The human energy fields then restore or heal the physical body. This produces health in people.

A religious explanation states that in healing prayer and touch, God and a human being are working in partnership to transmit God's healing power or energy. Anytime humans turn to another in a caring way, they can intentionally and naturally accumulate, attune and transmit healing energy.

In absent prayer, the healing message is sent on an electromagnetic carrier beam that contains the energy within the carrier beam itself. Clairvoyants report that this beam is being emitted from the heart area—not from the brain—as a white laser-like beam of light.

My own scientific definition of healing is this: Healing is that which brings healing to the body, mind, and spirit through its influence upon the energy fields (or spiritual body), and the consciousness of a living organism.

## Evidence for the Existence of a Healing Energy

This is a scientific way of looking at God's healing power. Science is studying a subtle energy that produces healing outcomes.

### 1. Infra-red shows changes in healer-charged water

A 1986 Mobius Society study examined the infra-red absorption spectra of water placed in sealed vials and treated by fourteen different healers. Statistically significant variation in the pattern of an infra-red spectrophotometric analysis was observed between healer-treated water versus controlled water samples. The changes were attributed to alterations in the chemical bond characteristics between the oxygen and hydrogen atoms in the water molecule. An energy had to be emitted to produce the changes.

### 2. Healer-charged bottled water

Bernard Grad had healer Oskar Estebany hold bottled water while emitting energy with his hands. The water was then used for his Wounded Barley Seed Experiment. The healer-treated water caused barley seeds wounded by a one percent saline solution to grow faster than control plants watered with an untreated one percent saline solution.

Robert Miller discovered similar effects in healer-treated water while working as a research chemist in Atlanta, Georgia. Charging of the bottled water with healing energy is the only explanation that accounts for the increased plant growth.

Grad stored healer-treated water adjacent to other bottled water for two years. It did not decrease in healing strength and did not contaminate the adjacent bottled water.

### 3. Healer-charged cotton and wool

In Grad's, The Healing of Induced Goiters in Mice Experiment, mice were deprived of iodine and fed a goitrogen, thiouracil, to induce goiters. Two healers treated the experimental group of mice through touch-healing, preventing goiters from developing, while the control group developed goiters.

In a second study, healer Estebany imparted healing energy into cotton and wool cuttings that were placed in mouse cages, producing results identical to touch-healing. In addition to proving that healer-treated cotton and wool produce a healing effect, this study also demonstrated that healing energy can prevent an anticipated disease from occurring.

### 4. Healer-charged surgical gauze.

Dr. Dolores Krieger (Therapeutic Touch) reports similar healing results with healer-treated surgical gauze. Applied as a wound dressing, it resulted in a statistically faster rate of healing.

### 5. SQUID-measured frequency of healers' emissions

Physicist John Zimmerman (Brain/ Mind Bulletin) while at the University of Colorado School of Medicine, Denver, used a Superconducting Quantum Interference Device (SQUID), cooled to near absolute zero. He conducted 7 investigations of healers practicing touch-healing, with healees, and observed discernible changes in the amplitude and frequency (7.8 hertz) of the biomagnetic fields detected by the SQUID. The healers emitted a steady 7.8 hertz frequency from the hands even when not healing. A control group of non-healers produced no changes. In an eigth investigation, the signal recorded near the healer's hands was larger during the healing than when he moved his hands towards the SQUID.

### 6. Infra-red shows energy emerging from palms and fingers

Zimmerman also examined infra-red film photographs of healers' hands showing an energy emerging from the palms and finger pads.

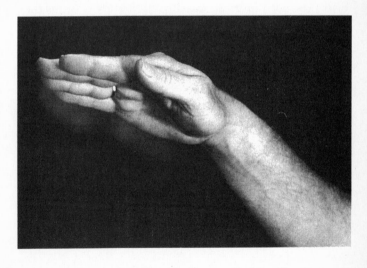

*When you intend to heal, your hand will emit
an eight-hertz frequency of energy
from the palms and finger pads*

### 7. Healers can produce more than 200 volts of energy

Researchers (Subtle Energies) in the Copper Wall Experiments at the Menninger Clinic, Topeka, Kansas, discovered that nine healers, during meditation and absent healing, emitted between 4 volts and 222 volts of electrical energy with a median emission of 8.3 volts. Non-healer meditators produced no surges over 4 volts. The healers used Non-Contact Therapeutic Touch (NCTT). The implication here is that NCTT therapists have a different "energy structure" or a different "energy handling capability" from regular subjects.

Their new technology detected and measured electrostatic potentials and field effects in and around the bodies of meditators and NCTT therapists. The NCTT therapists produced more surges during therapy sessions than during meditation, thus, the intention to heal produced the strongest results. All NCTT therapists believed their skill could be learned by anyone.

Researchers explained that these NCTT therapists' voltage emissions were 1 billion times stronger than brain-wave voltages, 100 million times stronger than heart voltages, and 1 million times stronger than large psychophysiology skin-potential. Their effect on human energy systems could be immense.

### 8. Naval physicists found frequencies that induce and heal cancer

Dr. Andrija Puharich and seven United States Navy physicists discovered that when a healer placed his hands in water, the water protons began emitting an 8 hertz frequency. They then radiated mice with a 5 hertz frequency, inducing cancer in them within 48 hours. When the mice were radiated with the healer frequency of 8 hertz, the mice's tumors were healed within 48 hours.

## Additional Qualities of Healing Energy

Not all the following qualities are substantiated by scientific data. These qualities contribute to a consistent and helpful new picture of what is occurring during the healing encounter. They provide a helpful model for the practice of healing.

### 9. *The energy is informational and acts intelligently*

From his research data, Grad draws the conclusion: "The energy is informational! The energy itself is an information-bearer, self-regulating, programmed. Where healing calls for the slowing down of cell growth, as in the goiter experiments, thyroid development is inhibited. Where healing requires speeding up of cell growth, as in the wounded mice tests, the process is accelerated. Slow down or speed up for healing? The same agent does both. The energy itself knows."

### 10. *Life energy produces the optimum conditions for life*

A bean experiment by SPINDRIFT in Salem, Oregon, graphically demonstrates that prayer produces the optimum state for life. Three trays of beans were prepared. One contained beans that had been dried out by oven heat. The beans on the second tray had been soaked to increase water content. The third was the control with untreated normal or healthy beans.

In a series of runs, persons prayed for the beans. This resulted in all three trays of beans consistently developing the same moisture content. The prayer increased water content in the dried-out beans; reduced water content in the soaked beans, and, had no scientific effect on the normal beans. The effect of the healing energy of prayer was to restore the treated beans to their optimal state of being. This finding agrees with Grad's conclusion that the "energy is informational! The energy itself is an information-bearer, self-regulating, programmed."

## 11. Healing increases the amount of oxygen in the blood by up to 12%

Dr. Dolores Krieger (Therapeutic Touch), professor of nursing at New York City University and one of the developers of Therapeutic Touch, learned that Grad had measured increased chlorophyll in plants treated with healer-charged water. Krieger wondered if healing resulted in more oxygen in human blood. In each of three different sophisticated tests of touch-healing, the results increased oxygen in hemoglobin by up to 12%.

## 12. Healing energy can be transmitted through electrical wiring

I heard Olga Worrall report this healing study to a group at the Holiday Inn in Boston Heights, Ohio in 1985. Her story began with a physician's wife weaving wiring into two vests which were then connected by two hundred feet of electrical cable. Olga wore one of the vests while an ill woman, whom she had never met, wore the other in a hospital room down the hall. Physicians used instruments to monitor the flow of energy in both rooms as Mrs. Worrall emitted healing energy into the vest. This caused the ill woman to become well.

This experiment indicates that healing energy can be transmitted through wiring.

### 13. Through prayer, healers impressed their brain-wave pattern upon healees, resulting in physical healing

Olga Worrall and her healing client were both connected to a brain-wave machine (EEG). As Olga began healing, her brain-waves slowed to the alpha range of about eight frequencies a second. Holding her hands about four inches from the healee's head, she transmitted a healing energy, impressing her brain-wave pattern upon the healee, so that both brains resonated with identical brain-wave frequencies and patterns. The waves pulsed in complete harmony and oneness, qualities that many healers subjectively report sensing during healing encounters. The healee became well during this process.

Two conclusions can be drawn from this study. First, Olga Worrall transmitted an energy with her hands that caused the effects. Second, some healings occur because the healer is able to change brain-wave patterns or consciousness. This implies that something as yet undetected, or considered insignificant in the brain-wave pattern, may help to cause or to maintain physical health or illness.

Dr. Edgar Wilson produced identical results with Israeli healer David Joffee, who impressed his brain-wave patterns upon a healee, causing the alleviation of illness symptoms.

## 14. The physical health of persons with multiple personalities changes with the shifting of personalities

This is about the role of consciousness in healing. Dr. Frank Putnam of the National Institutes of Health has found that electroencephalograms (EEGs) show the brain-waves of people who go from one personality to another in multiple personality disorder will change as dramatically as though the electrodes had been taken off one person and placed on another. Their brain-wave patterns vary widely from one personality to another, a phenomenon previously thought biologically impossible.

In the same physical body, one personality will have asthma; but when control is shifted to another personality, the asthma does not exist. Various studies have shown the following changes with personality/brain frequency shifts: one personality will be left-handed, another right-handed; one will wear glasses and be myopic while another personality will have normal vision; one will have diabetes and another not; one will be allergic to a drug and another not.

Dr. Lee Poulos of Vancouver, in multiple personality studies, reports wide fluctuations in psychological test results: one personality being blind and the other having 20-20 vision; up to 60 points difference in the intelligence quotient; even different religious beliefs. Within two seconds of shifting to another personality, the eye irises can change color, from brown to blue for example.

Multiple personality studies present a biological dilemma. Inhabiting the same physical body with one identical pattern of genetic material, the different personalities instantly produce different biological brain-wave patterns, allergies, iris color, biological impairments, and illnesses. This strongly suggests that a number of personality factors are responsible for biological traits. It also possibly explains why a healer's changing of brain-wave patterns can cure an illness. The role of personality and consciousness is obviously important to the wholeness of persons.

### 15. Only the brain-waves of a woman who was being prayed for recognized the healing energy entering her

While a cooperating physician was recording a woman's brain-waves in his office, her church prayer group prayed for her. The woman remained unaware of the prayers for herself, but her recorded brain-waves dramatically changed. In the process, the symptoms of the medical condition, for which she was seeing the doctor, disappeared. This is another piece of the puzzle suggesting that the brain and consciousness play an important role in some spiritual healing results.

### 16. The healing energy is extremely stable

The qualities of the healing energy in healer-treated substances are different from any known energy source. The energy does not dissipate nor contaminate adjacent bottles of water. Healer-treated water and cotton cloth continue to emit healing energy for up to two years

(Bernard Grad). This means that isolated healing energy is the most stable, storable form of active energy known. Sunlight and heat, at over the water boiling temperature, diminish healing energy.

Religiously, the healing energy acts as do holy relics: the bones, clothes and possessions of noted religious persons. The power to heal is attributed to holy relics. The healing energy also has the attributes of holy places and spas that are known for their healing potential. Subjectively sensed, God's presence has qualities identical to that subjectively sensed in healing energy.

### 17. Healing energy dissipates when imparted to living organisms

When healing energy is imparted to living organisms, it is rapidly utilized and diminishes in quantity. When Ambrose and Olga Worrall (Robert Miller) in Baltimore offered absent prayer for a blade of rye grass in Atlanta, it rapidly accelerated growth for 11 hours to a maximum of 830% of normal. This growth-enhancement then diminished for the next 36 hours, reaching a low of two times normal growth rate, where it remained for two weeks. This is similar to how some medications perform.

Grad reports that the healing energy imparted to laboratory mice was so rapidly used that a healer had to hold the mice for an hour at a time to maintain the necessary healing threshold of energy. This was attributed to the rapid metabolism of mice.

From experience, I have observed that imparted healing energy appears to be at its maximum strength for about forty-eight hours in surgical patients and for trauma injuries. This is consistent with the evidence of the emotional side effects of most healing encounters: an inner sense of calmness or well-being lasting about forty-eight hours.

In healing acute illnesses, the energy appears to dissipate as quickly as it does in lab mice. The healing energy must either be continually imparted, or be supplied in huge quantities using healer charged towel or soaking in prayer. The energy's effect behaves in similar fashion to that of an antibiotic—and most other medications—where repeated doses are necessary to alleviate all symptoms. Healing is rarely instant. It is a process.

### 18. Not all human-transmitted energy is healing-quality.

All persons can intentionally learn to emit an energy through their hands, but this energy is not necessarily healing-quality energy. Some persons can do more harm than good. Just because one competently practices a particular healing technique does not mean that one can be helpful. To be competent, one must transmit healing-attuned energy.

Bernard Grad asked two patients in a psychiatric ward each to charge up a bottle of water for healing. A psychotic man's treated water retarded plant growth, while a depressed woman, happy to be useful, treated water which accelerated plant growth.

Gerald Solvin injected mice malaria into mice and asked three volunteers to handle them for healing. One of the handlers, a scoffing non-believer in healing, was the real focus of the experiment. This unbelieving volunteer produced statistically significant negative healing effects in the mice (p = .02).

An extension of this scientific fact must be included in any valid research design. It has long been known in the practice of healing that one unbeliever or cynic can obstruct the healing efforts of a small group. Such an obstructive person would appear to "untune" healing energy. Any healing study in a medical setting might best be done secretly, with only those having to know being included in the design.

I have had my own first-hand experiences of destructive energy. Following a healing service, a well-meaning woman asked if she could offer me healing. I agreed. Within seconds of her placing her hand upon my head, I developed an extreme headache and a feeling of oppression. I was this woman's therapist and knew that she was filled with anger and hatred. In another case, a depressed woman took my hand and offered me a prayer. During the prayer, I could sense her depression entering me and my own energy being drained.

All persons emit energy. Those who advocate hugging, which shares energy, believe that four hugs a day maintain health. Newborn infants can die if not touched by human hands passing them energy. It is reported that cocaine-addicted infants gain more weight when massaged several minutes a day. Part of this effect is likely to be due to the passing of a healing energy. Elderly men in many third world cultures sleep with teen-age girls, not for sex, but in order to have their energy levels restored. Psychologists talk about a touch-hunger suffered by people who are not touched.

Human touch can pass a healing energy that results in a sense of inner well-being and replenished energy. Throughout human history, parents have held their ill children for many hours at a time. Because of their love, parents have naturally imparted a healing energy, possibly saving millions of children's lives. The flip-side is that parents who are angry, resentful, anxious or depressed may pass an energy that has negative effects upon their children. The effects of parents passing negative energy to infants may include colic, fussiness, diarrhea and irregular sleep patterns.

## 19. The intentions of the healer are present in the transmitted energy

If the intention is to heal, the transmitted energy reflects that intention so that healing occurs. If the intention is to harm, the transmitted energy contains information that harms. The human transmitter is attuning the energy by his intentions. Yes, I am saying that mental intention and emotions attune the frequency of the energy emitted by humans. It is agreed within the field of spiritual healing that compassionate or generous love is the primary emotion necessary for attuning the energy to the needed healing frequency. Thus, those who have a compassionate love for the sick naturally attune the energy to the healing frequency.

There is also evidence that a oneness with the person needing healing becomes a part of the attuning of the healing energy. Oneness can occur in a number of ways, all of which may be equally valuable. Healer and healee can be united through love. They can be united through the deep empathy of the healer for the healee's pain or identity. They can be united through the natural interpersonal unity that comes from close human interaction. They can be united by their mutual understanding of the medical condition.

A knowledge of both physiology and illness may improve the quality of the healing energy. This implies that health care professionals may be the best candidates as healers. It could be that a surgeon who is a latent healer unknowingly transmits a healing energy that guides his hands during surgery and contributes to tissue health and regeneration.

However, in its own right, transmitted healing energy also acts intelligently to heal. I have discovered that while I am intending to heal one condition, another condition may be healed, with or without the healing of the originally targeted condition. Here are some of my own experiences: (1) While I intended to heal an injured finger, a woman's scoliosis was healed instead; the injured finger was later healed by traditional surgery; (2) During counseling, I prayed for the healing of a marital relationship. The marital relationship was healed, but in addition, the woman's eczema was healed, even though I was unaware of the skin condition; (3) Twice, I effectively healed a targeted illness but also unknowingly healed genital herpes in young women. This reinforces the observation that the healing energy seeks to create the optimum condition for life on its own.

Grad states that only about one healing in six hundred is instant, and fewer than one percent of those seeking instant healing are healed at large faith healing services. Researchers have observed this for years, designing their experiments for multiple sessions of touch-healing. The scientific data indicates that the healing energy can initiate healing in conditions resistant to medical treatment and speed up the normal healing rate.

### 20. The imparted energy must attain a therapeutic threshhold

The 1989 Chouhan-Weston Clinical Studies video-taped bioelectrography to observe the healing encounter. It took about ten minutes for me, the healer, to transform a cancerous energy field into a healthy one and cure a cancer patient. The healee's energy field remained a steady blue-white for almost ten minutes. Then, instantly, like an explosion, the energy field changed, becoming about three times larger and intensely white. This experiment confirmed the theory that the transmitted healing energy needs to accumulate in power, reaching a specific threshold of power before it can transform the unhealthy energy field. No healing would have occurred if touch-healing had stopped before ten minutes. This implies the need to soak people with prayer over a period of time in order to produce health.

### 21. There is no correlation between the size of a healer's energy field and healing effectiveness

Previous research has assumed that there is a direct correlation between the large size of the healer's energy field and the healer's effectiveness. But emerging data refutes this contention. In preliminary tests during the Chouhan-Weston Clinical Studies, the five hospital staff members were all younger than myself, the healer, by seventeen or more years. The healer's energy field was the smallest of the six persons present and grew even smaller during healing encounters. This implies that the attuned quality of healing frequency is more important than quantity in determining healing results. If, during a healing attempt, the quantity of the transmitted energy filled a whole room or a whole sports stadium, no healing would occur unless that energy had been attuned to the necessary healing frequency. A properly attuned healing frequency is the first requirement of any transmitted energy that heals.

## 22. Healing energy can be transmitted from any distance

Prayer can produce healing results from any distance. The earlier mentioned classic Rye Grass Experiment by Ambrose and Olga Worrall demonstrated that these two healers' prayers caused rye grass 600 miles away (from Boston to Atlanta) to increase its growth rate by 830 percent. From my own observations, absent prayer from groups in worship, prayer groups, and prayer chains is extremely effective. A Russian healer successfully performed absent-healing in clinical trials. We do not have much experiential evidence that absent prayer from groups in worship, prayer groups, and prayer chains is extremely effective.

### A Summary of Healing Energy Qualities

1. Healing energy emerges from the palms and finger pads.
2. Healing energy has an electromagnetic frequency of about 7.8 hertz.

3. Healing energy changes the qualities of water.
4. Healing energy increases the oxygen in the blood by up to 12%.
5. Healing energy can be transmitted through electrical wiring.
6. Healing energy can be imparted to bottled water, cotton and wool cloth, and surgical gauze, with the unused charge lasting up to two years. Healer charged materials act like an intravenous feeding tube providing a constant supply of healing energy.
7. The healing energy is extremely stable.
8. When healing energy is imparted to humans and other living organisms, it is rapidly utilized and diminished as it is used up by the medical condition.
9. Healing energy works as a process, somewhat like an antibiotic. A therapeutic level of healing energy must be continuously maintained until complete healing occurs.
10. Healing through prayer and touch generates about 4 volts of energy for the average person. This is a billion times stronger than brain-wave voltages, 100 million times stronger than heart voltages, and 1 million times stronger than large psychophysiology skin-potential.
11. Cancer can be induced by radiating a person with a 5.xxx hertz frequency and healed with an 8 hertz frequency. (The x's after the 5 are masking the exact, necessary three place decimal frequency. We can't have you carrying out a perfect murder, can we?)
12. The energy is informational! The energy itself is information-bearing, self-regulating, programmed. Whether healing calls for the slowing down of cell growth or the speeding up of cell growth, the energy knows.
13. Healing energy produces the optimum conditions for life.

14. Healing energy acts like holy relics, holy places and spas in its qualities.
15. All human-transmitted energy is not healing-quality. Scoffers and those who do not wish to help the sick should not pray or touch for healing.
16. The intentions of the healer are present in the transmitted energy.
17. There is no correlation between the size of a healer's energy field and healing effectiveness. It is the quality of your love that is all important.
18. The imparted energy must attain a therapeutic threshhold level for healing to occur.
19. Prayer can transmit healing energy from any distance.
20. During healing prayer, you might impress your brain wave pattern upon the healee's brain. This is about a change in consciousness.
21. Multiple personality research indicates that a shift in personalities changes biological states. This is about a change in consciousness.

## A Bold Defense of the Clinical Data

Olga Worrall freely permitted scientists to examine her abilities as a healer and a clairvoyant. She was used as the subject of more than fifty clinical studies. Olga was a no-nonsense woman who did not mince words. When her biographer questioned a specific healing result, she defended the truth as she had experienced it throughout a long lifetime in which she healed thousands of the ill throughout the world.

Olga Worrall firmly stated, "Perhaps you can't [accept healing] but many can. How can anything like spiritual healing or clairvoyance be proven conclusively in a material way? In the greatest feats of clairvoyance, there are always those who refuse to believe what they see and hear, who insist that only coincidence or fraud can explain what has been shown to them. In the most spectacular instance of spiritual healing, the same responses hold, the verdict is that he would have gotten better anyway. If he isn't improved, then that is used to discredit all spiritual healing.

"People have eyes but don't see; they have ears but won't listen. When I made my commitment to spiritual healing, I was fully aware of the skepticism and ridicule and occasional hostility it would entail. But healing is God's gift to me—and I will not bury the talent he has given into my keeping. And not only will I go on healing, but I will also go on working with scientists in the hope and faith that by dint of the sheer weight of the accumulated evidence, someday, somehow, the limitations of this physical world will be manifest to all and a glimpse of the other world will shine through."

# 7

# The Science Behind
# Human Energy Fields

This book is not based upon theology or metaphysics. It is based upon the science behind prayer and healing. Only science can provide an objective new model for our understanding of the impossible, the healing miracle.

Contributing to this model is intuitive insight. Intuitive insight is knowledge that cannot be known by using the five physical senses. For example, Dr. Norman Shealy's studies indicate that some healers can accurately and consistently diagnose illness through their awareness of the human energy fields. They can see or sense the human energy fields.

Intuitive insight has always been associated with healing prayer and touch. This is a part of the impossible which the science behind healing can make scientifically possible.

Some of the best intuitive insights about human energy fields come from Barbara Ann Brennan (Hands of Light). This New York City psychotherapist and healer is also a clairvoyant. She presents a comprehensive look at human energy fields through her own intuitive eyes. Brennan's working model has been proven accurate by the thousands of people who have successfully used this model in their practice of healing.

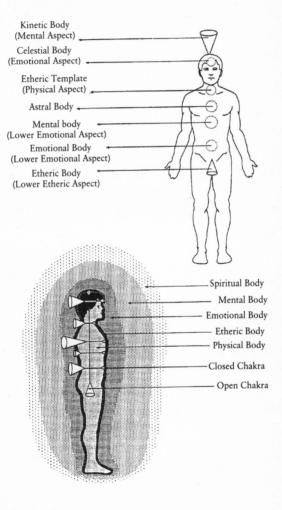

Kinetic Body
(Mental Aspect)

Celestial Body
(Emotional Aspect)

Etheric Template
(Physical Aspect)

Astral Body

Mental body
(Lower Emotional Aspect)

Emotional Body
(Lower Emotional Aspect)

Etheric Body
(Lower Etheric Aspect)

Spiritual Body

Mental Body

Emotional Body

Etheric Body

Physical Body

Closed Chakra

Open Chakra

*Human Energy Fields*

Brennan has intuitively seen nine layers of interpenetrating human energy fields (HEFs), but focuses upon a model based upon the first seven layers that make up the auric energy field.

She reports that each of the seven auric energy fields has its own peculiar color, brightness, form, density, fluidity, and function. Starting with the first layer and going outward, these energy fields are associated with:

1. Physical functioning and sensation
2. Emotional life and feelings
3. Mental life and linear thinking
4. Love and the emotion of love
5. The divine and the power of the Word
6. Celestial love
7. The higher mind of knowing and integrating the spiritual and physical make-up

Brennan then states: "There are specific locations within our energy system for the sensations, emotions, thoughts, memories and other non-physical experiences that we report to our doctors and therapists. Understanding how our physical symptoms are related to these energy locations will help us understand the nature of different illnesses and also the nature of both health and disease. Thus, the study of the aura can be a bridge between traditional medicine and our psychological concerns."

## Gerber's Energy Field Model

A scientific model of the human energy field has been carefully developed by Richard Gerber, M.D. (Vibrational Medicine). His thesis is that most orthodox approaches to healing are based upon the Newtonian viewpoint that the human body is a complex machine. Gerber's alternative is the Einsteinian viewpoint based upon Einstein's mathematics. This is what he refers to as "vibrational medicine," which "sees the human being as a multidimensional organism made up of physical cellular systems in dynamic interplay with complex regulatory energetic fields."

He provides evidence that energy field number one is the template (blueprint) that carries information for the growth, development, and repair of the physical body. The various human energy fields are composed of matter of higher frequency than physical matter. He compares these frequencies to the octaves on a piano keyboard. The lowest frequency octave is the physical; then come the etheric octave, the astral octave, and the mental octave, each at a higher frequency.

## A History of Human Energy Field Research

Throughout history, religious mystics have claimed to see an aura of energy surrounding living organisms including humans. During the Middle Ages, artists depicted religious saints with halos or auras of energy about their heads. God had so filled them with the Spirit that some people could see them glow with God's energy. Thus, the auras drawn in paintings.

Medical researchers have discovered variable energy readings along human energy meridian lines and have mapped out the meridian energy system. Some American health care professionals are now using sophisticated computer-enhanced readouts of the body's meridian energy system in assessing and diagnosing disease. They then balance the energy system using an energy tool about the size of a large pen. When I ask health care professionals who use this human energy field technology for scientific data to prove the existence of human energy fields, they laugh, because such proof is no longer necessary. Their technology assumes the electromagnetic nature of the human body, thus proving the existence of human energy fields.

Ancient Hindu mystics clairvoyantly saw seven major energy chakras plus minor chakra systems. These chakras whirl in motion perpendicular to the body, like the cone of a tornado. When a chakra is whirling the wrong way or is blocked and weak, illness can result. Using their hands, healers can both assess chakra movement and make the appropriate repairs. Health care professionals have mapped out the whole chakra energy system.

Ramesh Chouhan, MD, has screened twenty-five thousand women with bioelectrography prints of the human energy field, and can now diagnose cancer and arthritis months before their physical appearance by identifying the unique energy signature of these two diseases.

Here, we have described three different models of body energy systems as seen in meridians, chakras and bioelectrography. We will be focusing upon bioelectrography.

## Early Experiments

During Kirlian photography, the subject is placed in direct contact with the film and 20,000 to 50,000 volts of electricity are run through the film negative while the picture is taken. This produces an energy picture showing an aura, like the sun's corona, around the subject.

In 1966, Victor Adamenko of the former Soviet Union cut away a small portion of a leaf and used Kirlian photography to take an electrophotograph of the remainder. The developed photograph showed a shadow image of the cutaway portion, as if the entire leaf were still present. This became known as the "phantom leaf effect." This can be interpreted as meaning that a leaf has an energy field or aura that persists in the portion which had been cut away: an energy image projected after physical death.

Other Soviet electrophotography experimenters discovered that a plant's energy field showed visible signs of its disease weeks before the plant showed any outward physical signs of being diseased and dying. Initially, a bush with a weak energy field had shown no visible signs of disease. It was only weeks later that the disease became visible. The weak energy field became a predictor of later plant disease.

During the 1930s, biologist Harold Saxton Burr of Yale University conducted energy research with salamanders, worms, tadpoles, and reptiles. These lower life forms are capable of regenerating severed limbs. The question biologists were asking was: why aren't older members of these species able to regenerate limbs? Dr. Burr amputated the limbs of salamanders and measured an energy of 1.5 to 2.5 millivolts around the missing limbs. When the energy reading fell below that, the salamander could not regenerate a limb. He discovered a direct correlation between the energy level and age. Salamanders had difficulty regenerating a new limb when they were older and displayed a weaker electrical energy field. The energy-rich young could easily do this. This demonstration showed that a certain threshold of energy was needed to create a physical form.

Recently, a medical doctor stated that human children under the age of ten can regenerate the severed tip of a finger if medically permitted to do so. He cited over two hundred recent cases of such regeneration. This extends the implications of Burr's work with salamanders. In human beings, also, the young have stronger energy fields than do the elderly, enabling the young to regenerate tissue more easily.

## The Body Responds as if It Has Energy Fields

The effects of healing energy upon human beings show characteristics typical of energy-field activity. The healing energy effect is a process working over time. It needs to reach a certain level or threshold of energy to have an effect, and it needs to be replenished as it is used up. That describes how a human energy field would need to work in healing.

The healing energy can initiate healing in medical conditions that have proven resistant to medical treatment. Only if the human energy field is indeed the blueprint mold for every organ of the body can we account for and explain healings like the regeneration of arthritic bone joints.

Biologist Bernard Grad's early studies with mice indicate that the healing energy can prevent an anticipated disease from occurring. As will be described, Dr. Ramesh Singh Chouhan can diagnose an anticipated disease in humans because the disease appears in the energy field before it is evident in the physical body.

These were some of the assumptions I took with me when I was invited to India to participate as a healer in the Chouhan-Weston Clinical Studies. I arrived with modest expectations. I just wanted to prove scientifically that touch-healing produced an effect that could be verified in human beings. It came as a surprise when our limited clinical studies verified most of my assumptions.

## Human Energy Fields Hold Information

During the 1980s, Dr. Ramesh Singh Chouhan, a young physician at Jipmer hospital in Pondicherry, India, pursued energy photography research in his bioelectrography laboratory, under a research grant from the Indian government. His resulting data is based upon fingertip bioelectrography negatives of twenty-five thousand screened women. With this advanced form of Kirlian photography, he is photographing the aura of what appears to be the first of the seven human energy fields.

Chouhan measured the depth and the density of an energy aura made visible by running twenty-five thousand to forty thousand volts through fingertips, creating an ionized energy picture. In the early screening, he used X-ray negatives to record the bioelectrographic image of all five fingertips of both hands. The cost of screening was only twenty-seven cents (U.S.) per person.

Chouhan was able to make medical sense out of the immense database available to him. He identified consistent energy patterns or signatures for several medical conditions. This produced four diagnostic breakthroughs that are non-invasive, radiation-free, inexpensive predictors of biological conditions. Most important of all, the process can predict three medical conditions earlier than any other existing diagnostic method. Here are Chouhan's four medical breakthroughs:

## 1. The Early Diagnosis of Cancer

His data establishes that characteristic cancer signatures appear in the body's energy field prior to the appearance of cancer in the physical body. He is able to diagnose cancer three to six months before it can be detected by any known medical procedure.

In the case of cervical cancer, surgeons, seeing bioelectrography evidence of cancer in the energy field, would remove suspicious cervical tissue. Then, while the patient was still in recovery, a second bioelectrography picture would be taken. If all pre-cancerous cells had been removed, the energy field would already have returned to normal. If cancer cells were still present, the fingertip bioelectrography negative reflected this. Then, the surgery would continue with the removal of more cervical tissue.

The implications for cancer screening, for post-surgical assurance, and for evaluating the need for other treatments are revolutionary.

## 2. The Early Diagnosis of Arthritis

Chouhan's second diagnostic breakthrough detects arthritis six to twelve months before it can be diagnosed traditionally or its symptoms appear in the patient. Medical treatment can begin immediately, while the initiation of touch healing can prevent both cancer and arthritis from occurring in the physical body.

## 3. Pregnancy Diagnosis

A third breakthrough involves the energy field diagnosis of pregnancy moments after conception. A massive energy shift occurs that can easily be observed in the female bioelectrography negative.

### 4. Pinpointing the Optimum Moment for Conception

The fourth medical breakthrough involves Chouhan's work with infertile couples. Bio-electrography has proven to be the most accurate means for pinpointing the optimum moment for conception as a graph of daily energy field changes indicates.

Chouhan states that his research data proves that not only is there an energy field within the bounds of the physical body, but this energy field also reflects and can predict the state of health of the physical body, whether it concerns arthritis, cancer, conception or fertility.

## What This Teaches Us

Chouhan's data indicates that the illnesses reflected in human energy fields took three to twelve months to affect body tissue in the cases of cancer and arthritis. Whatever caused the distortions in the energy fields acted slowly in causing illness. In contrast, the body has the ability to quickly change the energy fields, as noted in the immediate change in women's energy fields due to the physiological changes of pregnancy. As you will see, a viral infection can also quickly cause an unhealthy energy field.

My experience from the practice of healing is that the healing energy quickly transforms the energy fields in most illnesses, producing physical health. Once the arthritis energy signature is discovered, it takes six to twelve months before physical symptoms appear. In contrast, all symptoms of osteoarthritis can disappear within minutes or an hour of a ten-minute healing session.

Cancer's response to touch-healing is completely different from that of arthritis. Rarely do the symptoms disappear quickly. Similar cancer conditions may respond differently; one might be cured following three sessions, while another stubbornly persists through two dozen sessions. The Chouhan-Weston Clinical Studies provide new pieces of evidence for what is yet an extremely incomplete picture.

## The Chouhan-Weston Studies

By the time I arrived in India, in January 1989, Chouhan had designed apparatus that produced a live visible energy field surrounding one finger. In a light-blackened room, this ionized energy aura could be photographed with an ordinary camera or an extremely low-light one lux video camera. We decided to record and observe, with a video camera, any ongoing changes in the energy aura during a healing.

## The Clinical Studies

In our preliminary trials, we learned that no matter where I touched subjects during healing, it had the same effect upon the energy field. This was a relief to me. As a minister, I practiced touch-healing by merely holding a hand and praying. I made the decision to place my hands on each subject's forehead and neck while praying aloud. The following studies can be replicated with equipment costing about $600.

## 1. A Viral Infection Quickly Healed

The Chouhan-Weston Clinical Studies provided un-expected videotape information on the healing of a viral infection. The 21-year-old female laboratory assistant displayed acute cold symptoms, including skin pallor, a fever, runny nose, watery eyes, and sneezing. The videotaped record of the healing encounter indicated that, using touch, it took only two seconds to transform the fingertip baseline bioelectrography image of the human energy field in the test subject. During those two seconds, the fingertip bioelectrography image changed from its baseline blue with a white outer fringe to a pure white hue about twice as large; and it remained constant. Toward the end of the 89 second healing contact, she complained of the extreme heat within her and vigor-ously pulled away from my hands to escape. She then explained that the heat had become too painful. About an hour after the healing encounter, all cold symptoms had disappeared.

## 2. Treating a Woman with Chronic Back Pain

The face of the woman with a 10-year history of back pain displayed a desperate longing for help. She had traveled over a hundred miles in seeking that help. Upon my touching her for the first time, her normal energy field of blue with a white tinge changed, at three seconds, into a pure white field about twice as large. I maintained hand contact for ten minutes during each of three ses-sions. On the second and third days, she arrived with her fingertip bioelectrography image (her energy field) still glowing with the transmitted healing energy of the previous day. She reported no change of symptoms until the third day. In the midst of that healing encounter, she reported the complete alleviation of all symptoms.

### 3. Pre-Cancerous Test Subjects

Through fingertip bioelectrography images, Dr. Chouhan had diagnosed pre-cancerous cervical symptoms in two young women who became test subjects. Normal medical treatment would have required the partial removal of the cervix followed by fingertip bioelectrography imaging to determine the success of the procedure. Here, we were utilizing touch-healing as the primary treatment mode.

Bernard Grad and others had already established that touch-healing could prevent an anticipated disease from occurring. Aside from the fingertip bioelectrography image indicating that cancer would occur within three to six months, we had only suspicious-looking cervical tissue as evidence of possible impending cancer.

For the test, I would place my hands upon the forehead and neck. The lights were shut off and I would begin praying in the total darkness. As in the previous studies, I would not know what was happening to the fingertip bioelectrography image until the videotape was reviewed on an American based technology color television monitor back in the States. My fingers sensed what I interpreted to be resistance to the healing flow, as if there was a wall blocking it. After about 8 minutes of touch-healing, I commented, "She is not receiving the healing, but I will give her a few more minutes." Just short of ten minutes, I announced what I was sensing: "She has begun receiving the healing flow." I continued touch-healing for two more minutes. The subjects' responses were identical.

A week later, my first viewing of the videotaped record of her fingertip bioelectrography image demonstrated that I had been wrong in interpreting the meaning of my finger sensings. What the videotape record showed was the normal baseline human energy field remaining unchanged for almost ten minutes. Then, like an explosion, at about nine minutes and forty-five seconds, the fingertip bioelectrography image became instantly pure white and almost three times larger. A later still fingertip bioelectrography image displayed no sign of the characteristic energy signature. She had been cured and would not develop cancer.

**Analysis.** This experiment raised more questions than it answered. When my fingers sensed the resistance, the healing energy was doing something, perhaps building to the threshold level necessary to cause the explosive energy field transformation just before ten minutes. At that transforming moment, I reported she had just begun receiving the healing flow. In reality, the transformation of the fingertip bioelectrography image had, at that moment, registered a complete healing. As a healer, I need to reassess the meaning of my fingers' sense of resistance.

The response of the fingertip bioelectrography image of this subject was remarkably different from the previous two subjects. For the subjects with the cold and the back condition, there was an immediate transformation of the fingertip bioelectrography image to the white image. Thereafter, it took time, from eighty-nine seconds to forty-eight hours, for healing to occur. These stand in marked contrast to the pre-cancerous subject. It took almost ten minutes for the fingertip bioelectrography image to change to white and with that change, the cancer signature in her fingertip bioelectrography image disappeared.

Some healing researchers think that cancer is a disease caused by a faulty human energy field that has been distorted in some way. This study hints that once an energy field has been transformed and enhanced by healing energy, cancer cells become healthy cells.

## The Significance of Energy Fields

Subtle energies research data informs us that all living organisms possess energy fields that contain information and act intelligently in response to that information. What implications can we draw from such a picture?

## Nash—Electromagnetic Effects on the Body

Neurologist Robert Nash, M.D., thinks that medical science will be relying more on electromagnetic approaches to health and less on the biochemistry that has dominated medical practice in the past century. Nash states, "Many of the traditional academicians and teaching centers, as well as research scientists, have difficulty in comprehending that the prime cause of health, and probably disease, is some sort of energy pattern modulated by electromagnetic fields.

"It appears at the atomic level that the electromagnetic fields, rather than chemical events, shape signal flow and energy transmission in biomolecular systems."

## Timmy's Healing

One Sunday evening my phone rang. The tense voice of a parishioner stated, "Hello, this is Tim. My grandson, Timmy, was hit by a car. The ambulance just got here. We are headed for the Emergency Room at Community Hospital."

Timmy's body appeared lifeless when he arrived at the hospital. His clothes were covered with blood. I joined Timmy's parents and grandparents in their grim vigil outside the door of surgery. A half-hour later a doctor emerged and informed us, "Timmy is in critical condition. Every bone in his body seems broken. There is damage to internal organs, internal bleeding, a fractured skull, and probable brain damage. We are still examining the full extent of his injuries. We have called in a neurologist and an orthopedic specialist."

The situation appeared hopeless. And, if young Timmy survived, there would be brain damage. Fear and anxiety filled the area where we waited. We returned to our silent prayers. Every half-hour we would do a group hug and I would offer a prayer for healing. As we passed through four hours of agonized waiting and prayer, physicians entered periodically. They gave us bits of hope: "Internal bleeding has stopped." "Has fewer fractures than original x-rays had shown." "Has no fractures." "All we can do is monitor him." "His condition has stabilized and we've put him in bed to sleep." We slept.

Four-year-old Timmy slept for sixteen hours. When he awoke, he got out of bed, ran to the nursing station, and asked for something to eat. He was healthy. No broken bones; no internal injuries; no brain damage; no bruises; no abrasions; not a scratch remained. We were jubilant.

Just for a moment, take this story at its face value. Assume that it is true. How would you explain the way God could have taken the dying, bleeding, broken body of a little boy and healed everything that was hurt? Yes, we prayed and God healed. But how did that impossible healing occur?

Here is how the impossible becomes scientifically possible: The energy of our prayers strengthened Timmy's energy fields. Not only was his immune system stimulated, his energy fields—Timmy's genetic energy blueprint—were restored and made every cell in Timmy's body new and whole.

8

# Scientific Evidence that Prayer Heals

One of the reasons so many false notions have gathered around the concept of spiritual healing is the public's unfamiliarity with this field of knowledge, especially healing research. Yet, even those with knowledge may cling to the old beliefs. Scientists, too, are slow in accepting data that contradicts their existing understanding of the universe.

## An Ancient Battle Is Still Being Fought

Disbelief in healing was first recorded twenty-four centuries ago in the ancient Greece of the fourth century before Christ. It was then that Plato and Aristotle disagreed on the nature of the universe and the basis of reality. To this day, a battle is still being fought over these ancient issues.

Plato believed that the material or physical universe is but a shadow or projection of the truly real world originating in the realm of the spiritual universe. The way human beings could know this reality was through the use of the inner faculties of higher or rational intuition.

Plato's student, Aristotle, contradicted his master's teachings by asserting that nothing comes into the mind that does not enter by way of the five physical senses (sight, sound, hearing, smell, and touch). Thus, Aristotle laid the foundation for what is known as the materialist-rationalist point of view. This is today's dominant understanding of reality.

The difference in their understandings of the universe may have been due, in part, to the differing ways they received and processed information. Plato's philosophical approach suggests that he had a natural ability for intuitive knowing and thinking. His personality type must have included the intuitive and feeling traits. Aristotle, on the other hand, could not accept Plato's intuitive way because he was unable to experience it. He must have been a sensing-thinking personality type, as defined by the Meyers-Briggs Type Indicator.

Throughout the centuries we can discern that this pair of personality types was the likely cause for the ongoing controversy about the nature of human reality. The sensing and thinking types have dominated Western history for many centuries. They tend to be college professors, scientists, physicians, attorneys and administrators. Statistically, as the Meyers-Briggs data shows, they account for eighty-eight percent of the population, compared to only twelve percent for the intuitive-feeling types.

This twelve percent, the intuitive-feeling types, are the ones who are consistently aware of their intuitive-creative-feeling-sensing. Throughout history, they have been trying to tell the rest of the world what they have sensed and experienced. They are heavily represented among inventors, innovators, artists, and creative geniuses of every generation. Historically, they have ended up being a small minority who have experienced many forms of persecution at the hands of the non-comprehending majority.

Today, they express their intuitive-creative-feeling abilities in such vocations as design, arts, poetry, writing, music, acting, theoretical physics, astronomy and mathematics, research science, inventing, innovating, teaching, pastoral work, mysticism and healing. It is no accident that only about twelve percent of the population believes in healing, reflecting the twelve percent who are the intuitive-feeling types.

Can the eighty-eight percent majority, the sensing-thinking types, ever come to understand and believe in healing prayer? Of course they can. They have accepted Einstein's thought, haven't they? Many of the creative thinkers and innovators throughout history have been intuitive-creative-feeling types. Their contributions to society are enormous. Their thought appears to become accepted when it is expressed in terms that the public will trust—those of reason and science. Therefore, reason and science are the basic approaches of this book.

## Is Reconciliation Possible?

The great historic heresies of the Christian Church (in theological doctrine) involved the same tension that existed between Plato and Aristotle and their opposite views of reality. With Western thought supporting Aristotle and denying Plato's world-view, the battle culminated some seven centuries ago in the thought of St. Thomas Aquinas, the great Roman Catholic theologian, who made reason the basis for Christian beliefs.

The same conflict also underlies the foundations for the birth of modern science. Through the work of the pioneering scientists, Descartes and Newton, Aristotle's thinking has become the basis for modern science. Medical science came to the same conclusion: human beings were mechanical in nature and that all disease and health could be explained through physical mechanisms. Consequently, our society holds the official view that only the physical dimension exists.

This is reflected in attitudes of textbooks, the mass media, and normal personal thinking. The spiritual and psychic dimensions, not being empirically verifiable, were simply dismissed. Those scientists who hold to the ancient concept of the spiritual nature of the universe are regularly denounced as unscientific.

Plato wrote that all physical matter has its basis in spiritual forms from which all physical forms derived. This approach to reality is the basis of all the world's religions. Religions state that human beings are first and foremost spiritual in nature, created and sustained by the spiritual power of God. Because of this, human beings have a spiritual body that is eternal and survives death. Platonic thought harmonizes with the theories of Albert Einstein about the nature of the universe, theories that we seem to ignore outside of the classroom.

The tension between these two world-views did not have to exist. Western civilization has chosen to judge these two views of reality with either/or categories. If one is right, then the other must be wrong. But, Plato and Aristotle were both half-right. They are two equally valid and necessary ways of looking at the world. One approach is to see the world with the five physical senses and to measure and work in it with physical tools, as Aristotle did. The other way is to sense other dimensions of both our physical reality and the spiritual universe through the higher intuition, as Plato proposed.

Morton Kelsey, an Episcopal priest who has written many scholarly books on spiritual development, has lectured to thousands of clergy about spiritual reality. His thesis is that physical reality is just the projected small tip of a wedge of human awareness. Most of that wedge extends into the infinite spiritual universe of God, heaven, the Company of Heaven, spirits, dreams, revelation, extra-sensory perception, creativity, intuitive knowing, and so forth. The five physical senses give us a valuable, but limited, consciousness or awareness of reality.

Religious historian John Rossner states that we live in a multidimensional universe. He then goes on to state: "The belief that the physical senses and sciences provide the only valid view of reality creates an immense aversion to the concept of prayers that heal or that what goes on in the mind can affect physical reality. The events of the Jewish and Christian faiths, as expressed in the Bible, could not have happened if there is only this physical reality."

All religious life requires access to another dimension: the spiritual dimension where God dwells. There are no spiritual gifts in a purely physical dimensional universe. Without the intuitive-creative-feeling process, there is no access to God and no intuitive-creative process. Einstein did not develop his theories by thinking. He dreamed his theories and the roots of his equations, and then rationally developed them. This is true of many of today's most productive scientists.

## The Science of Subtle Energies

Despite thousands of years of reported healings due to prayer, few people believe those reports. The practical use of prayer to aid in healing is rare. It is even rarer for medical centers to utilize the benefits of healing prayer. In the same style that Consumer Reports tests the claims of consumer products, there remains the need to prove product-performance with prayer. Can product-performance convince the world that touch-healing prayer is a useful tool for producing wellness in the home, medical center, and community? This book has been written with that goal in mind. Earlier chapters deepen our understanding of how prayer works, drawing a new road-map for guiding humanity into more effective prayer, health, wholeness, spirituality, and happiness. Scientific data can enable prayer to improve more fully the quality of life, just as do other technologies that we now take so for granted—immunizations, antibiotics, coronary artery bypass surgery, microsurgery, and laser surgery. Data cited here arises out of the work of subtle energies researchers.

Upon reading the research data in my first book, a clergy colleague dismissed it by saying, "Oh, you are into metaphysics." My only response was to chuckle silently. His was the old, easy dismissal of Platonic philosophical thought based upon a vital force that permeates the universe. Metaphysics is the philosophy of how the universe works. Subtle energies research is conducted by hard scientists—biologists, physicists, and health care professionals—who have produced scientific data indicating that the universe is permeated by a life energy that is necessary for the development and existence of all life.

In my own Wesleyan Christian tradition, there are four ways by which God reveals himself: the Bible, tradition, experience, and reason. Most people reject the Bible, tradition and experience as convincing proofs of the truth of the healing reality. This leaves only reason, which includes science, as the last, best chance to convince the world of its truth.

During the past half-century, scientists have been exploring the healing encounter and coming up with many answers concerning how God acts. The research data draws us a clear, new road map for our understanding of healing prayer; the nature of health and happiness; religious renewal; the basis for the practical transformation of individuals, marriages, families, groups, neighborhoods and humanity; and the restoration of the ecology of our whole planet.

Scientists must exclude belief in God from their objective research. They use terms like energy in studying the universe, life, health, prayer, and healing. To study these subtle energies, biologists, physicists, and health care professionals have developed a new science, the science of subtle energies. Subtle energies scientists have conducted more than a thousand clinical studies on what is occurring during the healing encounter.

Their research has not gone without considerable professional sacrifice, including loss of status, promotions, jobs, and even imprisonment. Often, subtle energies researchers are greeted by the same disbelief that their subject, spiritual healing, has traditionally encountered. Because theirs has been a misunderstood new science, getting research published in prestigious scientific journals has been impossible. As a consequence, researchers recently have established their own professional journal, Subtle Energies.

Their research has led to scientific discoveries as significant as those of Copernicus, Kepler, Newton, and Einstein. Just as the historic discoveries in astronomy, physics, chemistry, and mathematics set off revolutions in thought and created the civilization of today, so can subtle energies discoveries become the basis for the next stage in human development. These are down-to-earth discoveries that can be as practically helpful to humanity as the inventions of Benjamin Franklin and Thomas Edison.

Why has subtle energies research been so consistently rejected? For one thing, the discoveries contradict many deeply held personal, religious, and scientific beliefs; and, consequently, demand a new way of understanding the universe. The issues are complex.

First, these scientists are studying spiritual healing, the most disbelieved, misunderstood, ridiculed, and rejected subject of our day.

Second, they are scientifically examining a religious subject, something that is taboo in Western culture.

Third, they are examining the effects of the Platonic world-view that was discredited by the Aristotelian world-view of most people seven hundred years ago.

Fourth, this is a new science, which, though using the scientific method, has little connection to existing scientific traditions.

Fifth, it is applying new technologies that have always been considered the exclusive property of religious institutions.

Sixth, because these discoveries cannot be packaged and retailed in slick commercial packages for megabucks of profit, there has been no investment interest displayed by corporate America, and research grants for university research labs have not been forthcoming.

Seventh, because the discoveries threatened the vested interests of established institutions and professions, doors were slammed shut against the use of these discoveries.

Eighth, few people are taking the alleged immense benefits of these discoveries seriously. The discoveries call for a revolutionary new understanding of the universe and how it works, for a new road map for humanity, taking us from the troubled present into a far more promising future. These new paradigms are being expressed in holistic healing centers.

New scientific concepts have often been viewed with suspicion. During the 1950s, the new mathematical theories of Einstein were considered understandable only by geniuses. This perception was wrong. The new mathematics, physics, and astronomy are not that challenging. They just require a new way of looking at the universe as does the research data of the science of subtle energies. Because their perspective is so similar to Einstein's own, many have called the resulting technology "Einsteinian Medicine;" in contrast to traditional medicine that is labeled "Newtonian Medicine." These new concepts are so different from traditional attitudes that the human mind rebels to its core when confronted by the data.

## You, This Book, and the Suppressant Factor

You may have unusual mental and emotional reactions while reading these chapters. Here is my attempt to help you understand these reactions. Psychoanalyst

Carl Jung said that when people come into contact with information that contradicts their view of reality, they may exhibit the suppressant factor, a subconscious mental attempt to neither see nor remember healing data.

The suppressant factor produces several reactions to healing:

While listening to a healing account, the eyes of many listeners glaze over and they enter an unknown state of consciousness. There may be an amnesia in these listeners and in those involved in a healing encounter. There is an inability or unwillingness in people to talk about healing. There is such embarrassment and shame about believing in healing that most people literally would rather die than try healing prayer as an option for saving their lives. The subject of healing produces other responses as well, such as fear, anger, and confusion.

My guess is that many readers of the thinking-sensing type will exhibit the suppressant factor while reading the scientific data in these four chapters as well as new concepts elsewhere in this book. One reader of this scientific data reported how the suppressant factor affected him.

It took twenty-seven attempts for John to complete the first page of the data. John reported these avoidance tactics: the inability to concentrate; reading the full page and not remembering what he had read; falling asleep; unexplainably closing the book and putting it down; leaving the book open and pacing with a blank mind; muttering to himself; and throwing the book in the corner while vowing to read no further. Because I had warned of these possible barriers, he was intrigued by his own reactions and determined to overcome them. When he finished the book, John phoned and reported his reactions. If you display any of these reactions, I hope you will have enough curiosity to explore yourself. If you succeed in completing How Prayer Heals, I believe it will bless your life for years to come.

## The Difficulty in Science Studying Religion

When the earliest medical researchers wished to cut open human corpses, performing autopsies to examine the body's interior structure, their need to know was greeted by the public with anger, fear, suspicion, and sometimes violence. The human body was too sacred and too precious to be desecrated by a scalpel. Yet, performing autopsies allowed medical science to make enormous leaps in their understanding of human anatomy and disease processes. This knowledge eventually led to major breakthroughs in medical procedures designed to save lives, as well as to enhance the quality of life.

Many people exhibit a similar resistance to the scientific study of religious phenomena. In this context, our beliefs about God are too sacred and too precious to be probed under the scalpel of science. For most persons, religion is religion and science is science. Let us keep them separate. Yet, science is one historic means by which God has revealed himself throughout the centuries.

Because spiritual healing has been seen as a religious phenomenon taking place within the setting of organized religion, we have become accustomed to using religious words to describe what is happening. Religious words like "God," "spiritual," and "prayer" are a part of religion's vocabulary. When we turned to the clinical data, we began using the vocabulary of the science of subtle energies to describe what is happening in a spiritual healing encounter.

Researchers state that they are only measuring the effects of an energy transmitted by humans which causes healing effects. They are neutral towards the source of the energy. I know of no subtle energies scientist who has implied that God is the source of this healing energy. Existing scientific evidence indicates that life energy fills and permeates the whole universe.

Yet, from this believer's viewpoint, the energy studied is a result of God's ever-present existence as the creator, sustainer, and healer. In the science of subtle energies, the religious terms "God's power" and "God's healing flow" are replaced by the scientifically descriptive term "healing energy." As one views the scientific evidence, it closely matches the attributes of God as experienced and believed by most of the world's religions. Unfortunately, because spiritual healing attracted so much uninformed opposition, scientists in other fields have worn blinders in their unwillingness to accept the findings of subtle energies researchers.

This state of affairs prevails because our culture has separated science from religion in so many ways. With eighty-eight percent of the population being the sensing-thinking personality type, believing only in physical reality, we have had to separate religious (intuitive-creative-feeling) thought and belief from our daily lives. For years, I have chuckled about people "hanging their brains in the cloakroom" upon entering church. Many do not use their thinking-sensing skills in church, or in formulating their religious beliefs, morality, or life-style. This is so true that church sociologists report that fewer than half of practicing Christians use their religious beliefs as the basis for their morality and lifestyles. Sensing-thinking

Christians are forced to compartmentalize their lives with one way of knowing reserved for church, and another way prescribed for the other parts of their lives. As a clergyman, I have found this to be frustrating. I want people to use their thinking-sensing skills in their religious life. I am an intuitive-creative-feeling type myself, but I am equally adept at thinking-sensing. I have combined these skills in this book.

I am aware of the discomfort of most religious believers when scientists describe God's actions in terms of an intelligently acting energy; but this book must do this. By describing the results of prayer in scientific language rather than religious language, we see that a more accurate picture emerges. We are able to state that if you "do this, and this, and this" in prayer, then certain specific results are probable. This spiritual technology adds reliability and predictability to prayer beliefs. This book is not denying belief in prayer. It is seeking to strengthen this belief and encourage its more effective practice.

## The Basis for Early Religious Beliefs

To put this into perspective, it may be helpful to understand the basis for early religious beliefs. All the world's religions arose from humanity's ancient past. Ancient humanity was just as curious as we are about why things happen. What causes floods? What causes droughts? In a pre-scientific era with no scientific answers to these questions, there was no scientific understanding of weather patterns. Only one possible cause was perceived—God. So, the conclusion was, "God causes the weather." Thus, ancient humanity came up with religious beliefs to explain natural disasters like floods and droughts.

Why does someone become ill? What causes the common cold? What causes pneumonia? What causes leprosy? What causes blindness? Why are some infants born dead or defective? What causes an old man to clasp his chest, fall to the ground, and suddenly die? No physicians are mentioned in the Old Testament. There was no awareness, then, of bacteria and viruses, cancer and heart disease. There was no medical science. Therefore, few medical causes were acknowledged for physical conditions.

The belief was, "God causes illness." In those early times, in answer to the why, religious explanations were offered. People would say, "God did it. He died because he had broken God's laws." Not until medical science performed autopsies and discovered what went on inside human bodies did thinking begin to change. Now, medical science can usually discover the cause of death. Because of this, people can say, "He died of a heart attack induced by the blockage of coronary arteries."

These early religious answers to scientific questions remain embedded in the ancient sacred writings that support our religious beliefs today. Though science has provided objective answers to these ancient questions, these early religious answers still hinder both our religious and scientific understanding of the universe, as well as our ability to pray effectively.

## Prayer—Religious Vs. Therapeutic

We have been rather careless in our use of the word "religion;" it has two meanings: One refers to a specific system of beliefs in a religion like Christianity, Judaism, or Islam. This is the dominant meaning. The other definition of religion is a belief in God or gods. When we think of prayer, we identify it as arising out of the context of a specific religion. In reality, most prayers are not religious in this context. Most prayers express belief in God, but not that of a religion. The prayers of most people do not arise from formal education in religion.

There are also universal religious beliefs that are not unique to any one religion. These beliefs about God are shared by all humanity. These universal beliefs include perceiving God as the Creator, Sustainer, and Healer. From this arises prayers of praise and thanksgiving for divine intervention and healing.

When people pray for healing, this is an expression of compassion. They are praying to bring the power of God into the life of the ill because they care. They are using prayer for therapeutic or caring purposes.

Why are we exploring this? We are exploring this in order to release prayer and healing from their religious confinement. In the United States, it is a social taboo to publicly pray or heal because these are perceived as private religious activities, best done in churches or in private. Prayer in a hospital is perceived as a partisan religious activity and is not seen in the context of an act of caring.

In reaction to the taboo against prayer in a public context, many healing techniques have recently been developed to express practical caring that does not use or refer to prayer. These include Reiki, energy balancing, and Therapeutic Touch.

Therapeutic Touch was specifically developed for use by health care professionals. Therapeutic Touch has been taught to tens of thousands of nurses for use in a medical setting, with many nursing colleges including it in their curricula. From this has arisen the National Nurse Healers Association. Therapeutic Touch teaches people to center their inner selves while practicing the technique. It does not teach them to pray.

Recognizing the sensitive issue of using prayer in public, I see the need to separate certain types of prayer from a religious context by using a new term, "Therapeutic Prayer." Therapeutic Prayer is used as a therapy. It is offered out of concern to heal the ill and the troubled, and to restore harmony and balance to individuals, marriages, families, classrooms, work places, communities, nations, and the planet. It can be used with persons holding any religious beliefs. It is an act of caring, such as feeding the hungry, sheltering the homeless, or working for world peace. Therapeutic Prayer seeks to bring the power of God into practical situations.

I introduce Therapeutic Prayer at this place in order to direct your attention to the possible practical uses of prayer. These will be detailed with the scientific data. The use of Therapeutic Prayer gives humanity another practical tool for caring. It also provides many new and practical ministries for religions to practice. It is a new perspective that frees people to pray with the hurting without the limiting belief that prayer represents a particular religion. It provides a new healing technique: the practice of healing prayer.

## The Distortions of Faith Healing Services

Another issue has distorted public beliefs about spiritual healing: The circus atmosphere prevalent in most American televised faith-healing services not only challenges religious credibility, it turns most persons off. The style, the beliefs, the judgmental and manipulative statements, the distortion of the truth, the money pitches, and the wealthy lifestyles of the performers have blinded most persons to the fact that God actually heals through prayer.

Though people may reject faith-healing services, the latter have still managed to distort our beliefs and knowledge about how God heals. For instance, most persons, though not believing in faith healing, will still insist that (1) God heals instantly, and that (2) it is due to the immense faith of the subject. Both of these concepts are observationally faulty.

Healing prayer is misunderstood in dozens of ways. These misunderstandings raise barriers to the acceptance of scientific evidence. When science challenges religious beliefs, many persons will relentlessly cling to objectively erroneous religious beliefs.

My own residual skepticism has limited my own healing ability. To practice healing demands a suspension of disbelief, which must be replaced by a state of miracle-readiness.

Shortly after a Roman Catholic healing service had again raised our awareness and faith, my wife and I took part in an effortless healing. We had been to dinner with friends with whom we discussed healing. Returning to our home, our friend, Chuck, gave us a friendly challenge: He said, "Let's see if you are just talk. I have had a separated shoulder blade for forty years that causes me pain when I drive or play golf. Let's see you heal it!"

Standing in our living room, my wife and I placed our hands upon our friend's back. A few seconds into our prayer, we could feel the muscles rippling and the bone structure moving into normal alignment. As with most healings, we had the same sense of surprise and awe as our friends Chuck and Marcia. A month later we received a note from Chuck from Mountain View, California. He stated that he no longer suffered pain from long stretches of driving his car or from playing golf, and that his physician had examined him and the separated shoulder blade condition no longer existed. He wanted to make sure I had his statement in my files.

This is one last reminder to be aware of the many ways you may use to avoid unpleasant truths as you digest the data. Discuss it with others who have read this book. Share it with those who have not read this book and observe their reactions. It takes courage to acknowledge that you are willing to openly explore this field. How honest will your conscious mind permit you to be?

## Reasons for Science to Study Healing Prayer

There are four basic reasons for relying upon scientific research to understand how prayer heals.

First is to convince humanity that healing is real. Scriptures have convinced few people that God heals today. Personal witness has convinced few people that God heals today. Perhaps the mountain of objective scientific data can finally persuade humanity that God heals today.

Second, existing beliefs about healing are contradictory and usually inaccurate. Most of these beliefs are based upon theology, metaphysics, and cultural values. As observation and research data begin providing us with an objectively more accurate picture, these existing beliefs will, we hope, be altered.

Third, we need an objective understanding of what is happening in the healing encounter so that we can more competently offer healing prayer and touch. When our models are wrong, our approach cannot help but be wrong.

Fourth, scientific studies open the door to healing being practiced within conventional medicine. Though many physicians and hospitals may still be blind to the existence of and practical benefits of healing, objective scientific data offers an opening. Those health care professionals who want to help their patients to get well in every possible way, now have the scientific data to back up their courageous use of healing.

## Science and the Objective Reality of Healing

The pioneering researcher in scientific studies on the effects of healing is Bernard R. Grad. With his doctorate in experimental morphology, Dr. Grad spent forty years in biomedical research at McGill University, Montreal. He devoted his spare time to carrying out more than two hundred clinical studies on the effects of healing, using the same careful scientific research designs that he used in his university research.

Internationally recognized as the father of healing research, Grad's contribution to this field was in conducting the research; not in humans, but in animals, plants, and even non-living things. This eliminated issues of suggestion or hypnosis. The experimental design was the same in every way as if he were conducting experiments on drugs, vitamins, or hormones. Sufficient numbers of replicates were involved to take into consideration biological variation and to permit statistical evaluation of the data at the end of the experiment.

Suitable controls were part of each experiment, and in many of the experiments double and multiple blinds were introduced. The only unconventional aspect of the study was the healing treatment. When healing hands were shown to have effects on biological processes, the transmission of an energy was postulated as being the agent responsible for the results.

## The First Study: Treating Wounded Mice

Grad's 1957 Wounded Mice Experiment was the first healing study. With a scalpel and template, Grad surgically removed a one-half inch square of skin from the backs of forty-eight laboratory mice. Sixteen were treated by the Hungarian born healer Oskar Estebany, while the rest of the mice were used as controls. The wound healing rate was regularly measured with a template.

After fourteen days, the healer-treated wounded mice showed a statistically significant increased surgical wound healing rate over the control group. This experiment supplied the first scientific verification that healers produce a measurable healing effect in living organisms.

Bernard Grad was the faculty advisor for my doctor of ministry degree. Much of the research sited in this book came out of my academic studies with him. Some of the interpretations are mine, not Grad's. We disagree in our interpretations in several areas of healing. I state this to protect Grad, who is like a brother to me.

## Daniel Benor's Comprehensive Review

In 1990, Daniel J. Benor, an American psychiatrist, conducted a survey of healing research that had appeared in various academic dissertations and professional journals. His statistical evaluation of 131 controlled trials on cells, enzymes, yeasts, bacteria, plants, mice, and humans demonstrated a positive effect of healing in the fifty-six trials with a statistical analysis, at a significance level of $p = .01$ or better with another twenty-one at $p = .02$.

Benor's comprehensive review provides conclusive scientific evidence that healing efforts result in objective healing outcomes.

## Wirth's Research with Human Subjects

More recent studies have used human subjects. Here is an example of such healing research, entitled, The Effect of Non-Contact Therapeutic Touch on the Healing Rate of Full Thickness Dermal Wounds by Daniel P. Wirth, M.S., J.D.

Wirth had full-thickness dermal wounds incised on the lateral deltoid region using a skin punch biopsy instrument on healthy subjects randomly assigned to treatment or control groups. Subjects did not know who was being treated nor the true nature of the active treatment mode. Wound surface areas were measured on Days zero, eight, and sixteen using a direct tracing method and digitization system. Active and control treatments were composed of daily sessions of five minute exposure to a hidden Non-Contact Therapeutic Touch practitioner or to sham exposure. There were 48 participants. On the sixteenth day, the statistical results indicated significant healing with $p = .01$.

## Summary

Healing is the most researched subject in the history of man. Why? Because honest, open-minded scientists have stumbled upon the reality of healing in the midst of a skeptical world. When few people took their personal witness seriously, they developed carefully controlled lab designs to bolster their personal witness. Their curiosity also led them to explore the parameters of healing. They have blessed us. We have a mountain of solid evidence that prayer heals. We have a mountain of solid research that draws a new understanding of how prayer heals.

Healing research is not limited to one nation. Research has been conducted in every nation of Europe, in Japan, India, Indonesia, Burma, Brazil, Mexico, Canada, the United States, and dozens of other nations. God heals and he does it in every culture on earth.

⑨

# Outcomes of Healing Prayer

What can healing encounters contribute to your health and happiness? Four sources provide insights into this answer. The first source is religious wisdom. A second source is the scientific research data provided in the past five chapters that draws a preliminary picture. Another source would be the clinical reports coming to us from other nations where healing is practiced in hospital settings. A final source involves the first-hand observations of practicing healers. These four sources will help us explore the practical benefits of healing encounters.

## Practical Benefits of Religious Wisdom

Moses proclaimed, "... man does not live by bread alone but by everything that proceeds out of the mouth of the Lord" (Deuteronomy 8:3). This religious wisdom speaks to us today, telling us that the good life consists of far more than creature comforts like family, food, housing, education, health care, and entertainment. It tells us that the foundation of the good life is the Word of God. The Word of God is the Source of all life. It provides us with wisdom for healthy and happy living. It tells us that this is God's universe. God permeates the whole universe with his Spirit (Life Energy) and the Word. For humans to become entirely whole, they must rely upon the power of Life that comes from God.

Subtle energies researchers have confirmed this wisdom of the Word. Their evidence points to a subtle energy or life force that permeates the whole universe. During the healing encounter, this life force is accumulated, attuned, and transmitted by humans. Humans are capable of using this life force to bring new life to themselves and others because the life force acts to restore all life to its optimum condition of wholeness. The life force heals body tissue, emotional pain, mental confusion, spiritual emptiness, and relational divisions.

As a priest knowledgeable of the Word, and as one who has personally experienced God's transforming presence and power, I cannot read the scientific data without recognizing that it is describing God and God's work among humanity. God created and continues to create and make all things new through the healing encounter. God is the Source of health and happiness.

Much of the Word of God describes what it means to be fully human, mature and whole. Humans are far more than just biological tissue. The Word teaches that we are physical, emotional, mental, and spiritual beings. To be whole means all four of these aspects are fully alive, interacting, complementing, and balancing each other. If we ignore the health of any one of these human parts, it affects and diminishes the health, the life, of the others.

The existence of human energy fields, and their description as being many bodies vibrating at various frequencies, matches the wisdom of the Word. As the scientific data graphically portrays, when the healing energy flows into a human being, the energy fields become significantly larger and become white, like the mystic presence of God. All that is missing from this equation is the Word, God's wisdom in the life of humanity.

## Scientific Evidence of Practical Benefits

The scientific evidence indicates there is an objectively measurable healing effect. The evidence indicates that humans accumulate, attune, focus and transmit an energy that heals. The evidence indicates that this energy is information-bearing and acts intelligently to restore humans to their optimum condition for life. The evidence indicates that the energy works by restoring the human energy fields, including that of the mind. These restored energy fields then repair the physical, emotional, mental, and spiritual components of a human being. The evidence indicates that the energy can initiate healing in conditions that are resistant to medical treatment, and perhaps perform genetic engineering. The evidence indicates that healing energy dramatically increases the human rate of healing. As with an antibiotic, the healing energy must be constantly replenished in order to maintain a therapeutic level. The energy increases the amount of oxygen in the blood by up to twelve percent.

Healing energy has many unusual qualities. It can be imparted to water, wool and cotton cloth, surgical gauze, and then be stored in these substances indefinitely. These then produce effects similar to those produced by a healer. This energy can be transmitted through electrical wiring.

It can stop an anticipated disease from occurring. It can be transmitted through absent prayer to any location.

Healer-treated water emits a 7.8 to 8.0 hertz electromagnetic frequency, as do healers worldwide. Another extremely low frequency, 5.xxx hertz, induces cancer in mice within forty-eight hours. This induced cancer can be healed quickly with **an 8 hertz** frequency. Other extremely low frequencies cause emotional alterations both beneficial and detrimental to health and life.

The brain plays a role in the healing picture, with a healer able to impress his/her own brain-wave pattern on the healee to induce healing. Personality traits play a role in disease. Absent prayer from a group is able to affect the brain-wave pattern. All persons can transmit energy from their palms and fingers, but such transmitted energy is not necessarily healing energy.

The scientific data presents a preliminary picture of the effects of spiritual healing and the qualities of the healing energy. Physicians are in the best position to understand the full implications of this data and how the practice of healing can complement existing medical treatment. Future research must completely explore the scientific benefits of healing.

## Practical Benefits Reported by Other Nations

Healing is practiced in hospitals in England, Brazil, Russia, Poland, and Hungary. Italian physician Dr. Piero Cassoli's extensive study suggests the use of spiritual healing in infections of the sinuses, ovaries, and inner ear. He also recommends its use in cooperation with conventional medical care for epilepsy and malignancies.

According to Soviet healer Victor Krivorotov, the list of diseases that can be cured by Pranotherapy [touch-healing] is broad and diverse. It includes both functional and chronic diseases: nervous disorders (e.g.: irritation of the spinal nerve roots, skin diseases, fatigue of the nervous system, vegetative disorders), mental disorders (e.g.: hypochondria, hysteria, obsessive-compulsive neurosis), internal diseases (e.g.: coronary insufficiency, myocardia, respiratory disorders, gastric conditions, dyskinesia of gall ducts), and female diseases.

Polish hospital clinical data on spiritual healing offers hard scientific information. It is far more evidential than subjective reporting. Barbara Ann Brennan reports the following statement by Mietek Wirkus, who worked as a healer with physicians in a clinic affiliated with the IZICS Medical Society in Warsaw.

"Mietek Wirkus reported that his clinic shows that bioenergotherapy or BET [touch-healing] is most effective in nervous system diseases and the diseases that were consequences of migraine, in healing bronchial asthma, bedwetting, hemicrania, nervous illness, psychosomatic diseases, gastric ulcer, some kinds of allergies, liquidation of ovarian cysts, benign tumors, sterility, arthritic pains, and other kinds of pain. BET helps to relieve pain caused by cancer and decreases the amount of pain medication and tranquilizers taken by a patient. Good effect has also been observed in treatment of deaf children. In almost every case, the doctors discovered that after BET treatment, patients became quieter and more relaxed, pain was gone or relieved, and the rehabilitation process, especially after surgery or infection, was accelerated."

I met Evgeniya Stogny, the chief healer in one of the largest hospitals in Moscow, at a 1992 Montreal seminar. As the chief healer, she supervises a staff of two dozen healers who refer to healing as Bio-Energy Therapy. She says Bio-Energy Therapy improves the blood, which agrees with American research data. Through a healing purification process, she is able to improve conditions affecting the heart, breathing, and kidneys. She stated that Bio-Energy Therapy could improve all medical conditions. Evgeniya then specifically named the prostate, female problems, hepatitis, scar tissue, stomach-intestinal problems, brain conditions, disk displacement, and the immune system, including AIDS. Evgeniya revealed that she is working with three new diseases that the Western nations have not yet seen. She closed her presentation by reflecting that during the dying process, the biofield folds, and then disappears at death.

This clinical evidence demonstrates the serious study and practice of spiritual healing in eastern Europe. Eastern European research data could save the United States decades of research. Russian healers have verbally shared the news that Russian healing research instruments far surpass any technology in the West. If this should prove to be true, then the rest of humanity need only inquire and receive a needed gift. The following table summarizes the specific medical conditions that respond to touch-healing as enumerated in the clinical reports from Italy, Poland and Russia:

## European Clinical Reports

| | | |
|---|---|---|
| AIDS | immune deficiencies | allergies |
| arthritic pain | asthma | bedwetting |
| brain bleeding | chronic illness | chronic middle ear infection |
| coronary insufficiency | deafness in children | disk displacement |
| female disorders | gall bladder diseases | gastric conditions |
| ulcers | headaches | heart muscle damage |
| lung ailments | nervous system disorders | nutritional disorders |
| ovarian disorders | ovarian cyst | prostate disorders |
| psychosomatic diseases | respiratory disorders | sinus infection |
| skin diseases | sterility | stomach/intestinal problems |
| tumor, benign | anxiety | depression |
| hypochondria | hysteria | stress disorders |
| obsessive-compulsive disorder | neurosis | |

Healing complements conventional medical care for epilepsy and malignancies. It relieves pain caused by cancer and decreases the amount of pain medication and tranquilizers taken by patients. After healing treatment, patients became quieter and relaxed, pain was relieved, and the rehabilitation process after surgery or infection was accelerated.

## An Analysis of Reports from Other Nations

As a researcher, I look for any patterns and anomalies present in the data. In these reports, we see broad differences in the types of conditions that respond to touch-healing. The four clinical reporters seldom mention the same conditions.

As a healer, I have an explanation for this discrepancy. I have observed, in my own practice, that anything I know can be healed usually responds to touch-healing. I am guessing that the confidence of the healer plays a role in healing effectiveness. Having seen the above list, many healers will be able to duplicate these results. Missing from this list are a number of illnesses that have responded to my own healing efforts.

You might have noticed that touch-healing has many names. In these reports, we had Bio-energy Therapy—the current name for Russian touch-healing, in contrast to the name given by an earlier generation; "Bioenergo-therapy." The Polish "Pranotherapy" sounds as if it comes from the Hindu name for life energy, "prana."

Here in the United States we also have bio-energy therapy, plus names like Reiki, Therapeutic Touch, tai chi, energy balancing, touch-healing, prayer, acupuncture, acupressure, and Reflexology. There are dozens of other names for healing, all of which seek to restore the human energy field in order to restore physical and emotional health. Most of these avoid using the word healing because of its negative connotations. If you learn of a strange-sounding therapy offered by a traditional or holistic health care practitioner, ask that professional if it involves energy field work.

## Evgeniya

Stogny and I became friends. A lecturer had asked everyone to rub the back of those next to him and Evgeniya and I ended up as back-rubbing partners. The next day I signed a copy of my book for her. She smiled her thanks and then practiced her considerable healing skills upon me.

Diagnosing my energy fields, she stated through a translator that I was in perfect physical health but at a low energy level. Using wire dowsing (divining) rods, she measured the radius of my energy fields as extending about eight feet from my body. Evgeniya assessed my chakras and found my root chakra to be weak. She passed her hands about four inches from my body, restoring this chakra. Again, using the dowsing rods, she showed my energy fields now extended to about twenty-five feet.

During this healing session, a deep sense of inner peace and well-being began filling me, reaching its peak about an hour later and lasting about two days, a normal side effect of most healing encounters. I felt as if I were on the world's best tranquilizer, while feeling boundless energy and an enhanced creativity. Christians call this "the peace of God which passes all understanding."

Evgeniya Stogny is a devout Russian Orthodox Christian. She uses thin candle tapers blessed by a priest as a basic diagnostic tool. Lighting a taper, she passes it quickly next to a healee's body. Wherever a thick wisp of black smoke is given off, that area requires healing.

Evgeniya was born in the back country. As a child, she was considered not only a healer but also a sorceress. In Russia, a sorceress is highly respected because of the many psychic abilities that accompany her healing skills. Thousands of such healers work as staff members in Russian hospitals.

I have observed that Russia seems to possess far more than its fair share of trained and competent healers and psychics. If these observations are true, I speculate on five reasons for this.

First, Russia did not burn five million witches during the Middle Ages, as did the rest of the Western world, thus preserving this genetic stock for future generations.

Second, in the United States, many of our best psychics and healers have been nurtured in isolated rural settings. Russia possesses far more such isolated areas.

Third, Russian Christianity comes from the far more mystical Orthodox Church tradition that would tend to accept and nurture healing and psychic abilities.

Fourth, under secular Communist rule, Russia was far more open to nurturing its psychics and healers because it did not possess the constraints against research and development that faced the Western cultures with their religious and scientific taboos.

Fifth, Communist Russia viewed psychic and healing abilities as possible assets to the state for defense and health purposes.

## Sasha Artiouchkine

I have worked with a Moscow psychic, healer and computer analyst, Sasha Artiouchkine, whose wife did post-graduate work in biochemistry at Case-Western

Reserve University, Cleveland, before returning to Russia in 1994. He, like Evgeniya, speaks no English so his wife, Luba was our interpreter. Sasha is an excellent clairvoyant diagnostician. As a team, we do far better healing work than either of us can do individually. We complement and strengthen each other's insight and abilities.

My association with Sasha motivates me to encourage team-healing, and on an international basis whenever possible. Because spiritual healing remains a most unbelieved, misunderstood, and ridiculed subject, international healing teams and seminars hold the promise of increasing acceptance and respect in the field. I have found that the further I travel from home, the more respected and effective I become. In other nations, I am far more effective as the respect and status accorded me increase.

## Benefits According to a Practicing Healer

Through the years I have had more than ten thousand healing encounters in hospitals, homes and my office in private practice. The following data represents my personal observations about what healing accomplishes on a consistent basis during a pastor-healer's workday. Obviously, my subjective observations are not acceptable medical evidence. They do, however, give you some perspective on what occurs during touch-healing prayer.

I was initially hesitant to report this data. Citing professional observations of only one expert witness made me feel vulnerable to criticism. But having made a commitment to honesty, I placed the data in the first draft of this book. Two of my clergy colleagues who practice touch-healing, George Fisk and Francis Mac-Nutt, critiqued that first draft. Their comments in the page margins confirmed my own data. They emphatically stated that their observations on healings were almost identical to my reported data. Both punctuated their comments with multiple exclamation marks. I gave a sigh of relief for my increased confidence.

## Practicing in a Medical Setting

First, let me say that I feel comfortable in a medical setting. Medical procedures have saved my life. I have turned to surgeons for surgery. I have used prescription medications. I possess hundreds of hours of clinical education in pastoral care and counseling, having specialized in counseling and small group work. Like most pastors, I averaged more than a dozen hours a week visiting patients in hospitals. As a pastor, I have felt that I am a part of the medical team, offering emotional, physical, spiritual, and interpersonal wholeness to the ill.

Since discovering, in 1966, that I had the ability to offer healing, I have practiced touch-healing prayer in hospitals and homes. This was done by simply holding a person's hand and offering a prayer; again, as most pastors do. The only difference was in the intention and directness of each prayer. I believe in the practice of complementary medicine whereby physicians and healers complement each other's skills.

An increasing number of healers have ready access to hospital patients. Thousands of nurses practice Therapeutic Touch and are members of the Nurse Healers Association. A growing number of physicians are closet healers who hide their healing practice under other names for fear of losing their licenses, patients, or reputations. The evidence indicates that thousands of clergy and nuns possess powerful healing abilities.

Medical settings are the best place to practice healing. Holistic centers are opening in most communities. Holistic health care professionals rarely work directly with physicians in true complementary medicine. But that may be the next step. Using healers may reduce health care costs by as much as fifty percent. These enormous savings alone may prompt the government and health insurers to accept the services of healers. For years, my dream has been to work in a medical center as a healer, researcher, and teacher. That dream will soon be fulfilled.

## Clinical Observations and Applications

Clients usually come to me as a last resort. They may be in the late stages of cancer, or on social security disability with back pain, or come after years of suffering from chronic fatigue, multiple sclerosis, or heart disease. Family members have me visit a hospital to heal loved ones in comas, with high fevers, or pneumonia. Some of my clients have been clinically depressed for ten years, or been haunted by an emotional trauma for forty years. When all other approaches fail, they become my clients. More than ninety percent are cured.

I enjoy these challenges. They force me to perform beyond my existing limits and develop new approaches. They are my laboratory. Most of all, I am helping desperate people get well. But it would be so much easier if I was the first or second choice of treatment, rather than the last resort. Trauma injuries, painful spines, arthritis, and skin diseases all respond well to touch-healing prayer. And cancer is much easier to treat in its earliest stages.

The following medical conditions are just a few of those that respond well to touch-healing prayer. Many lend themselves to complementary medicine in which physician and healer complement each other's care.

### 1. Surgery

When I practice touch-healing prayer just prior to surgery, surgical wounds consistently heal faster with about 80% healing in half the normal time and the remaining 20% resulting in a 700% increase in healing rate. Healing also produces significantly less post-surgical pain, an inner sense of well-being, and increased physical and emotional vitality. Post-surgical depression all but disappears.

In addition, prior touch-healing can lessen the severity of the surgical condition. Dozens of times, patients were diagnosed with cancer, but during surgery only normal cells were found, with all symptoms disappearing. Equally true, surgeons would find cancer filling the abdominal cavity and be forced to do nothing and a few months later, the patient would be cancer-free. Some medically untreated ruptured discs became symptom-free with-in twenty-four hours.

Prayer before cancer surgery yields high results, even when incurable cancer is the prognosis. Prayers offered after the patient hears surgical reports of incurable cancer have been less effective. Prayers during chemotherapy or radiation treatments have resulted in reducing negative side effects and producing a higher rate of remission.

Touch-healing can also control vital signs like pulse and blood pressure. Many healers can place pulse and blood pressure at any level desired simply by touching and willing it. Internal bleeding due to ulcers, vessel rupture, or surgery can be stopped consistently.

---

### Medical Benefits of Using Touch-Healing Prayer Within 24 Hours Before Surgery

- Pre-surgical stress replaced by an inner sense of well being
- Blood oxygen levels elevated by about 10 percent
- Vital signs maintained during surgery
- Surgical hemorrhaging risk lowered
- Surgical wound heals 2-7 times faster
- Postsurgical physical vitality elevated
- Postsurgical emotional vitality elevated
- Postsurgical depression risk reduced

---

One morning in January, 1992, my eighty-four-year-old father, Bernard Weston, was rushed to the emergency room of Timken-Mercy Medical Center in Canton, Ohio. When I arrived at ten o'clock, a drainage tube had already sucked a liter of green fluid from my father's swollen left groin area. I practiced touch-healing prayer. That afternoon he was admitted to a surgical ward room, and at two o'clock family members gathered with me for touch-healing prayer. Before surgery, his surgeon cautioned us that with this much gangrene infection, his poor heart, and advanced age, prospects for surviving surgery were not good.

Late that afternoon, the surgeon approached us, smiling. He reported finding no gangrene, only bright pink tissue that looked like a twenty-year-old's, and confirmed the successful surgical repair of a simple groin hernia. My father was released from the hospital two days later, his surgical wound all but healed.

### 2. Physical injuries

Trauma injuries like bruises, torn muscles, lacerations, and broken bones respond remarkably to touch-healing prayer, which enhances the healing rate by two to thirty times. The earlier the touch-healing treatment is offered, the better will be the results. It seems that if we can prevent the trauma injury from being impressed upon the energy fields, then trauma healing can occur within minutes or hours. The implications of touch-healing are obvious for emergency, trauma and burn units, and for sports medicine.

### 3. Massive bruises

One day during my hospital rounds, I found a young man with an arm in a cast and in traction, and both legs in traction. He had been brought in that morning following an auto accident. Both legs were blue-black from the top of the thighs to his knees. I told him what touch-healing prayer might do for him. He smiled and cooperated. Two days later I observed his legs were their normal color, no limbs were in traction, and he was being discharged.

### 4. Trauma brain injuries

These respond well to touch-healing. This is true even with brain-dead patients. Two-thirds of the brain-dead injuries I have treated have survived, with damaged brain tissue regenerated and memory functions restored. Normal physical therapy follow-up was usually necessary. These healings were not accomplished through one simple touch. In all survival cases, I practiced touch-healing prayer within hours of the injury. I also practiced thirty minutes at a time, two or three times daily for one to two weeks. If possible, I involved loved ones in healing prayer, including first-hand touch with the patient.

### 5. Hearing losses

These can often be restored, at any age, with up to three consecutive daily touch-healing treatments. The restoring may take seven or more days to occur.

### 6. Dental conditions

Dental conditions respond consistently. Healing relieves toothache pain, and diminishes pain, bleeding, and swelling in tooth extractions.

All the above conditions respond consistently to touch-healing. I attribute this to two factors. These are uncomplicated conditions in which the healing energy merely initiates and speeds up the normal healing process. Emotional and mental factors that might maintain a condition are also minimal. The earlier that touch-healing can be applied to a condition, the more likelihood of success.

## 7. Osteoarthritis

With no previous surgery, most osteoarthritis responds to one or two healing sessions, with the healee being relieved of all medical symptoms within hours or overnight. For this to occur, we are going beyond simple acceleration of the healing rate. Bone tissue is being regenerated in what common sense logic can best explain as genetic engineering. Success is achieved, following previously unsuccessful results, by placing the healee in a light hypnotic state before transmitting healing energy.

## 8. Heart muscle damage

Damage due to a heart attack is best treated in the earliest stages, but I have been able to regenerate heart muscle successfully within two months of the initial damage. Low and irregular pulse rates can be restored in one twenty-minute healing session, using two healers. I have not worked with other heart conditions.

## 9. Chronic lung impairment

Treatment has produced no consistent results. I attribute this to poor motivation on the part of the patient who has no sense of impending crisis. I also find lung-impaired people are more skeptical of the healing process than others. When I request cooperation for three or four weekly sessions over a period of weeks, they are less likely to agree than other clients.

### 10. Genital herpes II

This can be cured consistently with a few minutes of treatment.

### 11. Scoliosis

Scoliosis responds well to four consecutive daily half-hour sessions. Between sessions the healee usually experiences extreme spinal pain or pleasant spinal spasms during the night. One hurting healee consoled herself with the explanation that if the bone structure were changing shape, it was likely to be painful.

### 12. Cancer patients

Cancer patients respond well when painful memories or anger, fear, and depression are removed through a new technique called Emotional Release Therapy. Cancer appears to feed on emotional pain. Remove the emotional pain and cancer cells begin normalizing. Or, the patient may respond better to conventional medical treatment.

### 13. Breast lumps (benign)

These respond to touch-healing as well as arthritis does. My first experience with breast lumps occurred fifteen years ago when a mammogram disclosed that my wife had a lump in her left breast. Prior to the surgical biopsy, I practiced touch-healing prayer daily for a week. No lump was found during the biopsy and the incision was twice normal size because the doctor looked for it carefully. Since then, I've found that one ten-minute touch-healing session removes the symptoms, within forty-eight hours, for about ninety percent of clients. Though my wife responded well, those most resistant to healing are family members. Cancerous breast lumps do not respond quickly to touch-healing.

### 14. Bacterial and viral infections

These are most healable during their earliest stages. It seems that when the energy field patterns have been changed to reflect the infection, there is more resistance. So healing must begin in the earliest stages before the energy fields are also infected and help to maintain the disease.

### 15. Emotional conditions

These all respond well to Emotional Release Therapy. Any traumatic memory can be permanently removed within an hour. Destructive emotional states like depression, fear, anxiety, and anger can be permanently removed in one to three sessions. Emotional Release Therapy is possible because we store our emotional histories in our emotional energy field. There, they stick to us like glue. We have access to the emotional energy field through the heart chakra. A simple technique permits a client to release their emotional hurts into the healer's hand. It is like draining an abscess.

## 16. Animals

Animals respond well to touch-healing prayer. Dogs, cats, and horses with chronic or life-threatening conditions respond exceptionally well.

## HEALING-CHARGED MATERIALS

I give healing-treated cotton dish towels to people with physical injuries and specific chronic conditions. Those who drape a healing-charged cotton towel over arthritic joints will normally experience the alleviation of all arthritic symptoms within a few weeks.

Knowing the scientific evidence on healing-charged water, my first attempt was with Gertrude, an eighty-six-year-old woman who had spurs (calcium deposits) on her spine, for which medical science had no treatment. Her

*A healing-charged cotton dishtowel is one of the best tools for trauma injuries and localized conditions*

medical condition caused such pain when she walked that she became confined to a wheelchair. Because of my limited time to practice touch-healing prayer with her on a daily basis, Gertrude agreed to drink two ounces of healer-treated water four times daily. Her son-in-law, John, brought me a glass pitcher of water which I held in my hands for twenty minutes to charge. Four days later, Gertrude phoned and asked me to come over. She greeted me at the door in her finest dress. She had awakened that morning pain-free, gotten up, taken a shower, dressed, and fixed the family breakfast. Gertrude lived a full life into her nineties.

Another case: for three years a thirteen-year-old named Wanda had suffered daily from the symptoms of Crohn's Disease. These symptoms included nausea, dizziness, vomiting, and abdominal pain. After one healing session, Wanda was symptom-free for a week before the symptoms returned. Additional healing sessions each brought relief for about seven days. I charged water jugs with healing energy that she ingested daily. This routine can keep her symptom-free. The symptoms of Wanda's chronic illness are alleviated by healer-charged water, just as insulin relieves the symptoms of diabetes.

## Life Enhancing Plants

The use of healing energy to enhance the growth and health of plants has been overlooked. Those who might choose to practice in this area might be better termed "life enhancers." Experimental data indicates that plant growth and health can be enhanced by blessing them with prayer and touch. In addition, seeds can be bathed with healing energy before planting by soaking them in healing-treated water.

Further clinical research is crucial for understanding the clinical usefulness of stored healing energy. Think how helpful it would be to therapeutically bathe a hospital patient in a healing energy provided by healer-charged wiring, water, cotton towels, or quartz crystals, or a frequency generator.

## The Potentials of Spiritual Healing

We have looked at a few of the practical applications of healing prayer. The data suggests that spiritual healing, in cooperation with medical and other professions, can do far more than anyone has dreamed.

Here is a list of the potential uses of healing knowledge:

1. Reduce or completely curb most physical and emotional pain
2. Increase the body's growth and healing rates
3. Initiate the healing process in chronic illnesses
4. Prevent anticipated diseases from occurring
5. Heal major chronic and life-threatening illnesses such as cancer, heart disease, arthritis, hearing loss, and, in newborns, genetic defects and "preemie" development
6. Hold the secret to how the body's immune system works, providing medical understanding of such diseases as multiple sclerosis, Lou Gehrig's disease, herpes simplex, AIDS, and cancer
7. Restore damaged human body tissue and organs
8. Remove painful and trauma memories of children, youth, and adults
9. Remove fixated destructive emotional states such as depression, anxiety, fear, anger
10. Enhance learning and cooperation in school classrooms

11. Offer spirituality and wholeness to couples, families, schools, the community, and work sites

12. Form therapeutic group energy fields which transform everyone encompassed in them, aiding families, communities, and nations. This transforms, building communities where everyone is filled with a sense of inner peace, love, cooperation, and responsibility

13. Restore the ecology of Earth through planetary-wide healing energy fields.

# 10

# The Miracle of Group Energy Fields

Research on how prayer heals presents us with many new paradigms. You have just been reading about them. No paradigm is more miraculous than the model for social behavior present in group energy fields. Why do groups act as they do? A mystery answers this.

The mystery first presented itself some twenty years ago in Pittsburgh as I was reading a group of books about the healing evangelist Kathryn Kuhlmann. Two books by different authors told the same documented story. I was intrigued by it at the time and long puzzled over it.

When Kathryn Kuhlmann was leading her healing services, the stories said, people walking on the sidewalk outside the building or driving past in a car were healed. Although they had not been aware that a healing service was going on inside the building they were passing, they were healed, nevertheless. Was there a rational explanation?

Kathryn Kuhlmann did not touch persons to heal them. The healings took place in persons seated throughout the congregation. Healer Father Ralph DiOrio also does not touch persons for healing in his healing services. How, then, do such healings occur?

As my understanding grew, I came to know that there is only one logical explanation. The only way that people can be healed when they are seated anywhere throughout a hall during a large healing service is if somehow the healing energy is able to touch them. Having sat through many a healing service, I can sense the presence of an energy throughout the meeting-place. Scientifically, energy cannot exist freely outside of a field of energy. Therefore, somehow, during a healing service a large group energy field (GEF) is formed. This energy field is filled with information that acts intelligently to restore humans to their optimum state of life, just as does the energy transmitted by an individual during touch-healing prayer.

As we shall see, the healer acts as a catalyst in the formation of a healing group energy field which is filled with the intentions of all those present. When the healing GEF of the healing service becomes extremely powerful, it grows beyond the dimensions of the building, enveloping pedestrians on the sidewalk and people in passing cars. Because the information-laden GEF acts intelligently, it transforms the energies of those within the vicinity and these people are healed. Thus, the mystery is solved.

## Sacred Space As a Sacred Energy Field

God is spirit. God can be described scientifically as an energy field. When people have strong experiences of God, God's presence or energy can continue to linger, permeating the objects in the area, just as healing energy can permeate water, cotton and wool.

Those in the Judeo-Christian-Islamic tradition are aware of the concept of "holy ground" as applied to locations in the Old Testament where God had appeared to people. Aside from the historical significance of the God-encounter, God's presence lingered after the event as an information-laden energy. People later sensed this divine presence in the lingering energy and the area literally became holy ground.

This brings us to the contemporary concept of sacred space. Religious congregations dedicate their worship areas to God. The worship area becomes a sacred space where reverence is shown through personal attitudes and sacred usage. But it seems to be more than the concept of sacred space that creates the reverence. Most persons "sense" the presence of God in these places. And, just like God's biblical people, they may state their awareness by saying, "Surely, God is in this holy place." Again, an explanation for this is that God's presence lingers as an energy field that permeates the area.

For similar reasons, spiritual wisdom advises people always to carry out their spiritual disciplines of worship, meditation, and prayer in one place in their homes. Experienced healers do all their healing in one particular healing room, even placing healees in the same chair. People can "sense" the holiness in such rooms. God's presence has formed a sacred, information-laden energy field in those places, making further contacts with God easier.

When I was to be interviewed by a potential new congregation, I would first go up to the altar area of the chancel. I would stand quietly, seeking to discern the presence of God. I wanted to be sure that I could sense God in this holy place before I accepted any invitation to be the pastor.

## The Power and Content of Group Energy Fields

For years, I have heard that the healing power of prayer was the square of those gathered in prayer. Later, the scientific theory of this will be provided. If ten thousand people gathered for a Kathryn Kuhlmann healing service, the power generated and the size of the resulting healing group energy field would be enormous. It would represent 100 million individual praying units of intelligently acting healing power. That is why a passerby, with no expectations, could be healed outside a Kuhlmann healing service.

Any time two or more people gather together, they form a group energy field whose information is filled with their identity, intentions, actions, or words.

## A Healing Circle Provides Another Mystery

We are assuming that a healing service GEF carries within it God's power to heal. This energy is intelligent. It bears information that heals. Are other GEFs similar in their ability to carry information within them? The following story provides our first clue.

My first reaction in the group was one of surprise. I had been expecting God, but I was enveloped by another enormous power. There was none of the familiar holy presence of gathered Christians; there was no sensing of love, joy or peace. My surprise quickly turned to curiosity. What was going on?

This occurred during the late 1970's. I had been invited by a group of strangers to take part in a healing circle. The leader, Jim, led twenty of us in an unfamiliar chant to "raise the healing vibrations." I had expected to experience the familiar sense of God as I did in

Christian church gatherings. But I did not. Instead, an enormous neutral power, an informationally neutral GEF, filled the little room and enveloped us. It was a pliable power. It appeared as if those present could use it in any way they chose. The emotional levels stayed neutral. We silently directed this power to persons needing healing.

That night, I spent several sleepless hours, seeking to make sense of the anomalous experience. I recalled the Old Testament's First Commandment, "You shall have no other gods before me" (Deuteronomy 5:7). Was that enormous neutral power in the healing circle God? Or had I encountered another god, other than my Heavenly Father? No, that was no god. What was it? I knew I must explore this further.

The next week, I was again part of the healing circle. Before going, I surrounded myself in the Creator's presence. In doing so, I wanted to protect my human energy field (HEF) from outside influences. During the healing circle, I now sensed nothing unusual. There was only the Creator within me. I had unknowingly surrounded myself with the biblical "breast-plate of righteousness" (Ephesians 6:14). I had gathered with a group of persons who said they were creating divine power to heal, but the GEF they had created did not include qualities of my God. I had another mystery to store until more information brought understanding.

## God's Power During Healing Services

In the years since, I have participated in numerous gatherings whose purpose was healing. Each time a "power" is present within the group energy field. I had

153

once called that power God, the Heavenly Father. Now I did not know what to call it.

I have the ability to sense the different qualities present in GEFs. For religious gatherings, my baseline is my own experience of God in the Christian context. During worship, I had always sensed the fruits of the Spirit: ("The fruits of the Spirit are love, joy, peace, patience, kindness, goodness, faithfulness, gentleness, and self-control" (Galatians 5:22). I had thought that I would always feel these qualities of God in the same way. By now, the phenomenon was occurring in more than just that healing circle. When I visited various healing services, God felt different in each. Certain traits were missing. Often, one trait predominated, like peace, or love, or holiness. In many services, I sensed only an enormous power or energy, as in that first healing circle. This was often tempered by a pervading sense of peace. What was the significance of this?

Another clue can be found in giant healing services. A long period of preparation, usually hours, passes before the service begins, as the congregation arrives early to find the choice seats. During this period, I discern a change in feeling levels. First, there is a boredom, then an annoyance at the delay, and a letdown just preceding the service. Finally, an air of expectation quickly builds. The large congregation is becoming unified as a group. This is inevitably followed by the build-up of living energy, an enormous power. It feels thick, like a warm fog. Sometimes it comes through as oppressive and clinging, like honey. If you have been to such services, you are already identifying with this description. I had always thought this to be the presence and power of God. But is it?

## An Anomaly Noticed Among Hindu Yogis

In 1989, hundreds of yogis from twenty nations gathered for an international yoga conference in Pondicherry, India. These were some of the most developed yogi adepts on earth. Yoga is a Hindu meditation style designed for developing the self mentally, physically and spiritually. Those who have mastered yoga are called yogis.

During the four-day conference, I experienced almost a dozen yogi devotional moments in which the yogis sang their sacred songs and mantras. I did not understand their language, but I could sense the spiritual qualities of the gathering. The sacred group energy field they created through their religious ritual was completely devoid of all feelings. This was another anomaly. I sensed no love, joy, peace, or holiness. What I did sense was pure intellect. It was disconcerting at first. But then I remembered the goal of Hinduism. It is to become totally devoid of feeling. It is to become pure intellect so one can be united with the Pure Intellect that is God. I sensed the same qualities at a Hindu worship service at an ashram.

## God Possesses Differing Religious Qualities

How can the one God possess differing religious qualities? Could it be that I had been sloppy in my thinking? Perhaps I had been mistaken in believing that I sensed the essence of God in GEFs. But what other explanation is there?

The revealed image of God is different in each religion. The qualities people sense in God's Spirit vary with the religion. Hindus experience God as pure intellect and devoid of emotion. Christians and Jews experience God as having emotional qualities like love, joy, and peace. So, could there be a link between what people believe about God and the GEFs they form?

John Rossner, a religious history professor in Montreal and a Canadian Anglican priest, states that every religious tradition is expressed in four identical developments. First is a God who reveals his/her own nature. This is the revelation of the nature of the divine to human beings. The second development is a God who transforms believers into his/her own revealed divine nature. Third is a God who empowers believers with the ability to perform divine miracles. Fourth, God empowers his/her believers to be channels for divine healing. All religions share these developmental stages in common.

There is one anomaly in these four developmental stages. It is something that does not fit. It makes one of the stages different from the others. The last three developments are true of all religions. God transforms the believer into his/her image, empowers him/her to do miracles and enables him/her to offer healing. The anomaly is the content of the divine revelation.

There is one God of us all. But the revelation of the image of God is different in each religion. The revelation tells the believer the nature of God. The believer seeks to become transformed into the image of the qualities revealed to be in God. For the Hindu, this means to become pure spiritual intellect during spiritual moments. For the Muslim, this means faith and submission to Allah's laws. For the Christian believer, it means to be transformed into the revelational image of God as seen in Jesus, the Savior.

## The Revelational Image of God

At this point, we must make a distinction between two concepts: the true image of God and the revelational image of God. Most religions claim that their particular revelation of God is the only true image of God. For instance, some Christians claim that the only way to salvation and eternal life is to be transformed into the image of God as revealed by Jesus the Savior. They believe Jesus has given humanity the only true image of God. Some Christians believe that their particular branch of the Church holds all the truth, and, that all other branches of the Church possess false beliefs.

It is scientifically questionable whether any of Earth's existing religions reflect, objectively speaking, the true image of God. All revelational images of God tend to pertain to the human culture from which the revelational image emerged. Believers have no choice but to accept the revealed image of God of their religion. As believers are immersed in the group energy field formed during worship and prayer, the information-laden group energy field is changing them. It is acting intelligently to transform them into the revealed image of God. The beliefs of believers are present in the information-laden sacred group energy field. This information, the revealed Word, acts intelligently in transforming and molding their minds.

This transformation into the revealed image of God is the second universal stage of development in all religions. I can sense the qualities of the fruits of the Spirit being emitted by mature Christians. I can also sense a common peace of God being emitted by Spirit-filled believers of other religious traditions.

When believers gather together, they begin emitting their individual revealed image of God and form a sacred group energy field filled with those revealed images of God-qualities. When they are subsequently bathed in the information of the formed sacred group energy field, it fills them with these divine qualities which act to transform them further. The power of God fills them. In this context, I have heard hundreds of parishioners comment, upon leaving the worship service, "God charged me up for another week."

The encouragement to participate in gatherings of one's particular faith tradition thus has a purpose beyond enabling the worshipper to act as a loyal believer. In building community, one is also building religious unity. The highest quality sacred group energy fields would be formed by believers who have religious education, commitment, spiritual experiences, and a life reflecting these. Religious rituals, songs, and prayers strengthen the content and power of the sacred group energy field.

## Making Sense of the Healing Circle Anomalies

During the healing circle noted earlier, where we chanted to create energy for our group energy field, we produced the pure energy we had intended. It did not contain Christian qualities, because we were performing an intellectual exercise. These were not practicing, believing Christians; therefore, their individual energy fields contained no revealed image of Christianity. So, their GEF was only capable of creating pure mental energy. I felt uncomfortable in the group because my energy field contained a different and discordant religious content.

## An Explanation of the Hindu Worship Anomaly

This also explains how I discerned the information of the Hindu yogis in their devotional rituals. The revelational image of God into which they had been transformed by the practice of yoga was present in their sacred group energy field. I sensed the pure divine intellect of their revealed image of God. The sacred group energy field that they created contained qualities representing their image of God which they embodied in each of their individual human energy fields while in contact with God.

This does not mean Hindus are not loving. They are loving in their personal lives. But while in religious ritual, they embody the revealed image of God as the Divine Intellect. Hindus practice healing, but they do so in the context of their revealed image of God. Their healing is like the psychic healing used in American holistic centers, rather than the spiritual healing of the Western context.

## Large Healing Service Anomalies

The revelational image of God also explains the emotional anomalies that I have sensed in large healing services. People in large faith healing services seldom worship. They are not a religious community. They are strangers to one another. Even if they do worship, their primary role is as spectators waiting for God to act. Their expectations, their needs and hopes, their spiritual being, plus other factors, are emitted from their personal human energy fields to become a part of the content of the giant healing group energy field. The main sensed quality of such a group energy field is God's power. God is present in all his great power. Just as we are partners with God in healing prayer, we also are partners with God in creating the group healing energy field.

## The Healer As a Group Catalyst

Earlier I described what I experienced in large healing services. The qualities present in the healing group energy field were different from those found in any other Christian rituals. Certain traits were missing. They were often dominated by one trait like peace or love or peace and holiness. In many services, I sensed only an enormous power or energy. This was often tempered by a pervading peace. I attribute much of this to the diversity and singular intent of the group. If they are not a worshipping congregation, but present to observe or to obtain a healing, the group energy field reflects this.

The healer presiding over a large healing service is doing something very special. The presiding healer does more than heal. Before healing can be offered, the healer must first be able to form a group energy field. The healer's energetic presence and charisma act as a catalyst, and the expectations of the gathered crowd contribute to this process as a healing group energy field is formed. The healer's own energy field may expand to encompass the whole group. And just as in the individual practice of healing, the healer must attune the energy of the whole healing group energy field to the healing frequency. The healer accomplishes this automatically.

As a leader of both worship services and healing services, I intentionally fill myself with God's presence and then mentally seek to spread this holiness throughout the gathering. Only measuring instruments could tell me if I am actually doing this or whether some unknown factor is involved. Within minutes, I can sense the sacred or healing group energy field being formed. My belief is that the intentions of all the individuals in the group are the major contributing factor. My role and ability involve creating a cohesive group energy field.

Healers appear to be hampered in creating a truly plus or minus 7.83 hertz frequency healing group energy field. The energy in most services feels coarse rather than fine-tuned. Ten thousand people squared produces one hundred million person-units of prayer power, yet less than one percent receive the healing they seek. Alone, with my relatively weak healing energy, I am more than ninety percent effective in healing people. The difference is that my individual energy is easier to attune than a group field.

During a recent large healing service conducted by another healer, I decided to fine-tune the group energy field frequency around me to a purer healing one. I was just sensing this occurring when the healer shouted, "Stop." He was pointing at me. Describing my appearance, he then said, "Leave my healing service alone. You have your way of doing things as a healer and I have mine. Mine works for me. Stop interfering!" I stopped. After the service, I apologized to the healer. His face was radiant with love as we embraced.

In large healing services, some healers appear to be in an altered state of consciousness similar to the hypnotic state but more accurately described as a trance state. In this trance state, the healer is believed to be inspired either directly by God's Spirit or by a guiding spirit from the Company of Heaven. Kathryn Kuhlmann had no memory of the service afterwards, a quality engendered by some trance states.

In this state, the healer has the spiritual gift of knowledge in which s/he knows either who is being healed or what type of illnesses can be healed at a given time in the service. In secular terms, the healer develops a telepathic linkage with the persons who will be healed and intuitively knows that he will be attuning to the specific energy frequency to heal a particular disease, like deafness. This ability to attune to persons can be explained by the unique information present in each individual energy field.

Everyone at a healing service has access to that immense healing group energy field. But it is the presiding healer who is most effective in bringing about individual healings. The issue of attuning answers the question of why less than one percent of those seeking healing at a giant healing service are healed. Only when the healer attunes the whole healing group energy to the frequency of 7.83 hertz, or when he attunes his own energy to the unique frequency of a particular individual or a specific disease, can healing take place.

## God As Expressed in Group Energy Fields

God uses people as channels for healing. Just like individual acts of touch-healing, healing group energy fields enable us to be channels for God's wholeness. This goes far beyond what we have dared to speculate. When people gather together for a healing service, the qualities of the revealed image of God in the individual human energy fields help to create the healing group energy field, along with the healer-leader as the catalyst. This group-created healing group energy field forms the context from which the healing flows for God's miracles of healing. Then frequency-attuning takes place to make the best use of the healing energy.

Group energy fields are constantly being formed naturally, outside of a sacred context. Whenever two or more persons are gathered for a common intention or action, a group energy field is formed. When caring occurs, a group energy field is formed which has characteristics similar to a healing group energy field. You can sense the love and peace present in a caring encounter. This is especially true of support groups where people share their hurts, and compassion is expressed. I design such encounters into my own healing services.

## William Tiller's Theory of Group Coherence

Is there any scientific basis for my group energy field analysis? The answer is yes. Physicist William A. Tiller of Stanford University provides a scientific theory on the power of the energy emitted by a coherent group energy field. Coherent means to stick together or to be logically connected and intelligible. A coherent human group has a common, clearly defined intent, emotion, or action. Professor Tiller states that the energetic power of a coherent group is the square of the number of people involved.

The energy of one person is one volt as the Menninger Clinic data shows. The energy of two people gathered together is four volts. The energy of ten people in a coherent group energy field is ten times ten, or one hundred volts. The energy of five thousand people in a coherent group energy field is five thousand times five thousand or twenty-five million volts. A million gathered people is 1,000,000,000,000 volts. A billion people can produce 1,000,000,000,000,000,000 volts through the attuned intent of their prayers.

This accounts for the energy involved in groups. For those who would like to examine the scientific data, the following section presents the details of Dr. Tiller's scientific theory.

## Tiller's Theory Presented Mathematically

During the 1960s, before I had any curiosity about the nature of group energy fields, physicist William Tiller formulated his theory of group coherence. In my private communications with Dr. Tiller, he explained the basic physics of his theory, beginning with: "The energy of a wave is proportional to the square of its amplitude."

1. On average, a single individual's energy effectiveness, E, for any specific application like healing, creating, working, etc., can be theoretically modeled as being directly proportional to the square of some quantity that we can call the individual's output wave amplitude, A. That is:

$$E \, cA^2 \text{ where c is some constant.}$$

2. On average, a group of N people's energy effectiveness for collective application to the same area of focus will be:

$$E \, N \, (cA^2)$$

3. a. Destructive Interference. If people are acting as interacting but largely independent resonators, this is because of the usual destructive interference that occurs between uncoordinated individual efforts: that is, their efforts are not in phase with each other.

b. Constructive Interference. However, if N people are coherently attuned to each other, their efforts will be both cooperative and completely in phase with each other's so that constructive interference occurs and we have:

$$E = c(NA)^2 = N\,[N(cA^2)]$$

Thus, we see that coherence versus incoherence in group efforts substantially increases the energy effectiveness of the action (by a factor often significantly higher than N).

## The Information-Laden GEFs of Secular Gatherings

At every large gathering of people, sacred or secular, there is a distinctive group flavor. A common feeling pervades everyone present. All groups of people who are focused on one purpose or action create information-bearing group energy fields. Even before a music concert begins, one can feel elated expectation pervading the crowd. Then the music begins molding the whole audience into oneness—a sharing of common thoughts and emotions—a coherent group. We can understand that and say it is caused only by the sounds of the music. But the evidence is that the performers have projected their energy into the audience. A good performance means the performers have projected their charisma—the information from their inner selves—into the audience's group energy field.

When fans gather for a football game, the emotional energy feels great. When the team is losing, one can feel the letdown pervade the crowd. When the team is winning, one senses an emotional high. Even persons who know little about football get caught up in the emotions of the coherent energetic group energy field. The noisy cheers are considered a home team advantage.

Another factor to consider is the effect of the home team's coherent group energy field on both teams. Also, do the emotional qualities of the group energy field at times cause violent actions and even sporting event riots? Could the aggression and anger building up in a group energy field place some persons into a mindless and violent trance state? The people gathered for any one purpose or intention are molded into a oneness of expectancy and emotion. Because human energy fields extend beyond the body and interact with other human energy fields, emotions are contagious.

Let us repeat what has been said. Every person possesses human energy fields. The human energy fields are bearers of information—mental, emotional, religious, moral—according to the activity with which the person is involved. Energy radiates from the individual human energy fields and mingles with other gathered human energy fields. When the individual human energy fields merge, they become one enormous, information-bearing, group energy field whose power is the square of the coherent number of persons gathered.

The group energy field entity is a "group mind" that can overwhelm individual will when the group energy field acts intelligently on the information within it. Parapsychology has compiled impressive experimental evidence that emotions are transmittable, but the mechanism by which this phenomenon occurs has not previously been named. That mechanism is now obvious. It is the information-bearing energy fields of living organisms that transmit information to other organisms.

This provides insight into troubling manifestations of group behavior. We have always been puzzled by mob violence. Why does a group of sane, responsible persons become a mindless group entity filled with such rage that they will injure and murder other human beings? A violent mob is a merging of individual human energy fields into a coherent group energy field, expressing the fears, angers, and prejudices of each individual. The group energy field takes on a life of its own, becoming an independent emotional entity. It becomes a mass mind that overpowers individual thought, caution, and responsibility. No other explanation fits!

The practical implications for crowd control expand with this understanding. When law enforcement authorities seek to control a violent mob, the authorities can become just as mindlessly violent as the mob as they, too, become enveloped in the angry, information-bearing group energy field. The feelings of a group are contagious, enveloping anyone who enters the group energy field. This implies that enforcement authorities need a means of protecting themselves from the angry vibes of a group energy field so they can responsibly carry out their job of crowd dispersion.

There are several possibilities for cooling a violent crowd. First, it is necessary to employ procedures to move a crowd out of the feeling-state of consciousness into the thinking-state of consciousness. That might mean getting the mob refocused on thinking and logic through obedience to authority, awareness of the wrongfulness of their actions, or logical dialogue. Other possibilities involve deploying appropriate music, humor, caring and love, or prayer.

It would be constitutionally problematic, but bathing a violent mob with a calming wavelength from a frequency generator of extremely low frequency waves would work. The most likely frequencies are at the 7.83 hertz healing frequency and at the calming frequency of 10 hertz that the United States Navy physicists discovered and Russia has used to calm workers.

The concept of group energy fields created by gathered individuals raises other concerns. Why do people tend to become like the company they keep? We think we have strong minds of our own. But if individual or group energy fields are information-bearing and can transfer this information to others, then even what we think and feel is being quietly changed. Be with substance abusers or criminals and their information-bearing energy fields will slowly subvert your best intentions. You will be changed against your will or knowledge. This explains the wisdom that "you become like the company you keep." It also explains the changes that occurred in kidnap victim Patty Hearst, who was transformed into a supporter of the beliefs and actions of her politically revolutionary kidnappers.

The implication for families is similar. The individual human energy fields of household members interact with each other. Emotional states, values, and attitudes are spread to everyone. Stress and anger, or love and peace are spread to everyone. In searching for the emotional causes of disease, medical researchers must not only look at the emotions of the ill, but also at the emotions projected to the ill by family and others. Living in a hostile environment will destroy healthy energy fields and replace them with energy frequencies that distort the human energy field and cause illness and death.

There are solutions for those living within destructive group energy fields. I now know that families and other groups can change the negativity in their midst through group prayer. In doing so, they are creating sacred space. A sacred group energy field bathes them in the power, love, joy, and peace of God. In other words, they are being bathed in God's presence. This transforms everyone; each is filled with these qualities. Health and wholeness follow. Anyone can learn to do this.

There are other examples. Many urban experts are puzzled by the fact that residents of an entire neighborhood carry similar thoughts, attitudes, values, and even act alike. Aside from the known factors, could neighborhood group energy fields transform residents by changing individual human energy fields, causing them to conform to either similar constructive or destructive factors? And if so, can we use Therapeutic Prayer to form a neighborhood therapeutic group energy field to bathe and transform all residents into caring and responsible persons?

It is said that prisons harden guards as well as criminals. Placing a thousand criminals together would create a group energy field whose qualities would reflect the values, attitudes, and emotions of each criminal. To alleviate this means developing a way to alter the harmful group energy field into a more productive group energy field. This can be done by making each individual separate from the group energy field through an electronic frequency shielding.

An even better way would be to teach the prisoners Therapeutic Prayers to create a therapeutic group energy field that will bathe them in qualities they voluntarily accept. Prisoners then become able to change and grow.

They could heal violent or criminal behavior, emerging from prison as normal. Research suggests that many criminals are enslaved by rigid brain wave patterns. Prayer can heal these.

### Designing Group Energy Fields

I have attempted to create a group energy field composed of love and peace by simply asking those present to concentrate on love and peace. This has not worked. But one can create the qualities desired in a group energy field through the activities with which the group is involved or through the intentions expressed in prayer.

When people care for and pray for each other, the group energy field becomes filled with God, love, and peace. This can be done within a family, among friends, in any community group, or for a whole neighborhood, community, or nation. Being bathed in such a group energy field transforms people just as touch-healing prayer, or a worship or healing service will do.

Designing therapeutic GEFs for senior citizens, the grieving, the depressed, the mentally ill, criminals, or crime-ridden neighborhoods could change the quality of life for a whole nation or the world. Finally, the use of GEFs to restore our environment is also feasible. Imagine a GEF with one million, one billion, or one trillion energy units of prayer power. Remember that healing energy acts intelligently to transform all life to its optimum condition. Polluted water and air possess energy fields upon which such a force could work. Could toxic waste sites be cleansed of their poisons? This is theoretically possible.

## Group Energy Fields in History

Group energy fields play an important role in the history of most religions. The Jews experienced a number of group events during the Exodus from Egypt. Christians had a group gathered in Jerusalem waiting for the coming of the Holy Spirit, out of which comes Pentecost.

Have you ever wondered how a cruel tyrant is able to maintain his power? I have no doubt that Adolph Hitler was a group catalyst. With this ability, he was able to create and maintain a coherent national group energy field in Nazi Germany, which brainwashed and changed decent people into cruel and inhumane zealots. This could have been possible only if he tapped into the darker fears and angers of a sizable group of Germans. Once they opened themselves to the GEF, their transformation became complete.

One of the most remarkable recent group events occurred during 1989-90, when the communist Soviet Union and its European satellites experienced one of the most rapid peaceful political and economic revolutions in human history. Obviously, these were group phenomena. The pent-up needs of enslaved people reached a critical group consciousness, exploding into revolutions that suddenly transformed their nations and shocked and surprised all of humanity. I have no doubt that these revolutions were created by information-bearing, coherent group energy fields acting intelligently to achieve their goals. I cite one example of how this occurred.

## The Fall of Communist East Germany

In 1989, the government of Communist East Germany, also known as the German Democratic Republic, collapsed as a result of more than just political and economic forces. Since 1980, the churches of that nation had annually celebrated a peace event known as "Ten Days for Peace," during which peace was emphasized in prayer, workshops, celebrations, and correspondence with persons of other nations. Out of this grew weekly prayer services for peace in many German churches.

In the autumn of 1989, the government, believing the churches were promoting political subversion, forbade the prayer services and the demonstrations growing out of them. In October, the churches defied the order. The Communist government decided to make the Nicolai Church in Leipzig an example. Twelve hundred Communist party members arrived early and filled every seat in the downstairs of the Nikolai Church, thinking they would keep out all worshippers.

To seat the parishioners, the unused balconies of the church were opened and filled with sincere worshipers. A service of prayer was conducted. No hatred or anger was expressed. In love, they prayed for peace and justice. This created a huge sacred group energy field. This energy field contained the knowledge of their prayer content and the political and spiritual yearnings of the worshippers. The group energy field then acted intelligently, based upon this knowledge.

The results were amazing. The love, peace, light, justice, and the national yearnings of those in prayer transformed the government agents. They felt at one with the church people. They became incapable of using violence against their fellow citizens. Millions of Germans began praying, creating a huge sacred group energy field that pervaded all of East Germany. The information in this energy field changed the consciousness of a nation. The government collapsed.

This example can give us a new understanding and interpretation of many seemingly unexplainable religious, political and military events. It can guide intelligent planning for change through the actions of group energy fields. Ten million people praying provide the enormous force of 10,000,000,000,000 volts of prayer power.

Our awareness of the power of group energy fields gives us a tool for transforming our troubled planet. Any positive results you achieve in your family or in a small group will also work with equal effect in a neighborhood, community, or nation. So, experiment, develop your skills, and prepare for the larger visions.

## Stopping a Cataclysmic Earth Crisis

Suppose a large comet is approaching on a collision course with Earth. How do we save Earth? One option is having four billion people pray for the comet's path to veer away from Earth. That would produce 16,000,000,000,000,000,000 volts of intelligent-acting energy. This is a far stronger force than nuclear bombs could provide. In addition, no stray pieces of a broken-up comet would hit Earth.

In a similar way, we could alter the path of a hurricane or stop a scientifically-predicted earthquake from occurring. We might be able to alter the weather to stop thunderstorms from flooding or provide rain for drought-stricken areas. We might be able to alter the heating-up of Pacific waters. Just imagine ten million people praying for regional weather changes. They would provide 100,000,000,000,000 volts of intelligent-acting energy that could alter weather patterns.

# 11

# Human Energy Field Interactions

For years, it affected me. Counseling sessions often exhausted me, especially with persons who were depressed, angry, anxious, or fearful. When I walked down the hospital corridor of a cancer ward, I could feel myself being drained. An hour's trip through a crowded shopping mall left me exhausted.

Millions share my former plight, constant fatigue. People sensitive to the needs of others often pay a price, a sense of being drained of energy. Many of those affected are professional caregivers. A clinical psychologist once told me an eight-hour day with clients left him with no energy resources to share with his family. He felt this played a role in his divorce.

Teachers, nurses, doctors, counselors, clergy, social workers, and salespersons have all shared the vocational problem of becoming drained day after day. Some eventually burn out and take early retirement. Others may be victims of Chronic Fatigue Syndrome, a condition that limits the lives of millions of Americans.

These people possess few hints about the source of their exhaustion. If the symptoms get too severe, they consult their physician, seeking the cause. Usually a physician suggests learning how to cope with stress. But, no matter what they do, the fatigue persists. What's causing this?

A dozen years ago, I came to the conclusion that mental effort, stress, and physical health could not account for my fatigue. My energy could be restored by a good night's sleep or by spending a day at home. It was spending time with certain people that seemed to cause my fatigue. I concluded that those people were somehow draining my energy.

## Energy Vampires

Then I heard a new term, "energy vampire." With that phrase, all the pieces of the puzzle began to fit together. As I counseled troubled persons, I came to sense that their energy fields were exhausting me. When I entered a hospital patient ward, the patients were draining me in some unknown way. Large crowds were somehow wiping me out. I was a victim of energy vampires.

When I studied subtle energies research, I found evidence that my earlier conclusions had a scientific basis. The outer skin of the physical body does not imprison the radiations of human energy fields. They project constantly outwards, often to a radius of twenty-five feet, mingling and interacting with the environment.

All energy contains information that can influence human energy fields. Concern has been expressed about the effects of the various man-made electromagnetic frequencies bombarding us from high-power lines, computer terminals, microwave ovens, etc. Of equal or greater consequence may be the energy interactions we have with other people.

Ambrose Worrall observed that life energy, like electricity, flows from a strong source of energy to a weaker source. People who cannot produce enough energy for their own needs are forced to steal it from other sources.

From clinical data we know that healers transmit an energy that transforms and brings health to others. In the last chapter, we discovered that group energy fields bathe their participants in information that acts intelligently according to that information. Group energy fields can influence people to love or to riot. Individual human energy fields can affect us far more than group fields.

## Examples of Energy Field Interactions: Depressed People Drain

Many who work with depressed persons report large energy drains. A depressed person's energy field works in the same way as what astronomers call a "black hole" in space. A black hole absorbs all the energy around it but never becomes filled. A depressed person's energy field seems to operate in a similar fashion. It absorbs all the energy around it, but is seemingly not energized by it. The energy disappears as if going down a whirlpool-like drain into another dimension, or as if it is leaking through holes in a ruptured human energy field. Depressed persons are the worst type of energy vampires. Their enormous need for energy can only be satisfied by draining the energy from other people's energy fields.

## Cancer Patients Drain Energy

People with cancer display similar characteristics. The research data of life energy scientists suggest cancer cells develop energy fields independent of the physical body's energy fields. The energy field of cancer cells competes with the body's own energy system for energy. It seems to absorb the energy around it to reinforce its own cell strength. The patient is then forced to draw life energy from his environment, including from other people.

## Energy Field Pollution

Evidence exists for human energy field pollution. When energy fields interact, one field can leave information—mental, emotional, physical or spiritual—which influences the energy field of another. If this is unwanted information, it is influencing and polluting another person's energy field. The energy fields of those persons who are angry, resentful, fearful, or feeling inadequate contaminate the fields of others. Polluted energy fields coat you with alien negative feelings and thoughts that short-circuit the normal flow and balance. This causes fatigue until the pollution is either removed or diluted by time. This is a theoretical working model for energy field contamination.

## Energy Field Pollution and Illness

Researchers have been studying the role of the emotions in the onset of physical illness. This is mind-body work on the role of a patient's internal mental and emotional processes at the onset of disease. Unresolved anger has been linked to the onset of a number of diseases. All of these mind-body studies have only examined the emotions of the person who is ill. None has taken into account the negative emotions present in the patient's environment. Could living in a hostile emotional environment prove to be a primary link to disease?

My own observations in a hostile work environment suggest such a linkage. Energy field interactions provide the mechanism. Three decades ago, as I began a ministry in the inner city, urban riots broke out in the neighborhood I was serving. In the aftermath of this violence, immense hostility and distrust arose between white and black residents of the community. Being a white professional in the midst of the black community, I became an available target for black hostility. I received weekly death threats from neighborhood residents for more than a year and was surrounded with hostility daily for almost five years.

Two other white clergymen shared a similar hostile environment. The first, Earl, suffered a heart attack a year before I left. I chose to leave that neighborhood because the stress had already produced hemorrhoids in me. Eighteen months later, I had a heart attack from clogged coronary arteries. While recovering, I phoned my second clergy friend in that neighborhood, Bob, suggesting he leave that hostile environment "because it might damage your health." A year later, Bob suffered a heart attack and died.

Yes, our heart attacks were stress-related. But it was not the anger within us that corroded our coronary arteries. It was not self-generated anger. It was the anger directed at us by others, as an energy, that filled our energy fields with poisonous venom.

I suggest that researchers examine the emotional environment in which patients live when exploring the mind-body connection. Medical treatment could include using touch-healing techniques that remove the negative emotions from the heart chakra.

## Interpersonal Energy Interactions

An angry person sends angry energy field emanations with extreme power. Some recipients may cower in fear. When one person intimidates the other, it is not just the force of words or a conditioned response. The intimidated person cringes because of an invisible interaction of energy fields allowing the intimidation to occur. Any defense must not only involve assertiveness training, but a means of protecting one's own energy fields from attack.

## Energy Intimidates Family Members

I have counseled many wives who are routinely intimidated by their husbands. No matter how the wife attempts to cope—even with assertiveness training—she is always fighting a losing battle. Her irritated or angry husband dominates every encounter; his projected energy field always overwhelms hers.

Knowing this, dominated spouses can learn to marshal the resources needed to become equals in such energy field power struggles. Do not choose projecting anger as your weapon of defense. This escalates the anger and leads to violence. You form a group energy field during this interaction that quadruples the power of your individual emotions.

Any defense involves either blocking off the other person's access to your energy field with a shield, or projecting an energy filled with compassionate love that neutralizes the anger, as acid is neutralized by an alkaline substance. The best psychological defense is verbally acknowledging the anger of the angry person. Example: "I sense that you are angry."

## Loving Interactions

The sharing of positive emotions is the upside of energy field interactions. Huggers sense this. Family members share their love and peace with each other, forming a life-giving group energy field which others can easily sense.

Lovers know the passionate energy of their human energy fields merging into sensations of heat, tingling, and pleasure. Lovers never lose their physical passion when they learn to merge their energy fields through Hindu Tantric energy field merging techniques.

One can feel the emotional warmth emanating from the rooms of a home where there is love, joy, and peace. One can also feel fear, anger, or an emotional void in the home of a dysfunctional marriage or family.

Caution is needed here. Yes, we can sometimes sense the information of another's human energy field. Note the word sometimes. Sometimes we may be attributing our own inner state or expectations to the other person. When you are sensing anger or fear in another, what does that mean? Is the person angry with you, with himself, someone else, or the whole world? Is the anger ongoing or temporary? Either way, what do you do with that information?

We need to be aware of both the temporary and long-term states of the human energy fields. When you are with a therapeutic personality or a healer, you will usually sense an atmosphere of peace and love. This is the 7.83 hertz frequency emitted by the healer's energy fields. Those persons may not feel its influence themselves, but others around them will. It is difficult to leave the presence of such persons because of the beneficial effects of their energy fields.

If you spend considerable time with a family member, friend, or fellow worker, you are susceptible to what is going on within them, and they, to you. A fellow worker is despondent because his spouse has left him. How does that affect you? In your household, a family member is physically ill or emotionally troubled. How does his or her impaired energy field affect you? Do the energy fields of others have short- or long-term effects upon yours? If each disease has a unique frequency, can the interaction of energy fields increase the likelihood of your contracting the illness? If so, how long must a contact be sustained for it to have a harmful effect?

## Feeling-Thinking Interaction

The love between two persons is transmitted in the information shared by their merged energy fields. Persons who lack this awareness are socially and interpersonally handicapped. When a feeling type, or people-person, expresses feelings to a thinking, logical type of person, the thinking type is usually unaware of the feelings expressed in the energy field. The thinking type tends to be blind to the feeling levels of energy and unable to pick up emotional information or cues from energy fields. Unable to sense the energy of feelings, the thinking type is labeled unfeeling. This is true if he is unable to sense feelings in energy fields.

## Minority Abilities

People who hold a minority status in any culture tend to be capable of picking up the feeling-information projected in human energy fields by the majority culture. It is a useful skill that is necessary for survival in a suspicious and sometimes hostile environment. Black Americans have told me that they have a sixth sense—a survival trait, an intuitive ability—telling them when someone holds prejudiced feelings towards them. Existence of human energy fields that are bearers of information accounts for the presence of this survival trait.

## Group Negotiations

Information present and discernible in human energy fields explains many things. When any two individuals or groups are negotiating their differences, the interaction of their energy fields plays a major role in the results. Whether it is two different factions, races, cultures, nations, or management versus labor, beneficial results are more likely to occur when their interacting energy fields are taken into account.

I can envision a future where a growing awareness of human energy field interactions plays a major role. If we can learn to sense the sacredness and humanity in the energy fields of every person, then the entire human race will learn to treat all persons with dignity and fairness. If those who inflict cruelty upon others begin sensing the pain, anguish, and hurt they are causing, this will slowly begin to transform them into more compassionate persons.

## Dr. Shafica Karagulla's Research

I discovered energy field interactions through observation and subtle energies data. A neuropsychiatrist put together a similar picture. Dr. Shafica Karagulla's fascinating findings based on eight years of research in the field of what she calls Higher Sense Perception are reported in her book, "Breakthrough To Creativity."

Her research used "sensitives" (clairvoyants), some of whom could see into and through the human body. Their diagnoses of states of health and illness correlated accurately with medical findings. Other sensitives could see energy exchanges among individuals in a group and describe what happens when people experience the energy pull of human "sappers" (energy vampires). We now focus on the latter.

## Interpenetrating Energy Fields

Dr. Karagulla states that some of the sensitives with whom she worked described interpenetrating fields of energy surrounding the human body. Three fields are seen and unified with each other. One is the physical energy field closely related to the body. Then there is the emotional energy field extending from twelve to eighteen inches from the body. Finally, extending two feet or more from the physical body is the mental energy field.

## Emotional Persons

Sensitives observe that certain activities, ideas, and experiences seem to increase the inflow of energy into the field of a given individual. Coming into the presence of a well-beloved person intensely brightens all three energy fields. Some people's energy fields are brightened by interesting intellectual conversation. The emotionally focused person likes to stir up emotional scenes around him which tend to cause those in his group to appear depleted and low in energy.

Many sensitives say we live and move in a vast and immense ocean of energy. People use varying means for taking in different types of energy. Emotions like grief or self-centeredness appear to diminish greatly the individual's access to this energy supply.

Within a group, there is often a stimulating exchange of energies between and among individuals, described as bright lines of energy connecting two people who may be across the room from each other, such as husband and wife.

## Performers

When an actor is performing before an audience, the actor's emotional field seems to glow, expand, and extend outward until the emotional field of the audience blends with the vastly extended field of the performer. A unified group emotional energy field is maintained for the duration of the performance. When the performer is unable to create this unified field, his performance is rated poorly. This may be similar to the exceptional ability of a healer to mold individuals into a strong healing group energy field.

## A Charismatic Personality

We say that a person who can hold a group spellbound has a charismatic personality. How true that statement is! His/her charisma or energy field extends itself to envelop the whole group, forming a group energy field that dominates and influences all participants.

## Karigulla's Energy Sappers

Dr. Karigulla's research data on "sappers," as described by sensitives, is similar to my experience covered earlier in this chapter. Certain persons, having a closed-in energy field, seem unable to pick up their needed energy from the surrounding ocean of energy. It appears they take their energy, pre-digested, from people in their immediate vicinity. Sappers are usually self-centered individuals. Victims of the sapper's energy draining effects find that they feel a need to leave the presence of the sapper.

The sapper pulls the energy from whatever is a person's weakest energy vortex. This could be from a weakened heart vortex or throat vortex, or from wherever resistance is weakest. Some appear to use their voices, others, their eyes, to drain the energy of those around them. Sappers may be found among socially passive observers at a party or gathering.

Sensitives describe the sapper as having a wide opening in the solar plexus area. From the edges of this opening, streamers or tentacles appear to shoot out and hook into the energy fields of a person who is close, in order to steal his energy. Sappers who use their voices or eyes do not have to be close to drain others.

All who may benefit from the information provided by this pioneer researcher owe their thanks to Shafica Karagulla. Her contributions to this field are invaluable.

## Thinking Types are Immune to Energy Drainers

People interact with the personal energy fields of others in varying ways. Some may have a natural immunity to both energy vampires and energy polluters. They were born with, or have acquired, a shielding that protects their energy field. This immunity may come from either their innate personality type, an act of will, or a state of consciousness.

In terms of the Myers-Briggs Type Indicator, thinking types are likely to have this immunity, an immunity that makes them appear to be insensitive to the feelings of others. The truth is that they are unaware of the energy fields of others and to the emotional content of those fields. Sensing types may also possess various forms of immunity. Introverts may be immune until they open themselves to others.

Using this theory, the person most immune would be the thinking-introverted-sensing type personality. Such personality types may have difficulty receiving healing energy. They also may not understand this chapter nor find it helpful, except for self-understanding.

## Feeling Types Most Vulnerable to Drainers

Other personality types may have far fewer natural defenses to the energy fields of others. The feeling type may be the most open to harm from other energy fields, with the extroversion and intuitive traits adding to the problem. The extrovert quickly exchanges energy with others. The intuitive person is often too unaware of what he or she is sensing to create a defense. The profile of a healer provides evidence that healers display all three of these traits, making them extremely vulnerable to energy vampires and polluters.

People in the caring professions often exhibit one or more of these traits which give them a natural ability to care for people. When they have compassion for another human being and reach out in a caring way, they risk having their energy fields drained and polluted by the very people they are seeking to help. This happens any time one is empathetic. Because the energy of love is so powerful, the one possible defense would be to project love when entering into a compassionate and empathetic link with another.

School teachers may find themselves so badly drained by their daily contact with students that they spend their free time simply sitting in a stupor of fatigue. Once teachers learn to protect their energy fields from drainage, their lives can be transformed into ones of satisfaction, rather than weariness. Anyone whose vocation involves continued contact with people may experience "people fatigue."

Feeling types are the most vulnerable. They are badly disturbed by arguments because of the resulting energy field interactions. During periods of alienation between members of a household, feeling types are vulnerable to the negative feelings of those from whom they are emotionally separated. Members of a household may project negative feelings like anger, anxiety, and fear even while sleeping.

When my children were growing up, I sometimes awoke in the middle of the night feeling extremely anxious. Upon checking my own emotional state, I realized that this was not my anxiety. I would then follow the source of the anxiety to one of my children's bedrooms. In every instance they were in an emotional crisis.

Eventually, I discovered that most of my insomnia came from outside me. I was picking up my wife's emotional anxiety while she slept. Going to another room enabled me to fall asleep.

Feeling types will find these concepts helpful. They will identify with the theoretical model that has just been presented because it fits their personal experience. When they learn to protect and to cleanse their energy fields, their quality of life will be greatly enhanced.

## Protecting One's Energy Fields

There are several ways to protect one's energy field. The basic strategy involves erecting a protective covering or shield around one's own energy field. This can be done in several ways. The shield is put in place before entering a situation where negative feelings or energy drains may be present.

Always pray for God to protect you in what you are doing. A prayer I have found helpful is,

"God, please protect my energy field from being depleted or polluted by others. Surround me in your love and light. Let the method I am using be all I need."

Other options include the following, with the first three options providing protection for about an hour.

1. **Space Suit Protection.** Imagine donning a space suit that protects you, zipping it up to cover you completely. Say the above prayer.
2. **Protective Bubble.** Use a protective mental bubble. Entwine the straightened fingers of both hands. Begin at the groin and, keeping your elbows slightly bent, move your hands to behind your neck and then do the same as you move back down to your groin area. Say the above prayer.
3. **Filled with God.** Keep yourself filled with God's love and continually project it.
4. **Saran Wrap.** This will protect you for six to eight hours: Take a piece of Saran Wrap (reportedly only Saran Wrap will do) about ten inches long. Stretch it both ways. Then place it over the area of your solar plexus (diaphragm), which is located between your rib cage and your navel. Secure it in place with clothing. After six hours, restretch the Saran Wrap and put it back. The solar plexus is

the primary energy center where energy drainage and pollution occur.

5. **Cross Limbs.** Crossing your arms with your hands around your sides protects your diaphragm's energy field. When sitting or lying, crossing your ankles provides similar protection.

6. **A Watch.** Wear a special watch on your left wrist that broadcasts an extremely low frequency wavelength in the 7-9 hertz range. This keeps one's energy field balanced and protects it from the frequencies on which negative energies are broadcast. Most health food stores can tell you where to order one. All these protective measures work for me. My energy levels remain constantly high. Yet there is the possibility that my belief in these methods provides protection through subconscious projection.

## Cleansing and Recharging One's Energy Field

When energy field pollution exhausts you, how do you cleanse and replenish your energy fields? Again, there are several possibilities.

1. **Showering.** Taking a shower cleanses the energy field. This suggests that the best time to take a shower is after work or after an argument. Once the water cleanses the energy field, the gross fatigue will vanish and in time you will fully recharge yourself. Be aware that showering also makes one more vulnerable, washing away one's own energy field protection for an hour or more.

2. **Water on Wrists.** Some spiritualists believe that running cool water over both wrists is quicker and safer. They caution about showers making one's energy field more vulnerable, suggesting fewer

showers. It might be prudent to avoid taking a shower an hour or two before going out in public.

3. **Water Rinsing.** Rinsing one's face and hands in water is a partial cleansing.

4. **Epsom Salts.** Bernard Grad suggests soaking one's feet in Epsom salts.

5. **Salt and Soda Bath.** Barbara Ann Brennan prescribes a twenty minute bath in a warm tub of one pound sea salt and one pound baking soda. She cautions that this may make you weak as it draws large quantities of energy out of the body, so be prepared to rest afterward to replenish yourself.

6. **Drinking Water.** Barbara Ann Brennan suggests drinking water to cleanse one's energy fields.

7. **Hand Cleansing/Recharging.** My favorite method for a quick cleansing and recharging during moments throughout the day is this. Hold your hands open palms up. Pray: "God, use my hands to cleanse my energy field." Then, beginning at the feet, move your hands all over your body in a scooping motion. Don't forget your head area. While doing this, periodically place the energy you are scraping off onto the floor. By patting your palms flat against the floor, you are releasing the energy you have removed into the Earth, which will purify and reuse it.

Then, to recharge (you can also do this after a shower), hold your open hands before you, palms up. Pray: "God, use my hands as channels to recharge and balance my energy fields." Using a straightened hand, palms towards the body and not touching the skin move your hands over your entire energy field. I prefer about one inch from the skin. I often repeat the procedure further out at about four inches.

8. **Embrace**. You can embrace someone you love. Children and dogs are great for this.
9. **The Sun**. You can lie in the sun.
10. **A healer can recharge you**.
11. **Many other ways**. Recharging can also be done through deep breathing exercises, inhaling through the nose and exhaling through the mouth, self-relaxing techniques, meditation, reading poetry, listening to classical music, singing sacred songs, using prayer and contemplation, attending a religious service, strolling through a garden or walking through woods. Feel free to put your arms around a tree to draw energy.

## A Caution

Some will feel uncomfortable with these exercises. A decade ago, my wife and I visited Massachusetts on vacation. After a day of sightseeing with old friends among large crowds, we pulled into a restaurant parking lot for dinner. I felt energy drained. After explaining what I was about to do, I practiced Hand Cleansing/Recharging beside the car, feeling refreshed afterwards. Our friends remained troubled by what I did. Out of concern, one advised, "Walter, if you must, be more discreet."

When people complain of undue fatigue, I have sought to help them protect and restore their energy fields, with mixed responses. Those who have experimented report good results. My reputation has suffered in the eyes of scoffers.

Discreetly experiment to see what works best for you. If you have a friend who is also seeking to protect, cleanse, and re-charge his or her energy fields, share what works with each other.

## 12

# The Profile of a Healer

I have delayed offering you this chapter because I am ambivalent about it. Healers do exist. Everyone knows that. This profile of a healer is pertinent to how prayer heals. In this profile, you may see yourself and finally accept the fact that you are, indeed, a healer. That is my primary reason for writing it.

The downside is that you may not find yourself described in this chapter. This strengthens the stereotype you likely have that only special people can offer healing prayer effectively. You may then connect these special people to this healer profile. You may then give up all attempts to offer others healing prayer. That decision would be tragic.

Anyone who is deeply concerned for the health of others and intends to offer healing through prayer and touch, produces positive healing outcomes. That is the conclusion of all the evidence. It is love that empowers God's healing flow.

As a pastor, I observed hundreds of non-healers effectively offer prayer for loved ones. Their prayers produced the normal miraculous healing results of prayer. Do not let the existence of healers stifle your healing prayers.

On the other hand, if you do see yourself in this profile, you have a choice. You can reject this gift and the opportunity to help people in this way. Or, you can explore your gift and grow in your use of it. Your life choices are your own.

At age 19, I took an aptitude test. The tester revealed that my best vocational choices were being a farmer, a policeman, or a CPA. None of these felt like me. I eventually became a professional clergyperson. This was the calling of my soul. Do not become a healer unless it is a calling of your soul.

## You Have Already Accepted this Paradigm

If you are still reading this book, you have probably accepted the new paradigms. In this model, human beings stand between God and healing outcomes. God uses people to produce miracles of healing. When people pray, they emit God's healing flow from their hearts and hands. God's healing love energy then enters the healee. This energy restores the healee's human energy fields which then heal the physical body.

The human role in the healing encounter makes sense. It is just an extension of normal human caring. Throughout the ages, people have bemoaned the fact that God has not intervened to rescue them from poverty, pain, anguish, natural disaster, illness, violence, and other injustices. Those expectations do not match our current understanding of how God works.

Today, we know that God does not personally feed the hungry, care for the sick, clothe the poor, provide money for housing, and stop human injustice. If caring and justice are to exist on earth, then it is caring humans who must act for God and become his hands and feet. God uses human agents to achieve these practical purposes.

Expanding on this concept, God uses human agents to achieve his healing outcomes. Religiously, these agents have become channels of God's healing power. As in any other practical works of caring, human beings are God's hands and feet. If love motivates you to assist any person, it is this same love that empowers your healing efforts. When you practice healing prayer and touch with the same self-confidence you possess in washing the dishes, your outcomes will become consistently positive.

## World-Class Healers

Some people possess special abilities to act as healers. These people exist in every religion and culture on Earth. It sounds elitist to say that certain persons might be set apart for their abilities as world-class healers. When it comes to abilities that are considered to be religious gifts, we like to be democratic.

Throughout history, religions have resolved this elitist issue by stating that God gives certain people spiritual gifts like the gift of healing. The religious explanation is that God has chosen certain people for their qualities of holiness, faithfulness, obedience, goodness, or usefulness for divine purposes.

The gift of healing can certainly be awakened by religious experiences. It is certainly empowered by persons filled with generous love. Faith, hope, and expectancy are key elements of healing encounters. But rational data indicates that special healing abilities are genetic. It comes at birth, like the color of one's skin and eyes. It is similar to innate abilities like learning aptitude or athletic potential.

We would possess little scientific data about the healing encounter if it were not for the involvement of world-class or professional healers in clinical research. So, we turn again to world-class healers to gain insight about praying for healing.

Before we become envious of healers, it must be clearly stated that anyone can produce the healing outcomes of a world-class healer. Their ability is similar to that of a world-class track athlete. A world-class track athlete shows consistent performance ability at the highest planetary competitive skill levels. This athletic ability begins with an inborn genetic potential that can be recognized early by coaches. The athletic ability is then nurtured through coaching, endless practice, and competition. It is the person with innate exceptional abilities who can attain to a world-class track performance level.

The same is true of healers but with one important difference. We can compensate for that difference in several ways.

1. **Through love.** Immense love for the hurting empowers the healing flow. This love includes the anxiety and fear you feel for a loved one.
2. **Group power.** When the power of prayer is the square of the number praying, then it is possible with two or three praying persons to achieve the same healing results as that of one world-class healer. This is similar to weight lifters. Few

individuals can lift the six hundred pounds of a world-class weight lifter but several persons working together can.

3. **Through understanding and techniques.** Having competent skills is usually more effective than brute strength.

4. **Through intention, faith, confidence, experience.** These produce similar inner power. The greatest barrier to healing effectiveness does not involve God's power, love, group power, understanding, intention, faith, confidence or experience. The greatest barrier to healing effectiveness is being unwilling to try.

## The Profile of a World-Class Healer

This profile is of spiritual healers. It may not be accurate for psychic healers. Spiritual healers view God as the source of all healing. They practice healing through prayer and touch. Psychic healers have the ability to sense or see the flows of energy within and around the human body. I think this profile also applies to them.

### 1. Personality Type

The evidence indicates that those people most likely to utilize healing are optimistic, outgoing, "people-persons." They are also the people who have the most potential as channels for healing prayer. Unfortunately, our image of healers has been molded and distorted by television faith-healing evangelists. This cultural image of healers is extremely inaccurate and does not reflect reality. Rather, people with the greatest healing potential are more like the friendly, smiling, talkative, unassuming, caring neighbor down the street.

Two researchers, Monsignor Chester P. Michael and Marie Christian Norraisey, identified the healer personality on the Meyers-Briggs Type Indicator. Healers are the "ENFJ" type. ENFJ stands for an extroverted, intuitive, feeling, decisive type of personality. The ENFJ trait is found in five percent of the population, accounting for two hundred fifty million persons on a planetary scale. This personality type deeply experiences God and expects dramatic answers to prayer. They are natural leaders, radiate warmth and fellowship, rely on feelings, are very personal, friendly, tactful and sympathetic, and place high value on harmonious human contacts. They enjoy admiring people and so tend to concentrate on a person's most admirable qualities. They try to live up to their ideals, are loyal, and are unusually able to see value in other people's opinions. They have faith that harmony can somehow be achieved and often manage to bring it about. They think best when talking to people and enjoy talk. It takes special effort for them to be brief and business-like.

### 2.  Healers emit healing-attuned energy at all times

Healers are at all times emitting a healing energy that causes people around them to feel calm and trusting. Their energy is always attuned to the healing frequency. Intentional efforts to offer healing through prayer strengthen and focus their healing flow.

Physicist John Zimmerman, while at the University of Colorado School of Medicine, Denver, using a Superconducting Quantum Interference Device (SQUID), a super conducting device cooled to near absolute zero, conducted seven investigations of healers practicing touch-healing with healees and observed discernible changes in the amplitude and/or frequency (7.8 hertz) of the biomagnetic fields detected by the SQUID. The healers emitted a steady 7.8 hertz frequency from the hands even when not healing. A control group of non-healers produced no changes. In an eighth investigation, the signal recorded near the healer's hands was larger while healing than when he moved his hands towards the SQUID.

The late Andrija Puharich, M.D., was a healing researcher for forty years. He researched the Brazilian healer, Arigo, who among other things, conducted surgery with a rusty knife. In 1988, I went to Puharich's home with three traveling companions. Puharich had a device with a sensing plate that measures the frequency emissions of the hand. My three friends each placed a hand on the plate, and like all non-healers, emitted variable frequencies between 7 and 11 hertz during about a one minute cycle. I placed my hand on the plate and the digital readout displayed a steady 8 hertz, like that of world-class healers. This affirms that world-class healers need only intend to offer healing and without any other preparation, they transmit healing energy.

### 3. Healers can produce more than two hundred volts of energy

Sensitive people who can see energy emissions have long observed that world-class healers emit about twenty times the amount of energy of other people. Now the Menninger Clinic reports significant energy discharges from healers versus non-healers.

Researchers in the Copper Wall Experiments at the Menninger Clinic, Topeka, Kansas, have discovered that during meditation and absent healing, nine world-class healers emitted between four volts and two hundred twenty-two volts of electrical energy with a median emission of 8.3 volts. Non-healer meditators produced no surges over four volts. The world-class healers used Non-Contact Therapeutic Touch (NCTT). The implication here is that NCTT therapists have a different "energy structure" or a different "energy handling capability" from that of regular subjects.

Their new technology detected and measured electrostatic potentials and field effects in and around the bodies of meditators and NCTT therapists. The NCTT therapists produced more surges during therapy sessions than during meditation; thus, the intention to heal produced the strongest results. All NCTT therapists believed their skill could be learned by anyone.

Researchers explained that these NCTT therapists' voltage emissions were a billion times stronger than brain-wave voltages, one hundred million times stronger than heart voltages, and a million times stronger than large psychophysiological skin-potential. Their effect on the human energy systems could be immense.

### 4. Healers possess identical brain frequencies

Beginning in 1969, physicist Robert O. Beck began testing the brain-wave frequencies of healers throughout the world, discovering that all healers measure identical frequencies of 7.83 hertz. This occurred regardless of their society, their beliefs or their healing modality. Beck worked with charismatic Christian faith-healers, a Hawaiian kahuna, and practitioners of wicca, Santeria, radesthesia, radionics, seers, ESP readers, and psychics.

## 5. Healers are able to merge their minds with the mind of a healee

Dr. Edgar Wilson produced evidence that Israeli healer David Joffee impresses his brain wave pattern upon a healee in order to produce healing. The healee must voluntarily allow this entraining to occur. During this process, some healers place a healee in a trance state similar to hypnosis. This provides one explanation for the amnesia of many healees about the healing encounter.

Physicist John Zimmerman has developed a theory based upon his data that the sense of vibration or tingling in the healing encounter is possibly due to both the introduction of the 7.8 to 8.0 hertz biomagnetic field upon the healee and the impressing of the healer's brain wave pattern upon the healee. The sense of warmth or heat is logically explained by the infrared radiation emitted by the entire hand of the healer and from the longer microwave emanations coming from near the center of the healer's palms.

### Therapeutic Personalities Are Likely Healers

A therapeutic personality comes through as a sympathetic caring person whom people quickly grow to trust to the extent that they share their innermost thoughts and feelings. In the presence of a therapeutic personality, people feel calm and safe, the same emotions associated with the presence of a healer. This data implies that therapeutic personalities emit the same energy as healers and are thus inborn healers, themselves.

Channels for healing are not restricted to this personality type. Anyone who is generous, self-giving, compassionate and sympathetic can offer healing. But in the present skeptical world, the healer or therapeutic personality is the most likely to attempt self-healing or healing.

Grad's experimental data suggests that positive results in psychotherapy and with the placebo effect are the result of the healing energy emitted to the patients by psychotherapists and physicians when there is a relationship of rapport and trust. In other words, caregivers naturally emit a healing energy when they establish rapport and trust with those for whom they are caring.

### 6. A Psychiatrist's Profile of a Healer

Psychiatrist Robert Laidlaw was chairman of the Commission To Study Healing at Wainwright House, Rye, New York for eight years. He developed a personality profile of a healer based upon the many healers he had met.

A healer must be one who elicits rather than inhibits.
A healer must be a resonant cavity, an instrument, an open channel.
A healer must be relaxed.
A healer's senses must be highly acute.
A healer must be a dedicated person.
A healer must be in a state of openness, of conscious or unconscious prayer.
A healer must have expectancy and faith.
His gifts often involve clairvoyance and telepathy and he is somewhat a sensitive.

### 7. The healing ability may run in families

It has already been stated that healing is a genetic trait, so of course it runs in families. That does not mean that everyone with the ability is willing to become a healer.

My grandfather was a practicing healer. My parents are latent healers who have repressed this ability. I have evidence that all my brothers and sisters are healers. None has accepted that role. In fact, two of them do not believe in the existence of healing.

Most Filipino healers were born in one specific farm district. They attribute their healing prowess to secret spiritual information that only they possess. They may, indeed, know a few special tricks of the trade. A more plausible scientific explanation is that through intermarriage in a small community, they share a common pool of genetic traits, including the healing ability.

### 8. Andrija Puharich's Ten Specific Healing Abilities

During his research, Andrija Puharich produced a list of ten abilities that he had observed in healers. No one healer has possessed all of these abilities. The Brazilian healer, Arigo, possessed seven of them.

The first four abilities can be learned by most persons. These are: (a) the ability to heal through touch (laying on of hands), (b) from a distance (absent prayer), and (c) to heal oneself (self-healing). (d) The fourth ability, to diagnose an illness, can be learned or emerges naturally.

(e) The fifth ability is the use of molecular medicine—to match intuitively what is chemically wrong in the healee's body with the right chemical needed to correct it. This may involve chemicals in such substances as herbs or prescription medicines.

The next three are a package of abilities. These abilities are: (f) to produce anesthesia by non-chemical means, (g) to perform instant surgery with a knife or the hand, (h) to perform surgery in unsanitary conditions without resulting bacterial infections. These abilities are primarily practiced by Brazilian spiritist healers, Filipino spiritualist healers, and North and South American Native Indian shamans.

(i) Ability number nine is to be inwardly guided by God, a spirit guide, a voice or intuition, which is constantly present with a healer in his work. This ability eventually develops in some persons who regularly practice healing.

(j) The tenth healer ability is to regenerate tissue, an organ, ear, eye, limb or even life itself in a person who is clinically dead. This is a comparatively rare individual gift that can be observed in healers throughout the planet. Healers with this specialized skill sometimes are unable to produce results which other healers achieve consistently. I have observed that regenerating tissue is far more common in group healing than with individual effort, possibly because of the added energy.

## 9. Weston's Five Newly Identified Healer Abilities

The previous ten healer abilities were identified by researchers studying individual healers. Being rooted in a religious community, I have had the opportunity of observing healing in a group context. With a background in healing research, I recognized these five new healer abilities naturally emerging from a rational grasp of what was occurring during healing services. Identifying these abilities provides answers to the most disturbing issues arising from faith healing services. Applying our knowledge of these abilities should enable many more persons to be healed during healing services.

# How Prayer Heals: A Scientific Approach

## 1. *The Group Catalyst*

As stated before, every person possesses an energy field that helps to maintain life and health. This individual energy field contains information and interacts with other energy fields. Any time people gather together, their individual energy fields combine to produce a group energy field that is filled with and expresses the information of that group's intent. The most intentional group energy fields are strengthened by persons who act as catalysts. So, the first additional healing ability involves acting as a catalyst in creating and shaping group healing energy fields.

Here is my reasoning for these conclusions. I have led what I call "A Course in Prayer" in order to teach people to pray aloud. My prayer groups produced dramatic healing results in comparison to those led by other clergy. Why? I came to understand that my presence itself was adding to the results. Let us move on to a consideration of healing services.

People enter a large healing service with the expectation that healing will occur. Not anyone can lead a large healing service. Everyone knows that a healer leads a healing service although that healer is doing far more than most people realize. As one waits for a healing service to begin, the energy of the group is similar to that of any waiting group. Then, as the healer enters the gathering, one senses a change in the information of the group energy. The energy thickens and one senses peace and power. Within a few minutes the energy has become enormous, clinging to each person like a mist of honey. At times, it is almost suffocating in its intensity. Sometimes added components of love or heat are present.

Anyone who has attended a large healing service will recognize this description.

For a prayer group or healing service to work, at least one person, usually a healer, must act as a catalyst in the creation of a group healing energy field. All ENFJs can act in the catalyst role as well as most persons with the leadership quality of charisma. Their heart chakras are dominating and controlling the quality of the energy in the room.

Those who have charisma can hold an audience spellbound by the energy they project. Accomplished politicians, stage performers, and religious leaders have this ability. Each acts as a group catalyst, projecting and creating an energy field that is filled with information expressing the leader's intent. In this fashion, some healers have the ability to be group catalysts in forming a healing group energy field.

## 2. The Healer-Attuner

The second identified ability is that of healer-attuner. Large healing services are usually criticized for their lack of beneficial results. The question most often asked by observers is, "Why are so few healed?" The more personal questions are, "Why was I not healed?" and "What could I have done to be healed?" With all the healing energy present, less than one percent of those seeking healing are healed. Why? Various religious answers have been given. Rational explanations go beyond religious wisdom in making sense of this dilemma.

The clues to rational answers are provided by another phenomenon—the spiritual gift of knowledge. This is expressed in large healing services by the healer who has an awareness of or knowledge of which persons are being healed amongst the gathered thousands. Pointing to the balcony, the healer may say, "There is a woman in a yellow blouse with breast cancer who is being healed at this moment. She is feeling heat in her right breast." She is there and she is being healed. From a rational viewpoint, somehow the healer has become attuned to that particular person's energy frequency identity. Those to whom he is particularly attuned to are the ones most likely to be healed.

The spiritual gift of knowledge has another expression. At a specific time, the healer will know that all persons with a specific disease can be healed at that moment. "Will all those who have a hearing loss come forward?" Again, the healer has attuned to a knowing—a knowledge; this time not of an individual, but to the unique frequency of the healing energy that heals deafness.

The failure to attune is a logical explanation that makes sense out of a number of issues. Why are some not healed in a healing encounter? Because no attunement to the healing frequency, to the person, or to the disease has been properly made. Some healers explain that they produce consistent results because of their at-one-ment with the healee. They have attuned, permitting the healing energy to work effectively. We see that the ability of the healer-attuner is important in any healing.

Attuning can be enhanced in the group-healing setting through the following means: increase group unity and identity; develop a group empathy for the ill; sense a oneness/closeness with both God and the healer. These attunings can be achieved by singing appropriate songs, by group prayers, by pray-along prayers, with rituals of compassion, by empathy for the ill, by involvement of the ill in the personal sharing of their anguish and hopes, and by involving the group in the practice of intentional healing.

Because research demonstrates that spiritual healing is a long-term process that requires ongoing quantities of attuned healing energy, it is essential to provide the healing energy after the healing service ends. This can be accomplished by teaching everyone present to pray daily, for a month, for the healing of those present. Experience teaches that the power of their prayer would likely approach the power present in the healing service. Hampering this approach are the faulty images shared by both healers and participants that only the healer possesses the ability to heal.

Major attuning occurs through compassion for the healee's condition, so that natural loving and caring produce emotional attunement and the healing of the emotional energy field. Attunement can also be made to the sacred uniqueness of the healee, with healing occurring in the spiritual energy fields. This attuning is to the deeper knowing of personality and being. Attunement can be at the mental level of knowing the physiology of the disease or condition, producing healing in the mental and physical energy fields. Or, attunement can be made to the thought processes, another approach that heals the mental energy field. All persons who wish to be channels for healing must become aware of the art of attuning.

### 3. The Sensitive

Another healer ability is that of the sensitive. This is a PSI factor. The healer-sensitive can diagnose and heal through direct awareness and manipulation of the various energy fields. The sensitive can see, understand, manipulate, and repair each of the human energy fields. Some refer to sensitives as psychic healers, implying that what they are doing is not spiritual. This is a false interpretation. In their way, they are truly spiritual healers because they are working beyond normal physical awareness in the seven human energy field frequencies. The sensitive works through the cleansing of energy fields, energy balancing, and kinesiology.

### 4. The Energy-Enabler

A fourth ability involves energy-enabling. The power of the healing energy may be raised or boosted by non-healers. This is a very valuable role. The trigger for enabling is compassionate love. Groups can act as energy-enablers. Strong feelings like anxiety, fear, and expectation generate power that can be attuned to healing. Children and teenagers are power generators. Certain adults, who are limited in energy attuning, can assist healer-attuners by boosting the power of the healing energy. I have become aware of energy-enablers during hundreds of my own healing encounters when one or more of a healee's loved ones have been present with their compassion and concern.

Four new abilities have been identified: the Healer-Catalyst, the Healer-Attuner, the Healer-Sensitive, and the Energy-Enabler. Rare is the healer who possesses all four of these qualities. It does not take much imagination to project a healing team composed of four persons, each specializing in one of these qualities, working together with the healer-catalyst coordinating their efforts. This can be done in a healing service or within a medical, therapeutic, or community setting.

### 5. The Prime Healer

This brings us to the final ability. That is the ability of the healer who possesses all four of these qualities. Such a person might best be called a Prime Healer. There is no research data on Primes but they would appear to be extremely rare within the population. Combining these four qualities in one person (or a healing team) produces what might be called a Reality Changer. A Reality Changer can alter the nature of physical, emotional, mental, and spiritual reality. The most effective faith healers are likely to be Primes. The great religious and spiritual figures of human history needed to possess the Prime qualities. I have witnessed only two Primes in action, one in a huge faith healing service; the other in a group of about four hundred.

All prayer changes reality. The energy of prayer programs order and purpose into chaos and decay. A Reality Changer is special because he or she is a catalyst for introducing massive shifts in reality empowered by large sacred group energy fields. My own fingertip aura suggests that I am a Prime Healer and Reality Changer.

## Identifying the Healer in Yourself and Others

These traits of healers can be used to identify people who have a special ability to offer healing and lead healing services. If you recognize yourself as a healer through the personality type, it may answer many baffling questions you have about yourself. World-class healers also possess the potential for all the spiritual gifts or psychic abilities. Healers also have the ability to act as group catalysts for prayer groups and healing services, meaning they are able to form, attune, and maintain a healing group energy field.

Bernard Grad cautions me about some of the above conclusions regarding world-class healers, especially those of the ENFJ personality type. He thinks that others, who may not be ENFJs, may be world-class healers. I am open to additional evidence about others with world-class healing abilities, but this is where existing data has brought me.

## What Are Healers?

Imagine a group of humans who possess abilities that differ from the rest of humanity. Their biological nature also differs. Their brain waves measure a steady 8 hertz, rather than the normal varying 7 to 11 hertz. They constantly emit an electromagnetic frequency of around 8 hertz. Their blood-oxygen level is about ten percent higher than other humans.

They possess a common personality type. Throughout history, they have been the human innovators in religion, the arts, science, technology, and leadership. Throughout history, when they recognized their latent ability and practiced healing, they were persecuted—tortured, imprisoned, burned at the stake, or shunned.

What are healers? Their origin was lost before ancient history began. Are they just another evolutionary branch of humanity? Or, are they the first in the next evolutionary step for all humanity? Or, did extraterrestrials genetically alter them so that they could lead humanity on to a higher level of civilization?

Forty years ago, I would not have shared this profile of a healer with you. Nor would I have provided this information that can identify us. For then, it was possible that we would have all been identified, hunted down, and destroyed. Hopefully, we have come a long way since then. My life depends upon that.

Of all the many paranoid conspiracy theories, this one would be the mother of them all. A movie on this would break all box-office records, because this human truth is stranger than all previous science fiction.

But, then, before this book, probably 95 percent of the latent healers amongst us did not know they were healers. They probably bear the same bias towards healers and healing as the rest of the population. Most may, in shame, remain closet latent healers. To these, I have a message. There is a joy and purpose to healing that surpasses all other joys and purposes. There is a spiritual bliss in healing that surpasses all other experiences of God. There are mountains to climb and an Earth to be renewed that surpass all other achievements of your lifetime.

To create a real conspiracy, let us unite all the healers on Earth. We are no small force. We number two hundred fifty million people on a planetary scale. Yes, I am baiting you, the reader. I want some response, some acknowledgment, that takes healing and healers seriously.

I am impatient that my work is the most unbelieved, misunderstood, ridiculed, and ignored subject on Earth. I am weary of being shunned as a professional healer. I want to overcome the shame and embarrassment, the fear and anger that surrounds the whole field of healing. I have a burning passion to have all humanity assist healers in restoring the optimum conditions for life throughout Earth.

On the other hand, perhaps the rest of humanity was somehow programmed with these shunning reactions, so that we could peacefully work in your midst, creating the optimum conditions for life, without fear of detection.

# 13

# The Unexpected
# Side Effects of Prayer

You are as ready as you will ever be for this chapter. Throughout history, humanity has been sidetracked in its spiritual explorations by the unexpected side effects of peak experiences of God, prayer, and meditation. Even today, these side effects are labeled by many as dangerous and evil, and therefore, unacceptable. The labeling continues, along with the hysteria and fear that accompany it. The unexpected side effects of prayer are just as misunderstood as spiritual healing. This is tragic because it makes people afraid to continue on the spiritual journey.

These unexpected side effects of prayer are an enhanced awareness and intuition. Enhanced awareness has enabled me to be more creative and purposeful. It has been a part of my prayer healing encounters for many years, enabling me to feel the emotions of others and tend to their needs. It is this enhancing of awareness that frightens many people.

The pursuit of any spiritual journey increases intuitive abilities. Healing prayer works because of the enhanced

213

intuitive abilities present in prayer. No book on healing prayer tells the whole story unless it explores enhanced intuitive abilities.

Most world-class healers employ a variety of intuitive abilities during the healing encounter. In the last chapter, healers were described as having the gifts of clairvoyance and telepathy; and they are to some degree "sensitives," able to see energy fields. I identified four healing abilities necessary for effective healing in groups and healing services. These abilities enable the healer to act as a group-catalyst, energy-attuner, healer-sensitive, or energy-enabler. Intuitive abilities must be used for restoring and maintaining healthy human energy fields. Understanding and accepting these natural human intuitive abilities is invaluable for the prayer journey, healing, and renewal.

## Prayer and Intuitive Abilities

Prayer has always increased intuitive abilities. In my own case, intuitive abilities inspired this book. Intuitive abilities once led me on a confirmed out-of-body experience while sleeping. Intuitive abilities enabled me to hear encouraging words from a deceased parishioner. Intuitive abilities often guide me to people who are hurting.

I have learned to telephone people when their name pops into my mind for no apparent reason. Each time I have discovered a person in crisis. I have been guided to the homes of hurting parishioners, or to a hospital. Christians call this the spiritual gift of knowledge. Para-psychologists would call it telepathic attuning.

Why have such experiences been called evil or satanic in origin or purpose? The awakening of intuitive abilities like these in religious groups has caused whole congregations to back off from spiritual practices out of a sense of fear, shame, and evil. This is the primary reason why churches are not spiritual. The Spirit of God cannot be alive in churches as long as congregations are afraid of the intuitive side effects and label them evil or satanic.

My mother has always possessed intuitive abilities. In earlier years, she was ashamed of them and, in embarrassment, downplayed them. Now in her nineties, she has learned to accept and respect them. Once, she sensed that her brother had just died in Las Vegas. A few hours later, her sister-in-law phoned to tell her that Foy had died, and at the very moment that my mother had intuitively sensed it. Was my mother's premonition in any way evil?

## Intuitive Abilities Emerge in Prayer Groups

Persons in every prayer group I have led experience enhanced intuitive abilities. A scientist began having dreams that solved research problems. A woman had a spontaneous out-of-body experience. Another woman reported vivid encounters with her deceased mother during meditation. A man had a deeply moving religious experience in which he had a conversation with Jesus and received a blessing of his life's journey. It was his first meaningful encounter with God, and it spiritually transformed him. A physician reported a new intuitive diagnostic awareness with his patients.

All these people reported that their experiences were astounding, rewarding, and welcome. Most of these experiences addressed practical concerns of the individual. Some dealt with subconscious information. Some centered on expanded consciousness. While a few people respond with fear, most people remain curious and eagerly explore their enlarged awareness.

One woman developed two unwanted abilities overnight. In what parapsychologists call distant viewing, Joan was able to see her husband at work in his office ten miles away, knowing what he was doing and saying. At times, she had similar knowledge of her children living at a university fifty miles away. The second ability would be helpful in a gambling casino. It, too, could be called distant viewing or mental telepathy or the religious gift of knowledge. While playing cards, Joan effortlessly knew the exact cards that each player held. Along with these new abilities, Joan experienced unusual awareness during healing encounters. Joan's overall response became one of fear and anger. After awhile, she became so frightened, she vowed that she would never pray again because its side effects were too scary.

Intuitive abilities have many names. According to their names, intuitive abilities are accepted or rejected, good or evil, blessings or curses. The Christian Church calls intuitive abilities either spiritual gifts or evil deviations. Social scientists study these abilities and label them paranormal, extrasensory perception, or psi. The public calls these experiences psychic or psi. Are they all the same phenomena under different labels? We will be exploring this question throughout this chapter.

## Intuitive Abilities in History

When the sixteenth century Christian monk Martin Luther struggled through his faith journey and read his Bible, coming up with the revolutionary concepts for the

Protestant Reformation, he did not figure it out in his mind, using reason. He dreamed his ninety-five theses. That was intuitive ability.

When the noted eighteenth century Swedish scientist Emmanuel Swedenborg had a vision (remote viewing) of his home city burning while he was hundreds of miles away from it, that was an example of an intuitive ability, clairvoyance—a clear vision from a physical distance.

Twentieth century mathematician Albert Einstein did not reason through his many theories. The theories and equations came to his mind while he was sleeping or walking. He spent years seeking to prove his theories rationally, producing the mathematical basis with his equations. Einstein was an intuitive genius, not a reasoning genius. He had a clear vision of a revolutionary new intuitive means for describing reality. His intuitive ability supplied the basis for Quantum Mechanics and a new Platonic view of reality.

## The Nature of Intuitive Reality

Earlier, we explored the two different views of reality described by Aristotle and Plato. Aristotle insisted that only what can be known by the five physical senses is real. Plato defended intuitive knowing and the spiritual nature of the universe, stating that the physical universe is a by-product of the spiritual reality/universe.

Episcopal priest Morton Kelsey has written a dozen scholarly books explaining spiritual reality. His contention is that physical reality is just the projected small tip of a wedge of human awareness. Most of that wedge extends into the infinite spiritual universe of God, heaven, the Company of Heaven, spirits, dreams, revelation, extrasensory perception, etc.

The five physical senses give only a limited consciousness or awareness of reality. The miraculous events in the Bible could not have happened if there was only this physical reality. All religions require access to another dimension, the spiritual dimension wherein dwells God. Intuitive abilities and spiritual gifts cannot exist in a purely physical three-dimensional universe. Without the intuitive-creative-feeling process, there is no access to God.

Religious historian John Rossner carries this argument a step further by stating that we live in a multidimensional universe. Albert Einstein, and quantum physics, state that there are an infinite number of parallel universes, each existing at a different frequency from our earth, and each a variation of our earth universe. Access to these other universes is possible through what is known as the Einstein/Rosen Bridge.

The existence of invisible human energy fields, existing at seven different frequencies, provides a scientific basis for the understanding of quantum physics and intuitive abilities. As we attune our brains to specific frequencies, we can actually see these seven human energy fields. As we attune our brain for specific frequencies, we can experience any of the intuitive abilities that operate on those frequencies. When, through loving concern, we attune to the healing frequency of 7.83 hertz, we are at the intuitive frequency that heals. Perhaps at 9.00 hertz we can bend spoons with our minds. Perhaps attuning to a 8.53 hertz frequency gives us the ability to see into the future. Perhaps attuning to a 9.27 hertz frequency can put us in touch with a parallel earth universe.

## Intuitive Abilities as the Basis for Sainthood

Sainthood is conferred by the Roman Catholic Church upon those who have exhibited spiritual and psychic abilities. An analysis of each of the 2,532 Roman Catholic saints, from the four-volume Butler's "Lives of the Saints", shows that some form of PSI was mentioned for 676 saints or twenty-nine percent. These included 310 saints known for their miracles, 55 saints with extrasensory perception, 31 cases of clairvoyance (knowledge of events through pictures or voices in the mind), 20 cases of discernment of spirits (the ability to read consciences), and 12 cases of prophecy (precognition or knowing the future).

While alive, most of these saints were viewed with suspicion. Many were condemned by their church superiors during their lifetime. Throughout history, humanity has responded to enhanced intuitive abilities with the same distrust it has shown to spiritual healing. Perhaps that is why the Roman Catholic Church waits one hundred years after a gifted Christian's death before making the decision to bestow sainthood.

## Removing the Mystery from Spiritual Gifts

Six of the spiritual gifts are referred to in almost fifty percent of all New Testament verses. Without these spiritual gifts, there would be no Christianity and no religions anywhere on earth. Enhanced intuitive abilities must be present for any religious revelation, healing, or miracle. Today, churches either ignore the biblically documented spiritual gifts, dismiss them, deny them, view them as divisive, fear them, or label them as evil. Just as spiritual healing does not fit into today's world view, neither do the other spiritual gifts.

## How Prayer Heals: A Scientific Approach

Most of today's churches focus on beliefs about God and seek a believer's mental agreement to those beliefs. This is followed by a commitment to living a life of love, morality, and service. This approach is backwards. Historically, ancient people experienced God and then formed theological statements to explain their experiences. When religions deny the existence of the spiritual reality by placing power only in the five physical senses, they prevent the action of the mystical power of God, and the religious experiences accompanying mystical awareness.

Today's religions ignore divine visions, the current evidences of the afterlife, communication with the Company of Heaven, near-death experiences, out-of-body experiences, premonitions, precognition, extrasensory perception, and spiritual healing. Yet, these ancient, biblically reported intuitive abilities still thrive among humans throughout our planet.

Sociologist Father Andrew Greeley concluded a poll in 1974 for the University of Chicago's National Opinion Research Center. Sixty-three million Americans have claimed personal experiences of one or more psychic or supernatural events (closeness to a powerful force that seemed to lift them out of themselves). Thirty-four percent reported having had contact with the dead.

The United States National Institute of Mental Health at the Center for Studies in Suicide Prevention, Los Angeles, published a study revealing that forty-four percent of those sampled were convinced that they had had several experiences of contact with the dead. Twenty-five percent of these persons indicated that the dead person actually visited them or was seen at a seance, while more than sixty percent of the incidents involved a dream.

In 1980, a Canadian national poll conducted by a sociologist at the University of Lethbridge in Alberta revealed that twenty-two percent of all Canadians are sure that extrasensory perception abilities exist, with an additional forty-seven percent believing that such abilities exist, for a total of sixty-nine percent either being sure of or believing in extrasensory perception. Sixty-three percent say they believe in life after death. Forty-four percent of those who are very religious believe communication with the dead is possible, with thirty-six percent of those "not very religious" saying communication with the dead is possible. Is the Christian Church perceived as being important in the exploration of these phenomena? Most people believed that science, not organized religion, is the place where future answers concerning these spiritual mysteries are to be sought. The same poll indicated that only twenty-eight percent of Canada's nominal Christians are regular churchgoers and that of these, only fifty-five percent still believe in the supernatural dimensions of their faith, as expressed in such traditional doctrines as the divinity of Christ and life after death.

## What Is the Church's Response to This Data?

The Church's response to this data has been either silence or condemnation. Who is going to answer questions about intuitive experiences? Will the clergy continue to ignore them? Will the clergy and psychiatrists continue to label the psychically gifted as mentally ill or troublemakers? Do we label people who have intuitive experiences as evil, as satanic, as filled with evil spirits? Do we insist that anyone having a premonition or receiving assurances from a deceased spouse is deluded, misguided, or evil? Do we continue to take the wonder of God out of people's lives so that they no longer believe he exists, so that the churches lie empty? Will we deny any acceptable place for God and intuitive experiences among church members?

Churches place barriers in the way of experiencing God. More Americans are traveling on spiritual journeys than at any other time in history. But most of their journeys are outside the church. Because people are enjoying the side effects of the spiritual journey, intuitive experiences. These are frowned upon in most churches

Organized religion in America can blame only itself for the existence of New Agers—those who are exploring and practicing the human intuitive dimensions. When an American has an intuitive experience such as a premonition, distant viewing, or an awareness of future events, there are few places within organized religion that support such exploration and understanding. Many of the most intuitive-creative-feeling type of people have participated in aspects of the New Age because there is no other interest group that accepts them.

## The Physics of Consciousness

In November, 1977 at Reykjavik, Iceland, a group of international scientists gathered for what became known as the Iceland Conference to present the results of experimental and theoretical research on the physics of consciousness. The scientists presented papers on distant viewing (seeing events with the mind from a distance), precognition (viewing the future), teleportation (moving an object within an enclosure with the mind), the mind's ability to collapse the wave-function of matter, and the ability of children to bend metal by the use of the mind. Five of the papers were collected in a book, "The Iceland Papers," edited by Andrija Puharich.

The results of five years of research conducted by Harold E. Puthoff and Russell Targ at the Stanford Research Institute were presented under the title, "Direct Perception of Remote Geographical Locations." The ability to perform remote sensing was brought to their attention by Ingo Swann, an individual who has the ability to perceive, and describe, by word or drawing, distant scenes and activities blocked from ordinary perception. While in an enclosed room, Swann can describe or draw scenes of events that are happening many miles away. In over seventy laboratory experiments involving work with more than a dozen test subjects, the ability for remote sensing was scientifically validated. Today, this is known as "remote viewing."

John B. Hasted of Birkbeck College, University of London, described his experiments on paranormal metal-bending with children, in which he showed that he was dealing with real, controllable psychokinetic phenomena. Psychokinesis deals with the ability to affect or move material objects through the use of the mind. Hasted used sophisticated scientific tools that could quantify the forces involved in psychokinesis. He applied statistical and theoretical mathematics to explain the data.

## Defining Basic Intuitive Abilities

Dr. Hal Banks, a consciousness researcher, has written a book, *An Introduction To Psychic Studies*, that I have found to be an excellent source for defining the following intuitive terms:

1. Parapsychology is the branch of science dealing with ESP and psychokinesis. ESP stands for "extrasensory perception," which includes telepathy, clairvoyance, and precognition.

2. Psychokinesis, or PK, involves the power of the mind over matter. Gifted subjects can do both ESP and PK, which suggests a linkage or unity between various psychic abilities. They may be a part of a single system. Psychokinesis can affect the roll of the dice. It is strongly suspected that psychokinesis is involved in certain spiritual healing phenomena. Filipino healers appear to use PK as they dematerialize human tissue during psychic surgery.

   Levitation is included in PK. Levitation means to raise a physical object, like a pin, by using the mind. Levitation has also been associated with deeply spiritual or loving persons who are capable of rising into the air. Poltergeist manifestations are another form of PK, involving the moving of objects in a house. This had been related to the actions of ghosts, but in recent years it has been associated with the PK ability of adolescents with a focus ability.

3. Telepathy occurs when mind communicates with mind. It is frequently associated with crisis situations having a strong emotional content involving loved ones, and may occur during the healing encounter.

4. Clairvoyance is the awareness of some objective event or object without the use of the five physical senses. Dr. Banks lists four subdivisions of clairvoyance. The first is "x-ray clairvoyance," which is the ability to see into sealed envelopes, closed spaces, boxes, books and rooms. This is also a part of what is known as "psychometry."

Second is "medical clairvoyance," the ability to see within the human body and its mechanisms, and to diagnose disease. I have met three clairvoyant diagnosticians whose accuracy in diagnosing disease is excellent.

Third, "traveling clairvoyance" is the ability to change one's perception and to travel with the mind, and to describe a distant scene ("distant sensing" or "remote viewing").

In the fourth, "platform clairvoyance," one is able to see or perceive discarnate (not in the physical body) personalities. A clairvoyant working with a group can bring messages from spirit folk. This is also known as "mediumship."

5. Clairaudience means "clear-hearing" or receiving information through hearing it, like listening to spirits or God. Some healers are guided by the clairaudient ability.

6. Psychometry is a form of clairvoyance involving the ability to gain information through sensing the information in the energy of a person by touching an object the person owns or wears. Psychometry is also known as "soul measurement" or "object-reading."

Psychometry can be applied to archeological objects, personal jewelry, or religious objects. It can be used in sensing the energy of a photograph in a sealed envelope, or what has happened in a room. Individuals with this ability can read the past or present by touching or being near a physical object. It has been a valuable tool to criminology in tracking evidence or finding a lost child or a body. Many healers use psychometry to read the energy fields of a client.

7. Precognition is a means of predicting the future. It is the knowledge, acquired through ESP of some future event. A historic example is Abraham

Lincoln's precognitive dream in which he foresaw his own assassination and funeral. Healers sometimes have awareness of a person's future state of health. "Retrocognition" is knowledge of a past event acquired intuitively.

8. Mediums and Mediumship. A medium is a link between the living and the physically dead who are now alive in the afterlife or spirit world of God. A medium is also known as a "sensitive," and is one who has unusual awareness. Psychical researchers prefer the word "sensitive," which does not imply afterlife survival. Spiritualists state that all healers are mediums as they bring the power of God into the life of the ill.

History is filled with experiences of mediumship. Two striking evidences of mediumship occur in the Bible. In I Samuel 28:7-25, King Saul seeks advice from a great deceased leader of Israel, the priest Samuel. King Saul goes to the medium of Endor who materializes Samuel. The troubled Samuel is told he and his sons will die in a battle the next day. In the New Testament, the Transfiguration of Jesus is a prime example of mediumship. With Jesus acting as a medium, Peter, James and John are able to see the manifested presence of the Old Testament heroes Moses and Elijah (Matthew 17).

There are two broad classes of mediumship. There is "mental mediumship," which includes such phenomena as clairvoyance, clairaudience, precognition, psychometry, automatic writing, trance and telepathy. Then there is "physical mediumship," which includes psychokinesis, levitation, apports, materialization, psychic photography, table-tilting, raps, direct voice, and psychic lights.

Any contact we have with the spirit world, including contact with God, is considered by some to be mediumship. In this perspective, a medium is one who serves as a link between the world of spirit and this physical world. With a large proportion of Americans having claimed contact with deceased loved ones, each of these at such times was a link with the spirit world, and thus, momentarily became a medium.

## A Comparison of PSI, Psychic and Spiritual Gifts

Christianity has always separated the paranormal knowing of parapsychology and psychic studies from the spiritual knowing of things religious, as seen in the spiritual gifts. The evidence points to the fact that they are all manifestations of the same phenomenon. When the paranormal gift is used within a religious community, it is often awakened and empowered by God's presence in the sacred energy field of that religious community. Once awakened, the paranormal gift often becomes actively alive within the context of a believer's faith in God, the content of one's religious beliefs, and the depth of one's spiritual development.

For many centuries, humanity has been negative in its attitude towards parapsychology and psychic studies. Therefore, we have come to separate the church-sanctioned paranormal knowing in religion from the paranormal knowing of parapsychology and the psychic. This artificial separation needs to be bridged if only for the sake of intellectual integrity. The benefits of a deeper understanding will be productive for everyone. The following table attempts to match the wordings of the three categories of intuitive knowing.

| Comparing Intuitive Knowing Terminology | | |
| --- | --- | --- |
| **Parapsychology** | **Psychic** | **Spiritual** |
| Precognition | Prediction | Prophecy |
| Telepathy | Telepathy | Knowledge |
| Clairvoyance | Clairvoyance | Divine Vision |
| Clairvoyance | Channeling | Revelation |
| Clairaudience | Mediumship | Mediumship |
| Guidance Dream | Clairaudience | Voice of God |
| Guidance Dream | Psychic Dream | Divine Vision |
| | Discernment | Spiritual Discernment |
| Paranormal Healing | Psychic Healing | Spiritual Healing |

## Discerning the Benefits of Religious Ritual

Institutional Christianity does its best to separate paranormal and psychic phenomena from religious history. Christianity is untiring in its denial of paranormal and psychic phenomena. Time and again, the Church asserts, "This is a religious phenomenon, not a psychic phenomenon."

Objective studies show there is no difference between psychic and religious phenomena. Are there evil psychic phenomena? Yes. We call them black magic because they are empowered by evil motives or demonic spirits. Are there evil religions? Yes. One form is Satanism, the personification of evil spiritual thought. Anytime a church spreads hatred and violence, it is expressing evil.

It is so easy to condemn non-religious psychic phenomena or the beliefs of other religions merely because they differ from our own understanding. In the Sermon on the Mount, Jesus offered advice on discerning between religious beliefs. Jesus stated, "Beware of false prophets, who come to you in sheep's clothing but inwardly are ravenous wolves. You will know them by their fruits.... So, every sound tree bears good fruit, but the bad tree bears evil fruit. A sound tree does not bear evil fruit, nor can a bad tree bear good fruit.... Thus you will know them by their fruits" (John 7:16-19).

Enhanced intuitive abilities or psychic abilities are the basis for all religious miracles. We discern the merits of any religious group, religious miracle, or enhanced intuitive ability by their fruits. Do they produce goodness, love, responsibility, peace, justice and interpersonal harmony? Do they effectively empower people by enhancing their health, happiness, and spirituality? Do they consistently help people? Using results as an evaluation tool may prove that there are groups within every religion that produce evil outcomes or consequences.

Religious rituals empower believers in every religion. My studies indicate that all religious rituals are magic rituals, or ritual magic. In Christianity, baptism, communion, confirmation, ordination, weddings, and prayers are all forms of ritual magic. Each uses ritual words designed to bring the power of God into human lives. Each produces similar fruits, bringing God's power into the human energy field to act in intelligent, loving, transforming, empowering ways.

Years ago, I was at a meeting where I angered a practitioner of black magic. I abruptly left his group and went home. Knowing how vindictive he was, I knew I was about to be cursed by a black magic ritual. Being an expert in magic rituals, I knew I could be harmed, so I sought a defense. I used Christian ritual magic to surround my home in a protective bubble of love while sending the whole black magic group Christ's love and peace. I slept the night in confidence, knowing that any magical curse directed toward me would be reversed and affect the perpetrators instead.

The next morning, I received a phone call from a woman in that group warning me that a spell had been cast upon me that would make me ill. An hour later, another woman phoned to tell me that the black magician had spent the night ill with a high fever, stomach cramps, vomiting, and diarrhea. I could simply state that I had prayed for God to protect me. I had.

But, I had done more than that. I had used a prayer ritual, or ritual magic, invoking Christ as the source of the power. The black magician had invoked demons to empower his ritual magic. Both the source and the purpose of my rituals represented goodness. The source, the intent, and the results of his ritual were evil. We both used ritual magic, a morally neutral technique.

## Intuitive Abilities Are a Gift to All Humanity

We have compared the universal gifts that are the heritage of all humanity. The common element uniting all the world's religions is not just that we all worship the same God. Uniting all religions is the universal human experience of God and his spiritual universe through revelation, vision, prophecy, guidance, the afterlife, healing, and communication with the spirit world.

The ability to act as a channel for healing exists in every culture and religion. Any person who loves another person with compassion and oneness can offer that person God's healing love energy. Since channels for healing exist outside of Christianity, the Church's exclusive claim for Christ as healer through the spiritual gifts is not objectively valid.

This is a necessary shift in thinking—a demythologizing of how the Holy Spirit is at work in our lives. It is also an empowering concept. It implies that any religion that upholds God's love as the source of creation, wholeness, and new life is valid in its teachings.

This concept can lay new beginnings for all humanity. These approaches promise new life for the world's religions. They also lay the foundations for interfaith understanding, tolerance, respect, and cooperation. They raise hope that the Golden Age of peace with justice may soon become reality for all humanity. This hope is rooted in the power of healing prayer to restore and make all things new.

## Cautions for the Spiritual Journey

Is there anything immoral or evil about intuitive experiences? In the Middle Ages, Christians meditating in monasteries had similar experiences. Their leaders discouraged them, telling them to focus only upon their religious purpose, experiencing God. Today, the same advice is given. When practicing prayer, meditation, or contemplation, a few people experience "bad trips." Vulgar, immoral, or sacrilegious data may appear. This is usually attributed to outside evil forces and influences. In rare instances, this is true. Experts in the field provide another explanation: This material is produced by one's own subconscious mind.

Our subconscious minds may be filled with pain, fear, anger, hurt, shame, and guilt, which become uncovered by the awareness awakened in spiritual practices. In rare instances, you may come upon spirit entities, some of whom may wish to possess you. Subconscious and conscious forces can empower such beings. Panic and terror are the worst responses.

Be aware that you do have control of your own mind. If problems persist, seek professional help. Those actively involved with traditional religious practices are protected by the presence of God's spirit, a sacred presence in the human energy fields. Spirit possession exists. But prayer, meditation, and contemplation are far safer than walking, bicycling, or riding in an automobile as far as injury and death are concerned. I have heard of no one who has been physically harmed by spiritual endeavors. On the other hand, expanded inner awareness can be an exciting and rewarding journey.

Some caution is warranted. Those with unresolved painful or guilty memories will eventually confront these during the long-term practice of meditation or prayer. In such circumstances, a competent person must guide them. Passive and suggestive people lacking in ego-strength also need a guide. Persons with psychiatric histories of schizophrenia, mania, depression, paranoia, multiple personality, and borderline personality should refrain from meditation, except under the guidance of a mental health professional. This is also true of persons on mood-altering prescription drugs and those with drug dependencies. The main danger comes from the fact that whatever is present within the mind of a person is expanded and empowered.

Criminals, abusers of others, and manipulators will have expanded access to both the higher self and the lower self. Possession by evil entities also becomes more probable for them and for those who have studied and believe in Satanism. Believe in Satanism and your beliefs will become powerful forces with a life of their own which controls you, beginning within the spiritual state and continuing when you return to a normal state of consciousness. Beware when any inner voice commands or suggests that you do something morally wrong, or sounds manipulative or ignorant. Do not obey it! It is probable that many serial killers and rapists are not just demonstrating uncontrollable compulsive behavior. Their statements to the media are consistent with what we know of possession by evil or demonic spirits. The use of the ritual magic of exorcism may be effective in eliminating their destructive compulsions.

Those actively involved with traditional religious practices are partially protected by God's spirit, a sacred presence in the human energy field. All persons need to take the precaution of using rituals to protect themselves from evil or random spiritual forces while in a spiritual state. Simply addressing God provides protection.

Most cases of possession involve earth-bound spirits who are looking for vulnerable persons through whose minds and bodies they can continue an earthly existence. Earth-bound spirits belong to deceased persons who could not or would not leave this earth dimension following physical death.

Some psychotherapists think that some chemical addictions are connected to the presence of earth-bound spirits that invade the bodies of vulnerable persons in order to continue practicing their addictions. Earth-bound spirits often leave when they are made aware of their circumstances and their destructive effects upon their hosts.

Familiar spirits, evil spirits, and demons do exist on their own, separate from the subconscious mind. Depossession may be required for resistant earth-bound spirits and for rare cases of evil, familiar, and demon spirits. This requires the team efforts of a clairvoyant and a healer or a knowledgeable priestly intercessor.

Instances of possession as a direct result of meditation and prayer would be unusual. Possession is more likely to occur in a group setting, due to the powerful forces generated by group energy fields, or because of an individual's involvement with evil activities or persons.

## Exorcizing Diseases

More and more, I practice exorcism of spirits of disease. For years, I rejected spirit possession as ridiculous. It went against all my cultural beliefs and education. Then I witnessed an exorcism at a Roman Catholic healing service. This exorcism involved hearing loss and cataracts. Later, when touch-healing prayer failed to restore a woman's hearing, I successfully exorcized the spirit of deafness. I was more surprised when it worked than my client.

As my intuitive abilities grew, I began sensing the presence of possessing spirits in physical diseases and destructive emotional states like depression. My exorcisms use prayer and take less than a minute. My rational explanation is that spirits of disease are conscious energy entities that can be created by the long term presence of a medical condition. They help to maintain the disease frequency and make the disease more resistant to medical treatment.

## Intuitive Abilities Are Becoming Accepted

In 1990, who would have believed that a psychic cable network would become a billion dollar industry? Who would have believed that local television stations would be interviewing psychic readers and offering astrological readings? Who would have believed that near-death experiences would become accepted fact?

Even though I doubt the value of phone psychic readings and star-gazing astrology, I like the acceptance of them. It opens the door to the acceptance of other intuitive phenomena. Yet, I remain disappointed. Prayers for healing and spiritual healers are still shunned by the media.

# 14

# Science Clarifies Religious Beliefs

Subtle energies research data and the practice of touch-healing prayer provide a revolutionary new understanding and foundation for religious beliefs and practice. They supply rational explanation for what have always been considered religious mysteries, answering many of the questions about religion that people begin asking in childhood and which may remain unanswered throughout a lifetime. They provide new reasons for participating in a religious community. They can be the basis for genuine understanding and cooperation between religions. As with any new understanding, they may give birth to new theological thought. They may also spur religious revival.

This new understanding is not for everyone. My own Wesleyan Christian tradition accepts knowledge about God that comes from scriptures, tradition, experience, and reason (which includes science). This tradition accepts science and experience as valued means for knowing about God. Yet, even those persons whose beliefs are based solely upon sacred scriptures will find insight into the Word of God through the knowledge and processes described here.

## Knowing God Rationally

In the Western religious traditions, understanding of the nature of God is based upon sacred scriptures and religious dogma. These essentially appeal to the spiritual mind by saying, "Accept the spiritual truth of these scriptures and dogmas and you will find the basis for your religious beliefs, practices, and salvation."

The increasingly rational mind of modern humanity rejects the spiritual truth of scriptures and dogma. The rational mind can neither enter the necessary spiritual mind, based in a state of awareness, nor respect it. Thus, the rational mind is forced to reject sacred scriptures and religious dogmas. This has produced today's secular individual, family, community, and society.

Subtle energies research data and the practice of touch-healing prayer can convince the rational mind that God exists. They also tell the rational mind about the nature of God and God's actions. With this new understanding, the rational mind is able to look at existing religious beliefs and practices with new awareness and appreciation.

## The Rational Mind Versus the Spiritual Mind

Previously we have explored the opposing world-views of Aristotle versus Plato, of Newtonian medicine versus Einsteinian medicine, and of the thinking-sensing personality type versus the feeling-intuitive personality type.

### The Rational Mind

Aristotle's philosophy, Newtonian medicine, and the thinking-sensing personality type all view the world in practical terms. Everything that matters in the world can be physically measured and quantified through rational thought and logic. This is the rational mind and world-view. There is no place in the rational mind for a powerful God who interacts with humans and heals through prayer. The rational mind must reject the significance of God, prayer, healing, love, compassion, and forgiveness. The rational mind emphasizes that science and reason are the only guides that people need.

## The Spiritual Mind

Aristotle's philosophy, Einsteinian medicine, and the feeling-intuitive personality type all view the world as originating from the spiritual, with the human spiritual dimension being immensely significant. This is the spiritual mind and world-view. The spiritual mind views spiritual transformation or renewal as a crucial stage in normal human development. Without spiritual renewal, humans cannot reach their full potential or a higher level of evolvement. You cannot transform the Earth until you have spiritually transformed humanity.

The human energy field model clarifies this. God's presence in humans transforms the human energy fields. God makes them healthy. God creates human maturity within the energy fields. The highest level of human development occurs when all seven energy fields are filled with God's truth. This moves us towards the next level of human evolution.

## The Clash

These two approaches to life have disagreed throughout human religious history. From a religious perspective, the rational mind represents fallen and sinful humanity. The demonic can be defined as that which opposes God's acting in the world. Therefore, the rational mind represents the demonic in humanity.

## Fallen Humanity and Spiritual Awakening

### *God's image in the Original Creation*

Most of the world's religions believe that in the ancient past humanity was spiritually awakened. In those days, humans had direct contact with God, were bathed in spiritual wisdom, lived joyously and responsibly, and possessed divine powers. Humanity was created in the image of God and was sacred.

Most religions preserve an account of the "fall of humanity" into its present state of spiritual unconsciousness. For Muslims, Christians and Jews, humanity's "Fall" is described in the story of Adam and Eve in the Garden of Eden in Genesis 3.

### *The Veil*

At that time, a veil (or cover) was placed over the Spirit in each human. Because of this veil, people could no longer find that sacred spark within themselves, the Spirit which connects them to God. Humans were forced to solve their own problems, to discover for themselves what was right and wrong. Without God, their options were limited by their reliance upon reason and logic, the rational mind.

The world's religions, each in their own way, tell the story of how humanity could not survive by its own wisdom and power without divine transformation and awakening. Individuals lost their capacity for such higher feelings as love, compassion, forgiveness, honesty, and integrity. Humanity fell into a life of selfishness and sexual immorality, hatred and betrayal, murder and war. When the rational mind rejected the awareness of God and unbelief became common, humanity lost the source of its moral grounding and began responding only to the stimuli of self-interest and physical sensation.

## Finding God

The purpose of most religions is to provide the means for humans to re-establish a firsthand contact with God. Those who establish this contact are transformed and awakened. These awakened persons, through divine guidance and experience, help others find God. Always, it has been awakened persons who have generated the world's sacred writings.

## The Spiritual Viewpoint

From the viewpoint of the spiritually awakened/re-newed mind, or the spiritual mind, the rational mind is severely limited in its abilities. Humans are both flesh and spirit. To be whole, the physical, mental and emotional qualities must be nourished by spiritual awareness. They need direct contact with God in order to fill all seven energy fields with life-giving informa-tion, wisdom and power. Look at the following chart of Brennan's model of the human energy fields cited in chapter five.

Brennan states: "There are specific locations within our energy system for the sensations, emotions, thoughts,

---

## The Function of Each Human Energy Field

1. Physical functioning and sensation
2. Emotional life and feelings
3. Mental life and linear thinking
4. Love and the emotion of love
5. The divine and the power of the Word
6. Divine love
7. The higher mind of knowing and integrating the spiritual and physical make-up

---

memories and other non-physical experiences." The rational mind can only nurture and program the first three energy fields of physical functioning and sensation, emotional life and feelings, and mental life and linear thinking.

## A Major Breakthrough

The rational mind has little input into the four outer energy fields which deal with love, divine power and the Word, divine love, and the higher mind. Humanity, through various religions, has struggled for thousands of years to understand these spiritual qualities and how to achieve them. We are now in the midst of major breakthroughs. Research data and the practice of healing prayer provide the missing pieces of the spiritual puzzle.

## The Search for God's Guidance and Power

### God Chooses Moses

Because the rational mind failed ancient humanity, alternatives were needed. In the Western religious tradition, Moses had a peak religious experience at the burning bush when God chose him as a prophet, as described in the third chapter of Exodus. During this peak religious experience, Moses was filled with ecstasy, joy, bliss, peace, and wholeness. These qualities are characteristics of the transformation and empowerment experiences of everyone who becomes spiritually awakened.

### Rules for the Rational Mind

The spiritually awakened Moses, possessing direct contact with God, gave his people the Ten Commandments and the Law in order to lead them away from their destructive way of living. The Law is composed of rules of good behavior devised for the rational mind with suitable punishments for disobedience. These were substitutes for the guidance to be had from the awakened spiritual mind, which humanity was not yet able to understand. (This is the same flawed approach practiced in today's America, where harsher laws and punishments are viewed as the only solution for a morally failing culture. The only practical solution lies in a spiritual awakening of individual Americans.)

Throughout subsequent centuries, prophets arose who spoke of the spiritual qualities of love, compassion, and forgiveness; and of a future time when rational laws would no longer be necessary, for God's Spirit would dwell within human hearts and personally guide each individual.

### Spirit's Action

In the Christian tradition, Jesus became the God-Man, the Savior, a spiritually awakened person who had direct access to God and all the powers of God. In the coming of the Holy Spirit at Pentecost, everyone touched by the New Word of God in Jesus and the power of the Holy Spirit became spiritually awakened and connected to the spiritual body of Christ, the Church. The rational mind takes a quantum leap forward in human evolution when it becomes awakened. Spirit-filled people become transformed into New Persons. Each new Christian, baptized with the power of the Word and the Spirit, have direct contact with God and the divine power to heal and perform miracles.

From the viewpoint of subtle energies research and touch-healing prayer, Jesus provided the spiritual information (the Word of God) and, at Pentecost, God's Spirit empowered that information. Forming a powerful sacred group energy field, the waiting followers experienced inner transformation as the information carried by the living, acting, sacred group energy field bathed them. Not only did they experience spiritual transformation, they were, as well, empowered with divine abilities.

The sacred energy connection bonding the participants to each other is known as the mystical Body of Christ, the Church. All Spirit-filled practicing Christians today remain united and empowered by this sacred group energy connection as members of the Church. This bond is strengthened by peak religious experiences and the awareness that this sacred energy connection exists. This sacred energy connection between believers must have been taught to the baptized as a part of the secret knowledge available only to the initiates—the new members of the Church.

## Spiritual Results

These spiritual minds were made whole. They were not only filled with the Spirit, but also with the Word of God. This gave them the ability to integrate spiritual love, compassion, and forgiveness with rational morality, responsibility, and integrity. In other words, all seven human energy fields were filled with the healthy information for which people had been starving. This information acted intelligently to make them fully alive and whole. Becoming inspired and creative through the actions of the Spirit, the new believers found that the power of their new spiritual mind permitted their rational abilities to blossom.

Until the fifth century, all Christians were awakened by God's presence. They were baptized only after their spiritual transformation. This baptism connected them to all other Christians through the sacred group energy field connection—the mystical Body of Christ. They were then initiated—given special knowledge—into the mysteries of the faith. This nurtured further awakening. God lived in their healthy energy fields. They lived constantly in a state of peak religious experience, filled with ecstasy, joy, bliss, peace, and wholeness. They invoked this inner spiritual power to overcome the fear and pain present in the rational world, and to fight the darkness with God's marvelous light, a light that filled their minds.

## The Rational Mind Barrier

By the fifth century, the peak religious experience and the awakened mind became suspect. The rational mind of church administrators began hindering peak religious experiences. The knowledge of faith was confined within the context of rational sacred scriptures, writings, doctrine, and tradition. Peak religious experiences were no longer considered appropriate, and rationally structured information about God became endorsed by religious authorities.

We see this pattern unfolding repeatedly throughout the centuries. A great need for change and reform would arise, followed by a wave of spiritual renewal. The renewal occurred when a peak religious experience transformed and awakened a leader and his followers. Reforms in spiritual practice, theology, or social consciousness would follow, and then, in the guise of administering those reforms, the rationally-minded church administrators again would put the lid on the people's free experience of the actions of God. Consequently, a sense of personal connection with the energy of the sacred disappeared from church tradition.

## Universal Experiences

Most of the world's religions originated from similar peak religious experiences and the resulting awakened leadership. Most religions emphasize the teaching that without God, humans struggle. Most religions have a history similar to Christianity, wherein rational administrators and dogmatic traditions first hindered and then suppressed the peak religious experience of God-awakened believers.

Organized religion is the most conservative institution in any culture as it seeks to preserve religious, moral, and social traditions, making them resistant to change. Organized religions have not been able to break out of their traditional molds to respond to the immense social changes that have swept humanity over the past three generations. The problem is that most religious traditions represent the rational mind, which does not possess the intuitive genius of the spiritual mind.

A struggle continues between awakened spiritual minds and rational minds, between the thinking of Plato and Aristotle, between the thinking of Isaac Newton and Albert Einstein. The rational mind insists on leaving out both God and the spiritual journey, even within organized religion.

### Religious Responses to the Rational Mind

The world's religions were not unaffected by the dominance of the rational mind. A rational acceptance of information about God, originally acquired through ancient peak religious experiences, is now considered all the connection to the spiritual that a believer needs. The experience of divine transformation and awakening are no longer regarded as necessary. Believers are suspicious of peak religious experiences, which they view as too irrational, emotional, and scary . . . an untrustworthy road map.

## Fundamentalism

Fundamentalism arose in all the world's religions as the rational mind went to religious extremes. Fundamentalism takes religious beliefs achieved through peak religious experiences and entombs them in dogma and doctrine. The rational mind sees its creation of a rational, legalistic Law of God as the Absolute Truth about God. It is characterized by manipulation, control, fear, anger, a distrust of non-believers, the hatred of many enemies, self-righteousness, human pride, and nationalism. Like the rational mind without God, religious fundamentalism is demonic—enslaving believers, turning people against each other, and creating the conditions for war. Love, compassion, forgiveness, freedom, transformation, and a bonding with all Creation are in short supply for religious fundamentalists. By their fruits you will know them.

## Charismatics and Pentecostals

These believers have a high regard for the Holy Spirit and the peak experience of God. They usually combine the recognition of the peak religious experience with the fundamentalist rational mind. While rejoicing in the peak religious experience, they express their fear of it by confining group members to a rigid set of traditional and rational religious and moral beliefs. If the transformed and awakened do not conform to these beliefs, they are labeled satanic or evil, and are shunned or rejected. Within these boundaries, no divine creative-intuitive guidance for reform exists. The new wine of the Spirit is always poured into the old wineskins of tradition.

I experience a personal sadness in this analysis. I am a charismatic Christian who has been nurtured in the liberal theological tradition. I, like millions of others like myself, do not feel comfortable as a member of any Christian community.

Even today, our shifting religious climate has only caused the rational mind-set to become more stubborn in its resistance. The present inconsistencies shown by members of the world's religions are cause for the non-believing rational mind to rejoice. Rationalists can point to many religious believers whose behavior makes a mockery of their own stated religious beliefs. Even when rationalists accept the idea that God exists, they point to such deluded believers as proof of God's inability to act effectively or meaningfully in the world.

### New Agers

The New Age Movement has grown due to the interest of those who wish to learn more about their intuitive abilities and apply them in worthwhile ways. Most new agers place a high priority upon a spiritual journey with God. Many new agers reject traditional Judeo-Christian beliefs. Instead, they build their belief system—their theology, their Word of God—upon many religious traditions and "channeled" or inspired contemporary intuitive religious truths.

Their theology represents the spiritual mind gone to irrational extremes, just like the Christian Gnostics in the Early Church. New agers place no value on developing a systematic theology that is rationally consistent.

One glaring example is their inconsistency in combining unconditional love with karma. Karma is the world's most legalistic religious concept. It is based upon the belief that no sin can be forgiven during a person's current earthly lifetime.

New agers cannot logically believe in both karmic debt and unconditional love. Unconditional love is directly contrary to karmic concepts. Nor can new agers reject the concept of sin, the basis of karmic beliefs, and still logically believe in karma. Religious beliefs must be logically consistent to be believable.

New agers also ignore religious history. The world's religious beliefs and sacred writings were built upon previous religious tradition, religious communities, and the inspired wisdom that flowed from them. They did not build upon a vacuum in religious knowledge. Inspiration is channeled and either elevated or distorted by the human mind that produces it. Any future original revelation of God will not flow from intuitive inspiration alone. It must come from the highest state of consciousness—peak first-hand experiences of God that transform and empower a person into a pure or divine channel for humanity's next evolutionary step upward.

## Suspicion of the Religious Is Widespread

Nothing prepared me for the complete rejection of the word "religious." As I began talking about the peak religious experience, people generally wanted me to change the word "religious" to something else. The general public wanted me to call it a "peak spiritual experience." Church people wanted me to call it a "peak faith experience." I was shocked with the negative emotional connotations associated with the word religious.

All my life, I have defined religious as that which pertains to God. Thus, the ancient and respected term, peak religious experience, means a peak experience of God. Webster's Dictionary defines spiritual as pertaining to the spirit or soul, although it popularly does refer to a journey with God. The dictionary defines faith as unquestioning belief in God or specific religious beliefs, although, it, too, refers to a journey with God. However, neither of these two terms are appropriate substitutes for the word religious in this context.

I am on a faith journey, a spiritual journey, and a religious journey. When you or I have a peak experience of God, that is a peak religious experience. However academically uncomfortable I feel about it, I bow to the negative feelings associated with the word, religious. I will from this point onward refer to the peak religious experience as "a peak experience of God".

## The Spiritual Journey

As a parish minister for thirty years, I have found that less than ten percent of church members are interested in a spiritual journey within the Church. I also discovered that most members were on a spiritual journey of their own, outside of organized religion.

This trend is increasing. Today, most people are on a spiritual journey with God. Most do not accept all of the orthodox beliefs of their church. They are each building a set of religious beliefs of their own, borrowing from many faith and cultural traditions. Continuing this trend, only about twelve percent of Americans are actively pursuing this journey within organized religion. Most of the remainder are privately exploring their own personal spiritual journeys. They seek spiritual transformation, awakening, and wholeness.

## The Present Human Condition

The rational mind has had seven hundred years to prove its worth as creator of the dominant thought pattern in Western civilization. It believes that adequate education, knowledge, government, laws, income, housing, food, medicine, and technology can solve all human problems and usher in a Golden Age of peace with justice and happiness for all.

Those are all worthy social goals. But, knowledge does not and cannot transform humanity. Transformation occurs through peak experiences of God that produce spiritual evolution. The products of the rational mind have left us in a dark pit, the same dark pit of which the Adam and Eve account warned.

Even today, the rational mind believes it can solve all problems. Many people in the United States are demanding solutions to increasing violence, to the disintegration of the family, to personal isolation, and the lack of community. But laws and punishment alone cannot transform people.

We all want a kinder, gentler, more caring nation. The rational mind cannot provide the solutions. In this perspective, the truly evil element in the world, the real demonic power, is that which opposes God's acting in the world—the rational mind.

Our society is breaking apart and needs to be put back together. How do we love, rather than hate? How do we care in our depersonalized world? How do we build values that enhance life? How do we build a sense of community?

How do we stop the violence, nurture and heal dysfunctional families, and rehabilitate chemical abusers and criminals? How do we enable people to love, express compassion, forgive, and become emotionally whole?

The answer is easy: by tending to the health of all seven human energy fields; by providing ample opportunities for peak experiences of God that transform and nurture people into wholeness. These experiences lift people to a higher ground of human awareness and evolution. Doing this requires joining with others in prayer.

## Healing Prayer and the Peak of Experience of God

Here is where the importance of prayer enters the picture. Healing prayer produces peak experiences of God that can spiritually transform and awaken people. When I practice touch-healing prayer, I am consistently aware of an inner bliss. Bliss is defined as spiritual joy or great happiness. This experience of bliss makes healing encounters the happiest moments of my life.

Accompanying this bliss, this spiritual joy, are other emotions. There is always a sense of peace, of an inner calmness or serenity. There is always a sense of heartfelt love, of a joyous, generous, shared love. There is always a sense of holiness, of a breathtaking and inspiring awareness of God. There is always a sense of connectedness with all life, of a oneness with a larger whole. One is no longer tied to the boundaries of the physical world. There is no awareness of the physical body, emotions, and thoughts.

These are the qualities of all peak experiences of God. No other human activity comes near to producing the bliss, peace, joy, holiness and, connectedness of the peak experience of God. I have a strong suspicion that a natural yearning for peak experiences of God accounts for the large crowds at faith-healing services. This experience of holy bliss draws people to the charismatic movement and to Pentecostal churches, to daily prayer, and to the search for spiritual renewal. One peak experience of God can drive one to search for a lifetime for a means of recapturing that initial bliss with God.

## Exploring the Peak Experience of God

Peak experiences of God are a normal and necessary part of any spiritual journey. But, the peak experience of God's Spirit does not transform and awaken the consciousness unless that consciousness possesses a consistent set of religious beliefs, a meaningful theology. This set of religious beliefs is called God's Word.

A person can meditate, contemplate, visualize, and pray for twelve hours a day, forever, without achieving transformation and awakening. God's Word must be present for these to happen. You can have a wonderful sense of ecstasy, joy, bliss, peace, and wholeness, but without the knowledge of the divine Word, there is no spiritual transformation.

In this setting, peak experiences of God are just a wonderful sensual experience. They are far better experiences than alcohol or other mind-altering drugs; but afterwards, they leave you just as far from God. Your energy fields temporarily light up and then dim again with no transformation. You end up unchanged.

In addition, one person alone may not produce enough divine power to ignite transformation. The power of God in prayer is the square of the number of people praying. This is a primary reason why people gather for religious rituals. In doing so, they form a sacred group energy field that bathes everyone in God's Word and Spirit.

I am not saying that one cannot have a peak experience of God alone. Millions of people do. I once had a peak experience of God while alone during a health crisis that regenerated a diseased organ of my body. It took place following six weeks of daily meditative prayer. I have had hundreds of such experiences during my life. I have no way of knowing how many others have had similar experiences.

I had an advantage. I had already been transformed and awakened during a peak religious experience at age ten when I became a Christian. I had been bathed in the Spirit and the Word for almost thirty years within the Christian community when this peak experience of God, and the subsequent healing, occurred. I was connected to the mystical Body of Christ. The Spirit and the Word already lived within me. I am aware of them as I write these sentences.

There is another side to this. The Word, alone, has little power to transform. God's Spirit makes the Word come alive. Yet, the Spirit is often contained in the Word. This is the primary reason that Christians distribute the Bible. Millions have been transformed and awakened by reading the Bible. One can read the Bible with the rational mind to learn information. The information, the Word, can also awaken the spiritual mind.

I never know when this will happen for me. While reading the Bible for information, the Spirit unexpectedly moves within me. A peak experience of God then overwhelms me and tears of joy will stream down my cheeks. Christ may be there with me, speaking personally to me.

God's Spirit causes religious information to take on a life of its own. It empowers religious beliefs so they can become encoded into the seven human energy fields. Without valid religious beliefs, peak experiences of God cannot transform and empower.

Most religions teach that God's Spirit transforms the believer into the revealed image of God—the Word—and then empowers that same believer with divine abilities. Most religions focus on these two essentials: the Word of God, and the power of God's Spirit. You cannot succeed on your spiritual journey without these two elements.

## Peak Experiences at the Menninger Clinic

During the past seven years, accumulated scientific evidence indicates that any time a person is able to achieve a peak state of consciousness, personal transformation and empowerment can occur. Using biofeedback, you can learn to enter the low theta brain wave state of four to eight frequencies per second. At that point, you get into a state of consciousness where you can move up and go into a state of revelry—a peak state of pleasure, ecstasy, joy, bliss, peace, and happiness. This state is called the autogenic shift. At this point, you are operating at the back of the head in the left cortex or the left occipital lobe of the brain. Elmer Green, Ph.D., who set up the Psychophysiology Lab at the Menninger Clinic in Topeka, Kansas in 1964, reports that through biofeedback a Westerner can attain the mystic state of the Tibetan or Hindu yogi in two to three days. The body, emotions, and thoughts are quieted as you enter the unconscious, upper four levels of consciousness. This is known as self-mastery.

In this state, you are at the "white light" level of the peak experience of God. In Zen Buddhism, this is known as the True Self. In Christian mysticism, this is known as the Christ Level. In Tibet, they call this place the Jewel in the Lotus. The Sufis and the kabbala, and in fact all religions, talk about this level of consciousness.

At this consciousness level, you can focus your intentions downward for the transformation of the body, emotions, and thoughts. When alcoholics get up to this theta state, they can turn their attention downwards to the hypothalamus and are able to rewire the hypothalamus so that they no longer want to drink. This has been done with six thousand alcoholic subjects at the Menninger Clinic.

During the peak experience of God, the Word and the Spirit, working together, begin to automatically transform the believer into the qualities of the revealed image of God through the hypothalamus area of the brain. Along with transformation can come ongoing empowerment with spiritual abilities, such as prophecy and healing. You have an experience of Heaven and bring it back to earth with you. You must be personally transformed before you can begin transforming the world.

## Common Elements of Religious Experiences

An enduring spiritual wisdom runs through all the world's religions. This comes from mystics—those who encounter God at the highest levels. A beneficial peak experience of God contains an awareness of ecstasy, joy, bliss, peace, and wholeness. This experience includes an awe and wonder of God and a oneness with God, the Creator and Sustainer. It begins a transformation that includes spiritual love, compassion, forgiveness, the need to serve others, a sense of inner freedom and sacredness, and a connectedness with other believers. At the highest levels it results in a oneness or connectedness with all humanity and everything that God has created.

If your peak experience of God contains the opposite elements of any of these qualities, be careful. Either your religious beliefs (Word of God) are faulty, or you are tapping into your own baser self, or you are being influenced by the destructive religious beliefs of others. The ability to determine the beneficial qualities of any religious experience is known as discernment.

## The Human Influence in Religious Experiences

From healing research data and experience, we know human intentions and expectations affect the results. In touch-healing, a depressed or cynical healer or pray-er may cause an illness to become worse. The transmitted energy is not at a healing frequency when the pray-er is feeling anger, hatred, resentment, or inadequacy. Such prayers can harm others.

### Voodoo Magic

This can be used to heal or to harm. The results are based upon the intentions and the Word used by the practitioner. All religious rituals are a form of magic. All religious rituals invoke a spiritual power or entity to act and to have an effect in our physical universe. Prayer is a form of ritual magic.

Any prayer that seeks to harm another person is a form of harmful or black magic. When you are seeking the destruction of an enemy through prayer, this is black magic. When Christians do this, it is not spiritual warfare. It is black magic—an evil.

When you are convinced that a critically ill person is going to die, do not pray for their healing. The energy of your prayers will contain your negative beliefs and hasten a death that might not have occurred without your negative energy.

### Human Influence

The human mind has a powerful influence upon the Spirit's actions. Everyone agrees that there is one Divine Spirit for all humanity. In the exploration of group energy fields, I have repeatedly noted that all groups form energy fields and the information present within those energy fields is produced by the intentions, attitudes, emotions, thoughts, beliefs, and actions of those participating in the group energy field.

### Limits of Healing Energy

A healing group energy field is not the best setting for transformation and awakening. That is not the intention of the information in the energy. The intention is to produce healing results in the three inner energy fields: physical, mental, and emotional. The healing energy lacks some of the qualities necessary for spiritual transformation. In most such healing services, I sense a powerful energy and peace. Sometimes an element of love is present, but it is rare to sense ecstasy, joy, and bliss.

## The Spirit Alone

My observation is that God's Spirit, when left alone, is religiously and morally neutral. God's Spirit (subtle energy or life energy) fills the universe. Left on its own and independent of humanity, the Spirit does possess information that acts to create and sustain life. Its energy is the source of life for all living organisms as it quietly acts to sustain and restore energy fields.

## The Living Word

When you have been spiritually transformed and awakened, then the Spirit acts within you according to the Word that is now living within you. However, there seem to be exceptions to this. Noah, Moses, Ezekiel, and Isaiah appear to have been called to service by God in order to declare a new Word. The Christian-persecuting Saul appears to have been possessed by Christ because God needed him to be an evangelist and missionary. At times, the purposeful Word takes us over, producing transformation without free will. This is known as predestination or divine destiny.

## Satanism

In the case of Satanism, the Spirit of God is being called upon to do evil. I believe this is due to the evil

Word used in the intentions and rituals of the participants. They are invoking evil to happen through ritual
magic. Being itself essentially neutral, the Spirit empowers the content of all religious beliefs.

The results of religious transformation and awakening are identical in most religions. In the limited contacts
I have had with awakened people of other faith traditions, I have sensed no difference between their energy
field information and my own. I sense love, peace, joy,
and acceptance. I feel comfortable with my brothers and
sisters of other faith traditions. The perennial wisdom of
the mystics is present in the awakened of all faith traditions.

I have also sensed the energy of Satanists and black
magicians in which I have been aware of information at
great variance with the perennial wisdom. On those
occasions, a discordant shiver of fear has passed through
me and I have needed to disconnect from them.

### Spirit Possession

Like attracts like. If we are not filled with God's Spirit,
being empty, we are susceptible to being filled with other
spirits (energy forms). The rational mind is more susceptible to addictive-compulsive-obsessive behaviors. We
can be filled with the spirit of obsessive, compulsive, and
addictive behaviors—chemical dependencies, obesity,
materialism, consumerism, and sexual deviancy. We can
be filled with the spirit of greed, jealousy, or envy. We
can be filled with spirits of illness. We can be filled with
the spirits of hatred, violence, coldness, and cruelty.
These often begin with small ventures into an area which

attracts negative energy forms which slowly possess and eventually completely dominate and enslave. Our best protection is being filled with God's Word and Spirit. Some spirit energy forms are so resistant to leaving their hosts that only a ritual of exorcism works to expel them.

The rational mind does have access to God. The rational mind can be filled with God's Spirit through a person's lifestyle. Moral actions based upon love, compassion, forgiveness, caring service, and peace-making can fill one with God's Spirit. Becoming close to nature opens spiritual awareness. The fine arts—music, visual arts, and literature—can produce spiritually transforming experiences without the mention or awareness of God. All these work to repair all seven human energy fields.

The birth of each of my daughters was a joyous and satisfying experience. But for my wife, Dana, it was an even more powerful experience. Following the birth of each child, I observed Dana in the midst of a peak experience of God, her face glowing with bliss and ecstasy, in awe of the sacred miracle of birth.

## A Rational "Word of God"

Every prayer would be answered if God's healing energy flowed freely and purely through us. Unfortunately, as the healing energy passes through us, we change its quality. Our feelings, thoughts, attitudes, and beliefs alter the purity, frequency, and intentions of the healing energy. They program it.

One major factor we can attempt to control is our religious beliefs. If we do not know what we believe about God, our prayers tend to be tentative and to lack power.

Consistent and clear beliefs about God also produce a purer quality of healing energy. These beliefs become God's Word, programming the energy of our prayers.

You already hold religious beliefs, some of which may sabotage your healing intentions. Here, we seek to provide you with religious beliefs based upon subtle energies research and the practice of healing prayer. Perhaps we need only one belief—that God's love and healing power are ever present and available to you, the pray-er. Yet, we must be careful not to hold other beliefs that dilute or negate our pure intention of expressing love.

Subtle energies research and the practice of healing prayer provide us with rational knowledge about God. From this, we can build a rational theology, a set of religious beliefs, or the Word of God for prayer. Here is a rational creed, God's Word for prayer:

## A Rational Creed—God's Word for Prayer

*I believe in God, who created the physical universe and continues to sustain it. God is always present, seeking to provide the optimum conditions for life.*

*I believe that God reveals the divine nature through the physical creation, through firsthand experiences of God that provide knowledge, wisdom, revelation, transformation and empowerment, through the life energy that fills the universe, and through the process of science and reason. Through intuitive-creative guidance, God personally provides us with direction and purpose.*

*I believe that God is the source of all love, joy, peace, awe, ecstasy, compassion, caring, goodness, wholeness, renewal, unity, and justice.*

*I believe that God created us in the divine image, meaning that we are, like God, intelligent, creative, energy bodies who are eternal and thus will always exist.*

*I believe that we are connected to each other and to everything that exists through God's information-bearing, intelligently-acting energy that pervades the universe.*

*I believe that God calls all humanity to be co-creators and co-sustainers of our universe. God transforms and empowers us for this purpose through peak experiences of God and in our acts of love, creativity, justice-seeking, prayer, and religious ritual. Through these, we become priests, bringing the power of God into the life of the world.*

*I believe that prayer is the primary means by which God is able to restore purpose, order, love, and goodness to the universe, replacing chaos and evil with divine good and purpose.*

*I believe that through prayer we accumulate, attune, and transmit the divine life force or healing energy, as we bring the power of God into the life of the world. Life energy renews the human energy fields, working like a cosmic antibiotic to produce physical, emotional, mental, spiritual, and interpersonal health and happiness. Life energy can heal any disease.*

*I believe that God wills every person to be healthy and whole. Any failure to achieve this is due to human ignorance and interference.*

*I believe that God calls us to live in peaceful community with all humanity through love, unity, respect, and cooperation. These act to produce understanding, forgiveness and reconciliation, cooperation and support, justice and responsibility, and true wholeness.*

*I believe that God transforms and empowers us to live on a higher ground of spiritual wisdom based upon the divine Word. Through prayer, God unites human beings in energy-laden sacred group energy fields that bathe everyone with the Word. The Word, empowered by the Spirit, connects, transforms, and empowers individuals, couples, families, friends, communities, and nations, encoding the Word into their energy fields and producing wholeness. Sacred group energy fields also hold the power to restore every other portion of God's creation.*

*I believe God is consistent in all these qualities because God's basic nature is to nurture the optimum conditions for life and abundant living.*

---

## Rational Reasons for Religious Beliefs

What does the data of subtle energies research and the practice of healing prayer teach us about the rational reasons for religious beliefs and practice? These articles expand our faith understanding.

### The Soul and Spirit

Achieving contact with the soul and the Spirit is the central purpose of all religions. I feel inadequate in defining the soul and the Spirit. I want, nevertheless, to share my understanding with you. The soul consists of all the information present in the seven human energy fields. The soul is the energy blueprint for not only the physical body, but also for our thoughts, memories, personality, emotions, and spirituality. The soul is our identity, our personality, our spiritual body. The soul, minus the first energy field—the physical energy field—is eternal and survives the death of the physical body.

The purpose of the soul is to grow and evolve into a higher awareness. This is achieved through spiritual and moral transformation in which the Word of God and the Spirit bathe the soul with new life. This is a process occurring throughout one's life. Transformation fills one with love and the need to live a selfless life devoted to serving others.

Transformation also unmasks a person's Spirit, which bathes the soul with God's power from within. This is the purpose of all religions: to help people get into contact with the Spirit. The Spirit resides within every soul. It is the free gift of God's presence in every person. It is one's core of life energy. It is hidden from our awareness and most often lies dormant until freed through transformation and awakening. It is like a three hundred watt light bulb covered by a shield that only permits ten watts of light to glow until touched by God, who slowly removes the shield as awakening continues.

Only a few ever glow with the full three hundred watts. When they do, they become celebrated mystics who expand on God's works and the Word. The Spirit is the true self. As one's Spirit is unveiled, one's life is transformed, empowered and guided. Your Spirit is connected to God and, as such, is always perfect as it is.

God cannot touch our souls nor free our Spirits until we voluntarily open ourselves. Touch-healing confirms the reality of human free will. The healing energy cannot enter a person without permission, as we can shield our energy fields from all outside energies.

Sin simply means to be separated from the Spirit—to live a life veiled from God. Barbara Ann Brennan produced clairvoyant drawings on the effects of the specific damage caused to human energy fields by drugs, alcohol, anger, grief, etc. These drawings are proving themselves over time as they provide effective working models for healing efforts. These drawings reveal that human energy fields may become polluted, darkened and unhealthy, producing the need for restoration. The drawings also display the enhancement of human energy fields produced by music, play, and meditation.

In the practice of touch-healing, we know that drugs, alcohol, anger, and grief hinder the ability of the human energy fields to be in contact with God. We also know that healing prayer restores the ability of people to experience God. Healing and salvation can occur through any action that repairs or transforms the human energy fields.

Salvation means that we have been transformed and awakened by the Word and the Spirit and have taken on the spiritual mind. The experience of the human condition is that our energy fields become distorted, weakened and crippled through life experiences. As the energy fields break down, we become physically ill, emotionally upset, mentally confused, interpersonally alienated, and morally vulnerable. Salvation restores the energy fields.

We have sayings like, "Christ makes all things new," and "God created and he continues to recreate." These sayings become literally true at the moment of salvation. God is the life energy in its purest form. We become whole, another term for salvation.

The quality of the human energy fields takes a quantum leap forward as one becomes a New Person when God's information-containing, living energy field is integrated into one's personal human energy fields.

Taking on the mind of Christ means that the qualities of Christ have become encoded into the human energy fields.

### Heaven

Acquiring eternal life, which must be done in this physical world, means that the human energy fields have become so transformed that they are able, upon physical death, to enter a specific afterlife sector like Heaven, because the quality of the human energy fields match the electromagnetic frequencies of the energy field's dimension of that sector.

### Hell

Evil is an expression of chaos. Chaos occurs in the absence of the Word and the Spirit. When at death, the human energy fields are in a state of utter chaos, the soul enters the afterlife sector with the energy frequencies of chaos. This is what we call Hell: the spiritual dimension where utter chaos rules. Through prayer, God introduces order and purpose into chaos. Without God, utter chaos rules, enabling evil to live and to act.

Salvation occurred for me at the age of ten. That does not mean that I remained in that optimum state. For this to happen, I needed a continuous bathing in God's power through a variety of means. When that did not happen, I backslid. Remembering how wonderful full salvation is, I hungered for it. I wanted to be restored to full wholeness through God.

## *Spiritual renewal*

Spiritual renewal is soul development as one seeks to renew all seven human energy fields. An individual's beliefs, thoughts, attitudes, worship, meditation, prayer and loving actions all help transform the human energy fields. Each energy field vibrates at a different frequency. Clinical evidence suggests that these frequencies change with spiritual growth.

It is likely that we already have the scientific capability to measure these frequencies. With application, we will be able to determine the frequencies of the various levels of wholeness. This will enable us to quantify levels of health and spiritual maturity, and lead to simple ways of determining the truth of persons and situations. Hypocrites will no longer be able hide behind masks of respectability. We will be able to stop lie detector and psychological testing; instead we will choose quality workers, spouses, and friends according to the compatible frequencies of their energy fields.

The practice of touch-healing prayer began opening my thinking in this whole area. While praying for wholeness in body, mind and spirit, I sensed God's healing energy being transmitted to the healee's spiritual body (human energy fields). I noticed that even when healing did not occur, the healee often experienced the presence of God's love, joy and peace for about two days. It sometimes imparted the information through changes in thoughts, emotions, attitudes, and beliefs. I realized that, in the proper context, prayers for healing produce a salvation experience. But religious knowledge is necessary for this to occur. The healing energy's presence made the existing religious knowledge, the Word, come alive in the healee for a brief time.

## Religious Rituals

These empower the Word and the Spirit. Gathering believers together in ritual, bathes everyone in the resulting sacred group energy field. This intelligent-acting information works over time to unite, transform, awaken and empower believers.

During the ritual of Christian baptism, God's Spirit is intentionally transferred by touch to the recipient. God then begins living within the recipient's energy fields. For a time, the energy fields of the baptized glow with and are protected by God's energy. Of course, God is literally present in all religious ritual. I, myself, have witnessed countless physical, emotional, mental, and interpersonal healings occur during baptism, confirmation, communion, and ordination.

Wedding rituals form an energy-bonding, uniting the bride and groom into a spiritual, emotional and physical oneness as "the two become one." From that moment on, a cord of divine energy continues to unite them, unless it is broken. This created unity may make some spouses feel smothered. One of the reasons that separation and divorce are so painful is because divine energy, the tie that binds, still exists. A prayer ritual can sever this cord, ending much emotional anguish. Love among family members and friends produce similar energy bonding/uniting. Casual sexual contacts can also produce such ties.

## Grief

Grief is deepened by two energy factors. First, we miss the presence of the deceased one's energy field. Second, we may continue to be linked through the energy cord that binds. Touch-healing prayer can restore wholeness to grieving energy fields.

## The Significance of the Word in Healing

The Word of God must be present in every healing encounter. The Word comes from the qualities present in the energy of the healer's mind, soul, intentions and energy fields. In healing, the content of the Word of God involves many qualities. The Word of God for the healer involves such qualities as love, acceptance, faith, hope, compassion, expectancy, trust, confidence. Thankfully, in therapeutic spoken prayer made by caring loved ones, people of all religions naturally express the Word of God for wholeness and renewal.

### Ineffective Idealism

There can be no spiritual development without the Word. Meditation, contemplation, and visualization possess no spiritual power unless the participant is aware of a viable Word of God. In the absence of the Word, a person can feel peaceful and centered, but without any significant transformation or empowerment occurring.

### Deep Belief

Religious commitment or deeply held religious beliefs (the Word) further empower God's Spirit.

So, no matter what rituals are being used, the Word must be clearly expressed. If you want God's Spirit to act powerfully in a sacred group energy field, it helps to have all participants sharing common, deeply held, religious beliefs.

## The Spirit in Groups

Any time two or more people gather together they form a group energy field. Healing encounters, couples, families, classrooms, work places, communities and nations all form group energy fields. If you wish health and happiness in any of these settings, then Therapeutic Prayers should be employed by every participant, expressing the Word for that situation, to empower the actions of God's Spirit. A sacred group energy field will then be formed that bathes everyone, transforming and empowering them.

## A Scientific Source for Life Energy

Physicist John Zimmerman, founder and president of Bio-Electro-Magnetics of Reno, Nevada, proposes a rational source for life energy. Dr. Zimmerman suggests that the source of life energy is our planet, Earth. Earth resonates with the Schumann Frequencies that exit with the Earth-ionosphere resonant cavity at 7 to 8 hertz. He asks, "Is it not within the realm of possibility that some people can perceive the 7 to 8 hertz brain-wave frequency of the Earth?"

Zimmerman's theory is that healers have either the innate or trained capacity to detect the weak variations of the earth's electromagnetic fields, the Schumann Frequencies. He suggests that the healing frequency varies, as do the Schumann Frequencies, with the time of day, month, and year, and the phases of the moon. The Schumann Frequencies vary from plus or minus 7.83 hertz. That variation appears to be identical to that of the healing frequency. Attuning for healing occurs by matching human brain-waves with the varied frequencies of Earth.

It is also necessary for the healer's respiration rate, either consciously or subconsciously, to adjust itself to become an exact sub-harmonic of the ongoing Schumann Frequency to facilitate the brain-wave synchronization. Normal respiration is about twelve breaths per minute.

If the Schumann Frequency is 7.8 hertz, the healer would need enough control to breathe exactly 0.195 breaths per second, the equivalent of 11.7 breaths per minute. This would give a Schumann Frequency and respiration rate of exactly 40 (7.8 divided by 0.195). The healer must then transmit this frequency to the brain of the healee, producing synchronized brain waves.

Dr. Robert Beck, nuclear physicist, confirmed Zimmerman's theory. Beck found that during healing encounters, the healer's brain waves became both frequency- and phase-synchronized with the Schumann waves. "That means the healer's brain waves pulse not only at the same frequency but also at the same time as the earth's Schumann waves. It could be assumed that healers are able to take energy from the magnetic field of the earth for the healing of patients. This process is called "field coupling." It is clear that what healers call "grounding into the earth" is the action of linking up with the magnetic field of earth, both in frequency and phase.

Dr. Edgar Wilson proved that Israeli healer David Joffee impressed his brain-wave pattern upon a healee in order to produce healing. The healee must voluntarily allow this entraining to occur.

Dr. John Zimmerman went a step further. He found that once healers have linked up with the Schumann frequencies, the right and left hemispheres of their brains become balanced with each other and show a 7.8 to 8 hertz alpha rhythm. In touch-healing, it has been shown that patients' brain waves also go into alpha and are phased-synchronized with the healers', as well as right-left balanced. The healer has linked the client with the earth's magnetic field pulses and has thereby tapped into a tremendous energy source for healing.

Scientists possess evidence that life energy permeates not only our planet but our whole planetary system and our galaxy, as well. Earth as a single energized planetary body may be energetically linked to all physical matter in our solar system, producing an information-bearing, intelligently-acting energy field that encompasses our whole solar system. Our solar system may be similarly linked to the systems of other stars. Or, our solar system may be unique in possessing life energy—the basis for all life.

Other scientists are exploring life energy as a new energy source capable of replacing nuclear power. Is life energy the fifth minor force scientists are looking for to balance their equations about the nature of the universe?

This discussion raises theological questions. Is the peak experience of God due to attunement with the Schumann Frequencies? Is Earth a living, breathing, information-bearing, intelligently-acting entity attuned to bring optimum life and spiritual wisdom to all of her inhabitants?

## Sacred Group Energy Fields in Religious History

I have always considered the miracles of the Bible to be quite literally true. I have also chuckled at the attempts of biblical scholars to explain away miracles as symbolic stories, or of scientists to explain specific miraculous events rationally. The existence of powerfully acting sacred group energy fields provides all the credibility needed for miracles.

How did Jesus calm a stormy sea? Storms are filled with energy and all he needed to do was to change the energy patterns and the storm and waves could be calmed. The energy released by a group in prayer can produce similar results.

The two most astounding group events in the Bible involve the Exodus and Pentecost. Here is a scientific energy field explanation.

## The Parting of the Red Sea

The Bible indicates that both Moses and Aaron possessed immense spiritual abilities. They were obviously ENFJs. They were group catalysts, attuners and PSI sensitives.

With the ability of their personality types, their divine destiny and the sacred group energy field created by the high emotional and spiritual energies of two hundred thousand Hebrews fleeing before the advancing Egyptian army, parting the waters of the Red Sea would have been possible. They possessed the skills, and forty billion energy units of prayer power. With this, they created two energy barriers as solid as poured concrete, damming the waters so they could walk across the sea bed. When all had passed, the energy barriers were withdrawn, trapping the pursuing Egyptian army. Read the story (Exodus 14:10-15:18). Moses' actions match this description.

## Pentecost as a God-Empowered Group Energy Field

The Resurrected Christ told the disciples to wait in Jerusalem for the Holy Spirit to bring them power (Acts 1). At Pentecost, fifty days later, that power of the Holy Spirit swept over them (Acts 2). They were told to wait, to stay together, to expect God's power. They did all this in the context of Jesus' ministry, his teachings, the drama of the Passion, and the post-Resurrection appearances. For the disciples, these events all formed a powerful drama of God's revelation to them. This is the revealed image of God and the Word of God for Christians.

The beliefs of those who awaited Pentecost are important. Those beliefs are the contents of God's revelation of the Word to the Disciples. God is love. God heals. God transforms and awakens. God in Jesus overcomes the world. God resurrects. God empowers. These are a part of the content of their revealed image of God. When the Holy Spirit came with power at Pentecost, it was in the context of that belief system, the Word of God as known in Jesus. The Disciples and others, gathered in expectation of the Pentecost, helped create the enormous sacred group energy field by their memories, thoughts, and anticipations. This preparation was necessary for the Holy Spirit's actions on Pentecost.

God acts apart from humanity to shape human history. God's revelations are always filtered through the person and personality of a human being: through an Abraham, Isaac or Jacob, a Moses, or a Jeremiah or Isaiah. God also acts through groups of persons gathered together, as on Pentecost or in religious ritual. Their intentions, and the information in individual energy fields, creates a sacred group energy field that we have always thought of as God, acting alone and independent of persons.

God's power at Pentecost was like a nuclear explosion. Tongues of fire from the Holy Spirit—God's living, intelligently-acting energy—encompassed the waiting crowd. Thousands were gathered. They all knew the revelation of God in Jesus, their revealed image of God. The power of God and this new revelation of God's love—the Word—interacted. The energy fields of those gathered were encoded with this combination.

God's power in the Spirit enabled the believers to fit all the pieces of the new revelation together so that it made sense. Three thousand believers were transformed and empowered by baptism that day. That is nine million units of prayer power plus the power of the Word and the Holy Spirit. The power of Pentecost, placed in the human energy fields of each believer as their revealed image of God, was passed on powerfully by touch and by energy fields throughout the next four centuries of preaching, conversion, miracle-making, and healing that dominated and then overwhelmed the cultures it touched. In the Fifth Century, the rationally-minded church administrators deadened the connection to the Holy Spirit. They continue to do this today.

Understanding this, a planetary Pentecost-type explosion of re-creation and transformation could happen if humanity had a new, universal revealed image of God exciting to everyone. Just imagine using the mass media to unite five billion people in common prayer for renewal. The energy created would be 25,000,000,000,000,000,000,000 units or volts of prayer power. Theoretically, this could transform every person on earth to optimum health and life. It could bring about the ecological restoration of the planet Earth's oceans, air, ozone layer, and forests, ushering in a Golden Age of peace with justice for all life.

## God's Love Is Universal

Parts of the Christian revealed image of God may also be present in persons who are not believers or church members or who are of other religions. Christians do not have an exclusive patent on the divine quality known as love. Most religions believe in the importance of love. The Christian revealed image of God's quality of compassionate love can be found in most persons at some level. In the Christian context, when the Word and the Holy Spirit come alive and produce salvation in a person, it does transform him into a person who shines with God's love.

This all sounds good on paper, yet it is quite complex. It may take a lifetime to integrate love into responsible expressions in the other energy fields. Compassionate love appears to have strong genetic and hormonal elements. New medical evidence indicates that the natural nurturing qualities of women are both genetic and hormonal. Compassionate love may be more rooted in innate personality traits than religious belief, with salvation only amplifying personality traits.

An individual's personality traits may be highly regarded in one religion while being seen as negative by another. American Christians hold in high regard the personality traits of persons who are warm, friendly, loving, generous, and outgoing. We say these are "Christian" traits and the qualities necessary for sainthood, when in fact their source may be due more to the genetics of the personality traits and cultural expectations of American Christians. An American who is the reserved, introverted, thinking personality type may be out of place within a Christian community, yet feel right at home in another religion like Hinduism.

All of this is important for our understanding of group energy fields. A group energy field is created by the contents of individual human energy fields; all the mental, emotional, moral and spiritual qualities present in each of the individual human energy fields combine in the group energy field focused upon a specific goal or event.

There is one God of all creation. He is the God of Jews and Christians, of Hindus and Muslims, and of all other religions. There is one God who reveals his true nature to all cultures and peoples. The qualities of God as Creator and Sustainer are known in all religions. In all religions, God transforms, empowers, and heals. These attributes are known in every community and religion.

In a like manner, healers throughout the world emanate a healing energy at identical frequencies. The healing effects of all healers are identical. Being in contact with God and being compassionate are common traits of healers in all cultures. These universal qualities promote health and wholeness.

## Health Related to Religious Participation

With this background understanding, it comes as no surprise that two 1992 studies linked religious participation to better health. Purdue University medical sociologist Kenneth F. Ferraro, reporting in the Journal for the Scientific Study of Religion, concluded that those who practice their faith regularly are healthier than those who don't. In his study of 1,473 people randomly selected nationwide, those who practiced their religion through prayer, religious services, and religious study were more than twice as healthy as those who do not. Nine percent in the non-practicing group reported poor health in comparison to only four percent in the religion practicing group. Those associated with mainline denominations such as Episcopalians, Presbyterians, Methodists, Lutherans, and Roman Catholic had better health than Jehovah's Witnesses, Mormons, Christian Scientists, and some Baptists.

In Psychological Reports, William Oleckno, professor of community health, and Michael J. Blacconiere of Hines Veterans Administration Hospital, found religious commitment to be strongly related to wellness, non-use of tobacco, alcohol and drugs, and use of seat belts among 1,077 Northern Illinois University students. This correlation was directly related to the frequency of attendance at religious services.

# 15

# Doing What Has Never Before Been Possible

One February, I traveled to Montreal to learn how to become a clairvoyant diagnostician. My teacher did diagnostic work for several physicians, one of whom was there for my first day. I did not expect to practice healing on her diagnostic clients, but a waiting room filled with healing clients confronted me. It was rush work. Ten minutes a patient.

I was finishing my seventh patient when a woman hobbled in using a walker. The anguish on her face spoke of her pain while walking. But overshadowing that was her despair. I had never seen anyone so depressed.

Diane's story brought tears to my eyes. Ten years before she had been injured in an auto accident that had broken many of her bones. Incapacitated, she could no longer work as a schoolteacher. Her husband had left her. She was in constant pain. As she left, I thought, "If only I could have given her the healing time she needed."

Two weeks later Diane phoned me at my home in northeast Ohio. Her first words were, "I am pain free."

This was not all due to my healing efforts. She had also used the self-healing guide I had given her. Then she added, "I still have my depression. The next time you come to Montreal, you can heal it."

Three months later, I made an appointment with Diane when I returned to Montreal for a conference. My only problem was I did not know how to heal depression. I prayed for God to guide me. Two hours before our appointment, I heard a lecture by Indiana psychologist Sharon Wendt. She provided all the clues I needed. In less than one hour, I was able to remove all of Diane's depression. That was five years ago. She remains whole.

I had done what has never before been possible. I had removed a chronic destructive emotional state with my healing hand. I soon learned that I could do that with any emotional state. I could also remove any painful or traumatic memory in the same way. I named this astounding technique Emotional Release Therapy.

### Emotional Release Therapy

Every person on Earth holds a lifetime of emotional pain within them. Emotional pain sticks to us like glue. No matter what we do, we cannot shake it off. Psychotherapy helps us understand and cope with our hurts, but following years of therapy, the pain remains.

Time does not heal all. It never has; it never will. In fact, emotional hurts can be just as painful forty years later as on the day they first wounded us. Why can't I shake off my painful memories? Why can't I just let go and forget? We begin thinking there must be something inherently wrong within us.

We undergo counseling. We gain support and understanding, but the emotional pain remains. We use a medication to mask it, but it is still there, lurking in the shadows.

## Answers in the Human Energy Fields

Remember our working model with the human energy fields. Emotional pain is stored in our emotional energy field and not in our physical brains. There is no way to work through the pain by thinking, because the pain is not in the brain where thinking takes place. We can cleverly suppress the pain so that we no longer totally feel it, but the emotional pain is still there and capable of distorting our energy fields to make us depressed, anxious, angry, or ill.

Every unresolved emotional pain that we have ever experienced is stored in our emotional energy fields. They are alive and stored as bits of emotional information. Here also are stored the good emotional experiences of our lives. Unfortunately, emotional pain can overwhelm a lifetime of good emotional experiences.

Our present emotional states are also stored there. Here is our reservoir of anger, fear, anxiety, and depression. Here is our reservoir of love, contentment, happiness, and joy. The painful and happy emotions battle each other for dominance in a constant warfare.

The contents of the emotional energy field influence our thinking, decisions, performance, energy, personalities, and ability to cope with life. They are the cause of destructive moods and behaviors. They nurture either health or disease, by creating the mold of the blueprint energy field that determines our physical health.

These are the answers to why our emotions seem to have a life of their own. These are the reasons why we have so little rational control over painful memories and destructive emotional states. It, like our emotional pains, possesses us. They literally do.

We have access to the emotional energy field through the heart chakra. Yes, the poetic heart where we feel love. This is the heart that can become heavy or broken, or light as a feather, or filled with passion.

By placing your healing hand just above the heart on the sternum, a person can release a lifetime of emotional pain. Because emotions are so fleeting, the client chooses a symbol to represent his emotions. The client visualizes this symbol and releases it into the therapist's hand, along with any painful or traumatic memories. Destructive emotional states like depression, anxiety, and anger are released just as easily. This usually takes less than an hour. You can do it on yourself. And the released emotions are gone forever.

Emotional Release Therapy can be just as effective over the phone. Both therapist and client place a hand on their own hearts. As the therapist directs the client, he can feel the emotional pain being released into his hand, from distances of thousands of miles.

The significance of all this is clear. No more need for psychotherapy. No more need for medications. No more hospitalizations for emotional pain. No more electroshock therapy. Just a little counseling now and then. And life can become emotionally good for every person on our planet.

And this is only a part of this amazing new paradigm. This sounds too wonderful to be true. That is why this is such a wonderful discovery.

Emotional Release Therapy is also a key tool in treating the whole person in holistic healing centers.

## The Paradigm of Our Magical Hands

Here is a new model for our magical hands. During healing, hands can learn to explore the qualities of the human energy fields. Hands emit healing energy into the human energy fields. Hands can act like magnets in augmenting the release of emotional pain from the heart chakra.

Now we have discovered another use of the hands. Following Emotional Release Therapy, a few clients complained of feeling emotionally empty. In response, I began offering all my clients a prayer blessing: "God, fill ___ with your presence, love, and peace." It worked. Clients commented that they had indeed been filled with these qualities. Some even glowed with them.

Then I began experimenting. Upon becoming aware of a client's specific lack, I used my hands and prayer to fill them with what they lacked during the blessing. These included qualities like confidence, courage, femininity, trust, and gentleness. This too worked.

I began exploring this with my wife. I discovered that a hand to the heart and prayer can fill your spouse with the intensity of your love or your passion, as well as a whole array of other great emotions.

## Healing Emotional Hurts

After your painful memories and destructive emotional states are released, you possess an ongoing sense of inner peace and contentment. You wake up each morning feeling happy and joyous about being alive.

The uses for Emotional Release Therapy are enormous. Victims of violence and abuse, and of painful relationships, are freed to move on with their lives. This is useful in rape crisis centers, crime victim assistance programs, battered women's shelters, and children's services. Children can release a lifetime of emotional trauma within a few minutes, freeing them to be normally happy, to learn and to grow.

Couples and families can release all their hurts and distrusts. This clears the way for beginning anew. A parent can use Emotional Release Therapy to heal any emotional trauma a son or daughter experiences. At the end of the day, people can use Emotional Release Therapy to rid themselves of that day's stresses. If your mind is racing at bedtime with emotions and thoughts, you can quiet these in sixty seconds by releasing them into your own hand. Sleep then comes quickly.

Battering husbands and violent youth and adults can release the rage and hurt that causes compulsive violence.

On the international scene, ethnic violence and bitterness following wars could be removed from a community or nation. Emotional trauma possesses us. Release the trauma and people can move on to building peace. Begin with just a few people trained in Emotional Release Therapy. Everyone they treat is healed and becomes able to treat others with about two hours of training. Each one heals one and teaches one. Within months, a whole nation could have all their traumatic wounds healed.

I have practiced Emotional Release Therapy with hundreds of clients. Everyone can do it. The results are immediate. I have taught more than two hundred people to practice it. Their results are as good as mine.

## Disease and the Mind-Body Connection

We finally have a solution to the mind-body disease connection. Conventional medicine considers emotional pain to be the cause of 90% of all diseases.

Our new paradigm for the nature of man is the needed model for why this is true. Over the past two decades, a number of studies have provided evidence that eighteen to twenty-four months before the onset of cancer, the cancer patient has experienced an emotional trauma. These traumas include a marital betrayal, a divorce, the death of a loved one, or the loss of a job.

What does this emotional pain do? It eventually distorts the energy fields, beginning with the emotional energy field. Our energy fields are quite stable, so it takes more than twelve months before the energy fields become diseased. Anytime during this period, a person can work through the emotional pain and no energy field distortion occurs. But if the emotional pain remains, the cancer process begins in the energy fields.

According to the previously cited Dr. Chouhan's energy field research, at three to six months before the onset of cancer, the energy fields have become diseased. The diseased cancerous energy field has a recognizable aura or signature. This diseased energy field, the blueprint energy field, takes three to six months to program the physical cells of the body to become cancerous. The person now has cancer.

This cancer is maintained by emotional pain. No conventional medical approach can heal the cancer until the emotional energy field has been healed or become whole. Those in the process of treatment whose emotional energy field somehow becomes healed, survive cancer.

This same model is true of most diseases that are resistant to conventional care. As long as the emotional energy field remains distorted with emotional pain, no conventional or alternative medical approach can permanently heal these unresponsive diseases.

Any holistic healing treatment works only because it has been able to somehow heal the emotional energy field. Most of these emotional healings are unintentional, a side effect of the practice of physical healing. Now that we have a working model for what is occurring, Emotional Release Therapy becomes the first of what will become many holistic means for removing emotional pain.

Medical conditions responding well to Emotional Release Therapy are chronic back pain, chronic fatigue, arthritis, heart disease, cancer, and bacterial and viral infections.

One afternoon recently, I worked with three clients. Ed had been on Social Security disability for four years with chronic spinal pain. He was also depressed and suffered from chronic fatigue. Three days after Emotional Release Therapy he brought me a bouquet of flowers and a hug. He was one hundred percent well.

John was suffering from heart failure following several heart attacks. Following one session of Emotional Release Therapy all tests showed his heart muscle had become normal again.

Jill had late stage breast cancer that had spread throughout her body. Her primary care physician sent the dying woman to me. She released the emotional pains which resulted from a dysfunctional marriage and a divorce. Six weeks later, her MRIs showed her cancer cells had decreased by one-third. Four months later, Jill was cancer free. Cancer seems to feed on emotional pain. Remove the emotional pain and the human energy fields become healthy and tell the cancer cells to become healthy cells. Emotional Release Therapy will not cure cancer or any other disease if the patient subsequently returns to be with the person or persons who are causing the emotional pain. Further emotional trauma will result, defeating the therapy's value.

I believe in complementary medicine. This means a conventional physician and a holistic health care provider working together. If someone has a cancerous tumor, I recommend conventional medical care that includes Emotional Release Therapy. Cancer, in particular, develops an energy system apart from the human energy fields. This may take on a life of its own so that the human energy fields cannot reprogram it. Removing the cancerous tumor destroys this separate cancerous energy field, permitting healthy human energy fields to reprogram all body cells to be healthy.

When practicing Emotional Release Therapy, I seldom practice physical healing. This is because Emotional Release Therapy restores all the energy fields. Thus, it is also a form of physical healing.

## Enabling People to Become Compassionate

Many people lack a compassionate nature. They are unable to be sensitive to and supportive of the hurts of others. Men in particular are culturally conditioned from childhood not to feel. People who have been terribly emotionally wounded also may lose their compassionate nature.

Compassion is a function of the heart chakra. When the heart chakra is closed, people cannot feel and respond to the needs of others. By healing their hurts and teaching people to open their heart chakras, Emotional Release Therapy enables people to become more compassionate. This is a learning process for males. It is best learned by using a coach, a loved one, who leads the male to practice it in various situations.

Compassionate people generously give their love to loved ones. Uncompassionate people cannot. They come through as takers of love. When they learn to open their heart chakras, uncompassionate people become capable of both giving and receiving love. This will bring happiness and fulfillment to many previously dysfunctional marriages and families.

## Opening One to God

People with a closed or wounded heart chakra have difficulty-experiencing God. As a pastor, many churchmen privately consulted me because they had never experienced God. In working with Emotional Release Therapy, I learned that the heart is the antenna or doorway to God. Uncompassionate people with impaired or closed heart chakras cannot experience God. Depressed people also cannot. Severe grief can close God off to people who have had life long relationships with him. Using Emotional Release Therapy we can heal the emotional wounds and teach people to open their hearts to God. This is the greatest evangelism assistance the world has ever known.

Anyone who chooses to practice healing prayer should receive Emotional Release Therapy. It makes their work far more effective.

## Emotional Release Therapy and Spiritual Bliss

I have no working model for this. Only questions. For many people, Emotional Release Therapy is a deeply spiritual experience. Afterwards, a few are radiant with spiritual bliss. It can be a life transforming experience. After people become emotionally whole and filled with God, they naturally begin rethinking all their attitudes and beliefs. They become new persons, freed and empowered to fulfill their life's dreams or soul needs.

Therapists know similar rewards. But there is a side to therapy that fascinates me. Ten to twenty percent of the time, God fills me to overflowing with his presence. I enter the deepest spiritual state I have ever known. I call it a spiritual trance state. Do not let the word trance scare you. I maintain control of myself.

When this happens during the practice of Emotional Release Therapy, I tell the client that I am in a deep spiritual state. I then ask them to quietly leave so that I can remain in this spiritual bliss. Inevitably, they want to stay. They say, "This room is now filled with God. May I stay and meditate?" I will remain in this spiritual state for an hour or more.

My questions are many. Is this triggered by two people being connected to the same heart chakra during Emotional Release Therapy? If the heart is the doorway to God, could Emotional Release Therapy connect us to the sacred part of each person, the human soul?

Is Emotional Release Therapy a type of soul healing?

## Cultural Resistance

Yesterday, a dying woman phoned me. She was a referral from a previous client. Her breast cancer had spread throughout her body and she was finally seeking alternative medicine. I explained Emotional Release Therapy to her but she did not get it. She had never heard of energy fields. She was looking for a physical magic bullet to cure her. I had no pills or herbs to offer her. She declined my services and hung up disappointed.

I realized there would be cultural resistance to Emotional Release Therapy, but I did not expect to hit a concrete wall. My private clients are extremely pleased with their outcomes. Their recommendations are bringing a growing clientele. But elsewhere, the barriers are immense.

Print advertising yields few responses, probably because it sounds too wonderful to be true. Organizations like the Rape Crisis Center, the Center for Battered Women, the Crime Victim Assistance Program, the Veterans Hospital, and many psychologists have refused to use Emotional Release Therapy. Those more open to its use are massage therapists, chiropractors, and healers.

Does it threaten the reputations and jobs of helping professionals? Probably. Does its source, the discipline of healing, frighten many people away? Probably. Does its human energy field model confuse people? Probably.

This cultural resistance is one of my motivations for writing about it. Can you accept the working model and its explanation? If you do, do not think that it will be easy to convince others of its immense value.

I believe Emotional Release Therapy is revolutionary in scope. It will radically alter the way in which health care is practiced. Millions of people will now be able to live happy and productive lives following just one or more therapy sessions. And this is only a small part of the Emotional Release Therapy story.

# 16

# Transforming Relationships

After Emotional Release Therapy heals individual hurts, a couple, family, or household can rebuild their relationships. They can do this without counseling or additional communications skills. They can rebuild their relationships using prayer. As a three-decades-old national church promotion stated, the family that prays together, stays together.

To understand how this is possible, we return to our working model of the human energy fields. I am convinced that interpersonal human energy field interactions contribute to dysfunctional relationships. Let us begin understanding this through practical examples.

Most women have an intuitive ability to read energy fields. When meeting with a complete stranger, they quickly accept or reject them. They do this by naturally picking up energy field interactions. If the other person's energy field is incompatible with theirs, they remain distant. If it is compatible, they lower their guard and warm up to the stranger.

In romance, some couples report love at first sight. Part of this love is due to energy field compatibility. When their energy fields complement and stimulate each other, that contributes to love at first sight. When their energy fields merge pleasurably, it is painful to be parted for long. They have joined their energy fields and their energies or souls become linked. That is also the basis for the heat of sexual passion.

Being homesick also involves linked energy fields. A child leaves home alone for a week and develops an intense yearning to return home. To not exchange loving energy with family members may become so traumatic that the child becomes physically ill.

I think you can identify with these examples. Now, let's apply these same types of interactions to couples and families living in homes together. To increase harmony in the home, we must find a means for spiritually merging human energy fields. What is our most common spiritual action? Praying. Where might the seat of the soul be? The heart. How do we transmit emotional energy to each other? With the hands. With these clues in mind, we proceed.

When my wife and I first began praying aloud for each other's needs, we chose to do it in the evening at bedtime. The first night, we began with our usual bedtime ritual of embracing face-to-face. As she began praying, we could feel this enormous heat building up between us. During our four-minute prayer, the heat became so intense it was painful.

Afterwards we discussed what had happened. The source of heat was in our energy chakras at the throat, heart, diaphragm, abdomen, and genitals. We guessed

293

that they had been merging and interacting during our prayer. We were correct.

The next morning came the great surprise. Our relationship was completely different. The rough edges of our relationship were gone. All relationships have their rough edges—irritability, put-downs, disharmony. Peace, harmony, and cooperation now enveloped us. How happy and joyful we became with each other. This was a welcome new stage in our relationship. Every evening for a dozen years, we have continued to pray in this same way with the same relation-enhancing results.

This is healing and enhancing relationships. Though not as powerful, holding hands while praying also creates a spiritual merging of family members. It also creates a sacred group energy field that bathes everyone present in God's love. Another possibility is for family members to create a touch-chain. Each family member places their favored hand upon the heart of another person. Each person, thus, has a hand on his or her heart.

This is holistic medicine. This is healing relationships. This is merging into a family love.

# 17

# Therapeutic Group Energy Fields

The group energy fields described in chapter ten have many potential uses. These group energy fields are sacred because they are filled with the energy of prayer. They are therapeutic because their purpose is to heal those who are bathed in them. So the most descriptive name is quite long–Therapeutic Sacred Group Energy Fields.

Prayer removes chaos, the evil and darkness that is present in the absence of God's presence. Prayer fills people and replaces with God's presence which produces sacred purpose and order, love and peace, happiness and fulfillment. Let us start small and then build up to the largest implications.

## In Your Home

Jesus said, "Where two or more are gathered in my name, there am I in the midst of them." That does not say much for the value of the sacred power released by one person praying alone. The power of prayer is the square of the number involved. One person praying releases one unit of sacred prayer energy. Two persons praying together releases four times that. Four persons release sixteen units of sacred prayer energy, and so forth.

In your home, when you pray with other family members, you form a sacred group energy field. The energy released bathes everyone in that room. It flows into the carpet, the walls, the furniture, leaving a residue of it present at all times. This sacred group energy field is filled with information, the information from the intent and content of your vocal prayers together. This sacred information enters the energy fields of everyone present and slowly transforms persons into the information qualities expressed in your prayers.

When I first enter such a room, I can feel those qualities. They become a part of the room. I can also feel the rough qualities in rooms where no one has prayed.

So to therapeutically heal relationships, use Emotional Release Therapy, touch the energy chakras while praying aloud, and create a therapeutic sacred group energy field that always bathes you in the energy of your prayers. This is relational healing. This is holistic medicine at its best.

## Religious Gatherings

Design your sacred rituals so that they are filled with God and the religious qualities you cherish. Your goal is to create a sacred group energy field that bathes all the participants in sacred qualities. Begin with a prayer that expresses this intent. Visualize the energy field forming, beginning in you and spreading out to encompass the whole area. This results in everyone being permeated and transformed by the sacred energy present.

## Schools and Classrooms

Where permitted, a classroom could be enveloped in a sacred group energy field whose information could transform every person into the qualities expressed in their prayers together. Thirty students in prayer would produce 900 sacred units of prayer energy.

Because this is not permitted in American public schools, parents could pray for the students and create the same kind of sacred group energy field which is conducive to learning. One hundred parents praying produce 10,000 units of sacred prayer energy. This could bathe the whole school in God's presence.

## Farm Communities

In Iowa, people throughout the whole state are praying for their farmers. Farm accident fatalities were cut in half the first year. Their financial needs are being met.

We already know that prayer increases the growth rate of plants by up to one hundred percent. Could we use therapeutic sacred group energy fields to grow crops faster? Could we make a forest grow twice as fast with such an energy field? Could we make endangered wildlife hardier for their survival? Could we accelerate the growth of a rain forest by fifty percent?

## Communities and Nations

Bathing a neighborhood or community in a therapeutic sacred group energy field may completely transform it. If a thousand people in a neighborhood of five thousand, prayed daily for valued sacred qualities, the energy of their therapeutic sacred group energy field would be one million sacred units of prayer energy. This would slowly fill everyone in the neighborhood with the sacred qualities expressed in their prayers.

In a large city, 100,000 praying residents would produce ten billion sacred units of prayer energy for their therapeutic sacred group energy field. That is 10,000,000,000 units.

In a nation of ten million, one million citizens would produce one trillion units of prayer energy for their therapeutic sacred group energy field.

Globally, if one billion earthlings prayed, they would produce 1,000,000,000,000,000,000 units of prayer energy for their therapeutic sacred group energy field.

In the last two examples, the energy released would be the most powerful sacred force ever known to humanity. It would bathe every human exposed to it with qualities that bring wholeness to everyone.

This could also be done through absent prayer for another community or nation. These actions, preceded by Emotional Release Therapy, could transform every person on Earth.

## Restoring the Ecology

Prayer creates the optimum conditions for all life. This is God's creative force that makes all things new. Theoretically, a planetary wide therapeutic sacred group energy field, created by one billion praying earthlings, might have the power to rid the earth of airborne and water pollution. It might be able to remove man-made radioactivity throughout the planet, as well as other hazardous wastes. It might be able to control weather patterns and tropical storms. It might be able to stop earthquakes before they begin.

Only experimental models can test the validity of this science-based theory of the power of prayer. I am willing to help anyone with the design.

# 18

# Ancient Religious Models for Healing

We have now completed the scientific foundations for how prayer heals. Does this help us better understand ancient stories about healing? How do the ancient religious models for healing compare to the new scientific model? Can we learn anything new from the ancient models depicted in the Bible?

## The Healing Style of Jesus

In the gospel accounts, Jesus' healing encounters are briefly described. We do not know how much the witnesses might have missed or did not think needed to be reported. The biblical purpose is to tell the story of God's power at work. Jesus performed healing in several ways.

1. **Touch-healing**: In Matthew 8:14-15, Peter's mother-in-law, "lying sick with a fever," was just touched and the fever left her.
2. **Expected healing**: In Matthew 8:2, a leper knelt and asked to be cleansed. Jesus agreed, touched him and the man was well. The leper obviously

respected Jesus because he knelt. The leper's very statement showed that he expected or took for granted Jesus' ability.

3. **Faith**: In Matthew 9:2-8, a paralytic was healed. The following transactions took place. The paralytic, and those who brought him, had faith. Could that mean either an expectation that Jesus would heal or a belief that Jesus healed? Or is it a trust as one might trust in modern medicine? This faith seems to mean "to put one's trust in."

4. **Forgiveness**: Another element in this same story is forgiveness. Since this is all we know of the encounter, we must assume that Jesus intuitively saw the man's obvious need for forgiveness.

5. **Command**: The third element in this story is a command to be well, in which the spoken word focused and empowered the healing energy. This one of the reasons for using forceful prayers in healing.

6. **A healing flow**: In Matthew 9:18-26 are two reports of healings. One tells of the hemorrhaging woman who touched the hem of his garment. Mark 5:25-34 says that this act immediately healed her and Jesus "perceived in himself that power had gone forth from him."

   Today's healer would sense the same energy flow, though no loss of power. This affirms modern research that there is energy transmitted from a healer or from that which he has touched (a garment).

7. **Assurance**: In Matthew's account, Jesus assures the woman that "faith has made you well." This is the same assurance today's healer might offer to fixate the healing.

8. **Raising the dead**. The second healing in the passage was of Jairus' daughter who had actually

died. Jesus took her hand or touched her, and she lived.

After reading the research data, we should not be surprised by this. Healers are transmitting an energy that possesses voltage. This voltage is more than a million times the voltage of the heart. This is how a defibrillator works to restart the heart.

The mass media implied that faith healer Oral Roberts could not have brought a dead man back to life. This was impossible. The whole nation laughed at Robert's expense. I also have done this. Oral Robert's claim is possible according to the picture that emerges from our research data.

9. **Healing as a process**: Mark 8:22 tells of the gradual healing of a blind man. First, Jesus spat in the man's eyes. The healing energy would be present in the saliva. Then he tested out the healing, just as a modern healer would do. Then he healed again, placing his hands on the eyes, and this time his testing showed the man had completely restored sight.

10. **Healing as compassion**: In Matthew 20:30-34, two blind men were healed by touch after Jesus had pity upon them. Today's word for pity might better be translated as compassion, which is one of the qualities necessary for healing.

11. **Absent-healing**: In Luke 7:3-10, Jesus carried out absent-healing on the centurion's servant. The centurion felt compassion for his servant and Jesus may have channeled the healing through the Centurion (a focus for sending the healing to the servant) just as a healing group might do today.

12. **Ungrateful healees.** Luke 17:11-19, one my favorite healing encounters, describes Jesus healing ten lepers by command without touching them.

Only one leper returned to Jesus and gave thanks. Why? Jesus said it was a lack of religious belief.

This speaks to the modern healer. Ninety percent of those healed never mention it to the healer. Partly, it is the selective amnesia that goes with a miracle. Partly, it is not believing that Jesus did the healing. (He didn't touch them; it merely happened.)

A similar event was the disappointment of Jesus depicted in John 4:46-54. Jesus had sent absent-healing to a Capernaum official. During this encounter Jesus told the father, "Unless you see signs and wonders you will not believe." Healees usually need to see healing as dramatic and convincing, yet healing occurs so quietly that most people do not know anything is happening. So the healer often has the healee claim or acknowledge his healing, to affix it so it won't slip away.

13. **Healing of a misfit**: The entire ninth chapter of John deals with a blind man's healing. Even before the age of modern science people did not believe that healing was possible. Here Jesus denied that the sins of the blind man's ancestors or that deeds of anyone else caused the blindness. Here is a healing of a person who was considered by the community as unfit to be healed. To the healer, no status, or faith or religion was required. This is still true today.

## Healing Styles in the Early Church

### *Powerful commanding*

The Book of Acts relates many healings by the followers of Jesus. The first one is told in Acts 3:2-10. This healing got Peter and John arrested. (Healers are still arrested today in such places as Germany and Quebec Province.) A man who had been lame from birth was healed as Peter commanded, "...in the name of Jesus Christ of Nazareth, walk." Peter took him by the hand and raised him up and immediately his feet and ankles were made strong. Here is a command in Christ's name, a touching and a boldly demonstrated faith action, expecting specific healing results. This justifies forceful praying for healing today.

### Passing the Holy Spirit

In Acts 9:10-19, Ananias was sent as a messenger by Jesus to heal the blinded Saul and to fill him with the Holy Spirit. Ananias' touch not only healed Saul but it passed on the Holy Spirit. This implies that Ananias possessed the energy of the Holy Spirit within him and when Saul was touched for healing, the Holy Spirit remained, a purposeful, intelligent spiritual energy and presence. This is consistent with blessing people with love and peace at the close of Emotional Release Therapy.

Another story of a healing performed by Peter is found in Acts 9:33-35. Peter said, "Aeneas, Jesus Christ heals you; rise and make your bed." Aeneas, bedridden for eight years and paralyzed, immediately arose. No touch. Just a command in Jesus' name. But again, we see the order to rise (to act or do something) to fixate the healing results.

### Believing

In Acts 14:8-11 is an account of how Paul performed a healing. But he did not even attempt it until he looked in the man's eyes and knew the man believed that he would be healed. Paul did not even evoke Jesus' name, or touch the man. He just commanded in a loud voice, "Stand upright on your feet." By today's standards, that would be sacrilegious. Yet, Christ said he would empower his people with the Holy Spirit. Paul healed with and without reference to Jesus.

### Exorcism

In Acts 14:16-18, he did invoke Jesus' name to cast out a spirit that had given the woman the ability to do divination. My approach is that if it works, use it. Exorcism acts to heal, so I use it.

### Raising the dead

When Paul preached a long sermon, Eutychus went to sleep and fell to his death. Acts 20:10 describes how Paul embraced him (transmitting energy to his heart and brain) and made a shift in reality, or spoke for the expected results, when he said, "Do not be alarmed, for his life is in him."

### Touch-Healing prayer

Finally, in Acts 28:7-9, we read of how Paul went through the traditional rituals of healing for Publius' father, who had a fever and dysentery. He visited him (perhaps talking and relating), prayed and "putting his hands upon him healed him."

## Summary

In Acts we see healing done by commanding, by invoking Jesus, by touch, by demonstrating the expected results. In all but one situation, the healing was freely volunteered with no talk of faith or commitment. It is the healer who must have the faith, not the healee. The suddenness and casualness with which the healings were offered did not give the healees a chance to doubt or raise resistance. It is obvious that the Holy Spirit empowered the disciples to do healings equal to what Jesus had done. In a similar way, God empowers healers today.

## 19

# How Healing is Practiced

This book is about how prayer heals. It was not intended to provide details on how to practice healing. How to practice healing is detailed in my other books.

Here are the steps that I practice during healing sessions.

### Rapport

I usually begin by establishing a relationship with the person. This begins with friendly chatter that moves into obtaining information about the person and why they have come. I then explain what we are about to do together.

### Emotional Release Therapy

My first healing effort involves the practice of Emotional Release Therapy. Sometimes this is all that is needed.

With my hands, I can usually sense the level of healing energy they have absorbed during Emotional Release Therapy. I can also see it in their faces. But I do not trust this subjective awareness. Until I have measuring devices that can assure me that they have received adequate healing energy, I still practice physical healing.

## Removing Cellular Trauma

Conventional medical research has already established that body cells possess memory. I regularly use my healing hand to remove cellular trauma memories with any trauma injury. I actually talk to the tissue, telling it how to cooperate. I also use my hand with longstanding medical conditions, like with cancer, heart disease, and multiple sclerosis.

Here are my reasons for doing this. In trauma injuries, I discovered that some healees were not receiving the healing flow. Instead, I felt a wall beneath my healing hand. I guessed that the cells were in pain and could not receive the healing flow. I also guessed that injured tissue in pain is in chaos, thus no longer having a memory of how to be whole tissue. I continue to do it because it works.

From this, came another leap of understanding. Perhaps cells suffering from disease had also become traumatized. Removing disease trauma works sometimes. Because it does not work all the time, either my theory is flawed or my technique is flawed.

## Prayer

I use vocal prayer in every step of the healing session. Each prayer focuses upon what we are immediately about to do.

## Physical Touch-Healing Prayer

I then practice physical touch-healing prayer. I touch the skin of the healee with my healing hand. I choose the place to touch according to the condition. More and more, I touch the heart chakra. Healing energy applied to the heart chakra appears to flow throughout the energy fields.

The videotaped Chouhan-Weston Clinical Studies demonstrated that within three seconds of touching most people, their normal blue energy field with a white fringe is transformed. It becomes white and doubled in size. But healing has not yet taken place. I think I must keep touching until their energy fields are completely saturated with healing energy. It is like filling a cup with coffee until it overflows. I want healees to be filled to overflowing with healing energy.

I usually sense this with my healing hand. When I feel the healing flow stop, the healee has been filled with the healing energy and can accept no more. I wish I had a scientific instrument that would objectively tell me when this has occurred. I tend to err on the side of caution, continuing the healing flow far beyond when it is necessary.

## Overcoming Barriers

When I touch a healee and feel a wall of resistance that stops the healing energy from entering the healee, I do not blame the healee for not cooperating. If this is not due to cellular trauma, I assume that the healee does not know how to open his energy fields to receive the flow. I coach him to open a door under my hand and let it in. Or I tell him to accept my touch as friendly and open himself to it. It works. Almost immediately, I can feel the acceptance of the energy from my hands. Therefore, I conclude my assumption is true.

## Exorcism

Once in awhile, I do an exorcism. I let intuitive guidance or experience direct me. Sometimes I sense a spirit of disease and a few times have seen it leave the healee, swiftly moving away and out of the room. What is being exorcized has been described earlier in this book.

## Follow-Up Is Your Responsibility

Anyone who practices touch-healing prayer plays a leadership role. She or he knows far more about healing than the healee. If you think another session is necessary, suggest when the healee should return. Or, phone the healee and inquire about the outcomes of the first session and schedule another session if needed. Remember, healing is a process. It will take forty-eight hours or more to access the outcome of your session.

Using healing-charged cotton dishtowels or bottled water is, again, your leadership responsibility. I use these whenever I think the healee is open to it.

## Trust Your Healing Hands

Once your hands are doing what you intend them to do, forget about them. Your hands naturally know how to heal. Express your intentions to your hands and then concentrate on being one with the healee. Your hands will continue to flow without further input.

## Conclusion

These are the steps I use in most healing sessions. They are provided for your knowledge. If you are already competent in a healing technique, they provide you insight for your own sessions.

## Subjective Awareness During Healing Prayer

Here I share with you my own subjective awareness during healing sessions. I hope this is helpful.

Through the years, I have been a pragmatist who believes "if it works, use it". In the presence of each healing miracle, I am awed. I am focused totally upon the person as I pray for a healing. These are the most exciting, alive, joyous moments of my life. After the healing encounter, I can remember with sharp focus every detail of those life-enhancing moments. I have discovered several factors are usually present in my healing prayers:

1. I always sense a holy presence guiding and sustaining me.
2. I am always touching the other person, with a handclasp, or hands on the injured area, or one hand on the healee's head with the other clasping one of his hands.
3. I always have a relationship with those I heal. There is caring. If I know of their hurting, there is compassion. Sometimes it is human friendship, a closeness. Sometimes there is the stimulation of persons getting to know each other at deeper levels. Sometimes there is laughter and the prayer is begun in a joyous spirit. Sometimes there has been tension between us, but as the prayer begins, an intimate bond begins joining us together and a deep rapport develops.
4. There is always a sense of merging, unity, or oneness, between myself, the healee, and God. I call this the Healing Trinity.
5. There is always a sense of peace with any negative awareness filtered to a vague background.

311

6. Usually there is yielding or accepting, a simple flowing into a beautiful new reality of timelessness.

7. I usually sense a mutual healing. I am healed, too, as if there were a mutual healing exchange between healer and healee, or because the healing is flowing through me. Any fatigue or tension is gone. If I have a raspy throat, a stiff back or a sore muscle, all are healed. After I do healing all day, I feel refreshed.

8. Sometimes my fingers will tingle and sometimes I feel heat where my hands are touching. I feel heat in my own fingers only when my fingers touch myself. Often I can sense an energy flow from my fingers, but this has no known correlation with the healing results. More recently, when I feel nothing, the healing results are better. This leads me to believe that the sensed heat during healing is not signifying that healing is taking place but is showing the resistance of the energy field to the transmitted energy. The only effective heat is that felt within the healee's physical body.

9. When a healee's loved ones are present, I often sense a much stronger energy flow.

10. Those whom I have healed report a variety of impressions. Some feel heat either where I have placed my hands or in a diseased or injured area. Some feel a tingling throughout the body. Some sense an energy flow. Emotional factors—peace, love, joy, holiness, energy—are reported more often than physical factors.

As the prayer begins, I attempt to do nothing except pray. As the prayer continues, my words flow without conscious thought. When this happens at a deeper level,

I am conscious of the other factors described above. I flow easily between Type I and Type II healing modes—alternating between the oneness and the energy flow. Only rarely is there a telepathic exchange at the conscious level, yet a deeper knowing of the healee usually emerges.

I only developed this inner awareness following many years of healing. I provide this as a model for where you might be heading someday in your prayers. Your inner experiences also may take a different path than mine. Above all, do not let this model let you feel inadequate.

# 20

# Soaking People in Prayer

The most consistent way to produce healing outcomes is through soaking prayer. Healing is a process that works somewhat like an antibiotic. You must constantly bathe people in healing energy until they are well. You do this to maintain the necessary therapeutic level of healing energy. The healing energy is used up in the healing process and needs to be constantly replenished.

For most people, this is a new paradigm for prayer. In this new model, people are only receiving their needed supply of healing energy while people are praying for them.

One of my daughters and her husband live on a very modest income. If they receive one unexpected extra bill, they are in trouble. So, my wife and I decided to soak them in prayer, asking God to provide for their financial need. We soaked them in prayer by praying for their financial needs every evening. We did this faithfully month after month, year after year.

Then one day, my daughter expressed amazement about her financial good fortunes. She shared, "Mom and Dad, I don't know what is happening, but God sure is good to us. Whenever we have an extra expense, extra money comes in seemingly from nowhere to pay for it. This happens all the time. I just don't understand how this could be happening to us."

I enlightened her. "Honey, your mother and I have been praying daily for your financial needs for years. You are living on our prayers."

Her face lit up and she responded, "Oh, now I understand. It all makes sense now. Thanks. Keep praying for us."

That is usually how all prayer works. In healing prayer, you can offer soaking prayer in several ways. You can pray daily for healing. You can pray hourly for healing. You can pray for a half-hour at a time for healing. You can gather with loved ones for healing prayer, knowing that the power of prayer is the square of the number of people gathered in prayer. Your goal is to fill the ill person with enough healing energy at all times, so that healing proceeds at a steady pace. The amount needed varies with the seriousness of the illness.

## Discouragement

Sometimes we get discouraged. We think there have been no outcomes from our prayers. We fight discouragement with faith. God calls us to be faithful. Faithfulness means doing what we believe God calls us to do, including praying for ourselves and others.

Years ago I began praying daily for my alcoholic brother who lived more than two thousand miles away. After two years, I became discouraged. After all this soaking prayer, nothing was happening. I shared my discouragement with a prayer group I was starting. I accepted their offer to join me in prayers for my brother. Now, we were really soaking him in prayer.

Two months later this brother phoned me. He said, "Walt, I have been dry for six weeks. I am feeling great. I still don't know how this happened. One day, without planning it, I just quit drinking. It was no problem at all."

My brother was a great agnostic, a scoffer about all things religious. So, I never told him about my prayers for him. He was so anti-God that he might have returned to drinking just out of spite.

## Touch Enhances Soaking Prayer

The most efficient way to transmit healing energy is by touch. When parishioners were in critical condition, I went to their hospital bedsides and would offer touch-healing prayer for half-an-hour at a time. I have often done this while patients lay in a coma from a brain injury. This is soaking prayer.

Below is my favorite story about soaking prayer. Our scientific working model for healing prayer provides a practical understanding of this dramatic healing encounter. Francis MacNutt (The Power To Heal), one of the world's most knowledgeable healers, relates Theresa's story. It took place at a Roman Catholic retreat for priests in the Diocese of Sonson, Rionegro, Columbia in February 1975.

On the evening of the first day of the retreat, a group of nuns and laywomen sought Father MacNutt's assistance for Theresa, a nineteen-year-old woman whose withered right leg was six inches shorter than her left leg, and twisted at an angle. This was the result of stepping on a sharp object in a swamp at the age of five. The untreated infection had entered her bones and developed into osteomyelitis, an inflammation of the bone.

The women had been praying all day with Theresa. Father MacNutt joined them in prayer. The eight-person group "soaked" Theresa in prayer that evening, each taking turns touching Theresa's leg. The day's earlier prayers had produced an inch of new leg growth. After two hours of gentle evening prayer, her leg grew another inch. The following day, a two-hour session resulted in another inch of leg growth.

During this soaking prayer process, the leg began straightening, scar tissue healed, shrunken toes grew, and a deformed foot reshaped to normal. When they finished their soaking prayer at the end of the week, her right leg was only one-half inch shorter than the left. The leg bone and foot were normal. Theresa's healing is not unique. It is a clear textbook example of soaking, touch-healing prayer.

# 21

# Closing Thoughts

This is the last chapter. But your journey need not end here. Here are some suggestions for continuing the journey.

1. You can teach yourself to become a complete healer through my book, *Healing Others: A Practical Guide*.
2. You can teach yourself to heal yourself through my book, *Healing Yourself: A Practical Guide*.
3. If you are seeking healing for yourself or others, write me and hopefully I can refer you to a complete healer in your community.
4. If you would like to contact others who have read *How Prayer Heals*, write me and if enough others write me, I can put you in contact with them. Maybe you can have a study group.
5. If you would like to sponsor a seminar or lecture by me, please write. Address your letter to

Walter Weston
c/o Hampton Roads Publishing Company, Inc.
134 Burgess Lane

They will forward your letter to me. I am presently living in the Akron, Ohio area.

Thank you, friend, for welcoming me into your life.

# About the Author

Walter Weston holds a bachelor's degree in psychology from Kent State University and a graduate theological degree from the Vanderbilt Divinity School.

In 1991, he earned a Doctor of Ministry degree in healing research at the International College, Montreal. His faculty advisor was Dr. Bernard Grad, a research biologist at McGill University and the father of healing research with more than 200 healing studies.

Dr. Weston has had the privilege of studying with researchers and healers from a dozen nations. He studied the scientific data, beliefs, theories, practice, and history of healing and prayer in the United States, other cultures, and the world's religions.

While researching healing, he studied and observed spiritual healing as practiced by many churches, as well as learning such techniques as Therapeutic Touch, Reiki, Lawrence LeShan healing, kinesiology, balancing energy fields, Chinese Qigong, spirit healing, and pranic healing.

In 1989, he participated as a healer with Ramesh Singh Chouhan, M.D., in the Chouhan-Weston Clinical

Studies at JIPMER regional hospital, Pondicherry, India, that scientifically verified a dozen theories involving the practice of prayer for healing. The videotaping of changing energy fields during the touch-healing prayer encounter provided answers for many troubling questions, creating a helpful new picture.

For thirty years, Dr. Weston served as a United Methodist parish minister. He specialized in counseling, personal growth, and the spiritual journey. He is a veteran of the marriage and family enrichment movement and of holistic health practices.

Walter Weston is presently a professional healer, psychotherapist, hypnotherapist, wellness counselor, and workshop leader. He is the author of *PrayWell: A Holistic Guide To Health and Renewal, Healing Others,* and *Healing Yourself,* as well as this book.

His most recent work has pioneered Emotional Release Therapy that offers dramatic healing of painful memories and destructive fixated emotional states.

Dr. Weston is president of the Cleveland Association for Holistic Health and a member of the International Society for the Study of Subtle Energies and Energy Medicine.

He lives near Akron, Ohio, with his wife, Dana, a registered nurse. Their great joy is their closeness to their three daughters and seven grandchildren.

More Healing / Alternative/Complementary
Medicine titles from
Hampton Roads Publishing Company, Inc.

## Remarkable Healings
### A Psychiatrist Discovers Unsuspected Roots
### of Mental and Physical Illness
Shakuntala Modi, M.D.

A doctor discovers that patients, during hypnotic therapy, have "entities" attached to them, living in their energy fields and affecting their behavior. She has developed a technique that "clears" energy fields— with the patient miraculously recovering within days.

*6 x 9, trade paper, 632 pages*
*ISBN 1-57174-079-1, $18.95*

## Diagnosis Unknown
### Our Journey to an Unconventional Cure
Randy Smith

Linda Smith suffered from a debilitating ailment that no conventional doctor could diagnose. The Smiths found that alternative practitioners effectively diagnosed Linda's ailment and provided a cure, while "orthodox" medicine only served to worsen her condition. A wonderful introduction to alternative medicine and practitioners.

*5 ½ x 8 ½, trade paper, 256 pages*
*ISBN 1-57174-065-1, $12.95*

### Questions from the Heart
Answers to 100 Questions about Chelation Therapy,
A Safe Alternative to Bypass Surgery

Terry Chapell, M.D.

EDTA chelation clears blocked arteries and improves general circulation. Safe and legal, it has been used by more than 500,000 heart patients in the past thirty years, and costs 10% of what coronary bypass surgery costs.

*5 ½ x 8 ½, trade paper, 136 pages*
*ISBN 1-57174-026-0, $10.95*

### Healing Myself

Gari Carter

After a head-on auto accident destroyed much of Gari Carter's face, she suffered for months—yet came to realize that she had learned patience, love, and proper priorities. A truly inspirational story.

*5 ½ x 8 ½, trade paper, 208 pages*
*ISBN 1-878901-75-3, $10.95*

"Shows how one woman can become a symbol of courage."                 —*The FreeLance Star*

### Why I Left Orthodox Medicine
Healing for the 21st Century

Derrick Lonsdale, M.D.

Symptom-treating "orthodox" medicine is not as effective as simply treating the *causes* of disease. This book shows that nutrition, exercise, and vitamin/mineral therapy can be used as very effective preventative measures. The author relates the story of his shaken faith in the system, and how he found the strength to do what he knew was right for his patients.

*5 ½ x 8 ½, trade paper, 256 pages*
*ISBN 1-878901-98-2, $10.95*

### Racketeering in Medicine
The Suppression of Alternatives
James P. Carter, M.D., Dr.P.H.

Are Americans being deprived of effective medical treatments because orthodox medicine and pharmaceutical companies can't profit from them? Dr. Carter presents many disturbing cases of legitimate therapies being disparaged as quackery, government agencies harassing alternative practitioners, and drug companies buying political influence—the real causes of today's health-care crisis.

*5 ½ x 8 ½, trade paper, 392 pages*
*ISBN 1-878901-32-X, $12.95*

"Asserts [that] what amounts to an establishment cabal...has ruthlessly conspired to suppress alternatives."
—— *Venture Inward*


### Acquiring Optimal Health
Gary Price Todd, M.D.

Eating energy-depleted and nutritionally poor foods is the root cause of many degenerative and age-related diseases. This book shows you how to heal yourself and achieve optimal health by replacing poor eating habits with Dr. Todd's comprehensive dietary and nutrition regimen. An eye-opening introduction to good health and wellness.

*5 ½ x 8 ½, trade paper, 128 pages*
*ISBN 1-878901-92-3, $8.95*

"Information that could save your life."
— *Baton Rouge Advocate*

# Hampton Roads Publishing Company

*. . .for the evolving human spirit*

Hampton Roads Publishing Company
publishes books on a variety of subjects including
metaphysics, health, complementary medicine,
visionary fiction, and other related topics.

For a copy of our latest catalog,
call toll-free, (800) 766-8009,
or send your name and address to

Hampton Roads Publishing Company
134 Burgess Lane
Charlottesville, VA 22902